Sarah Brennand
Balancing Act

Sarah Brennand

Balancing Act

———

Mastering Work, Wealth and Wellbeing

DE GRUYTER

ISBN 978-3-11-168026-2
e-ISBN (PDF) 978-3-11-168027-9
e-ISBN (EPUB) 978-3-11-168078-1

Library of Congress Control Number: 2025943923

Bibliographic information published by the Deutsche Nationalbibliothek
The Deutsche Nationalbibliothek lists this publication in the Deutsche Nationalbibliografie; detailed bibliographic data are available on the internet at http://dnb.dnb.de.

© 2026 Walter de Gruyter GmbH, Berlin/Boston, Genthiner Straße 13, 10785 Berlin
Cover image: Banphote Kamolsanei/iStock/Getty Images Plus
Illustrations: Luisa Phillips
Typesetting: Integra Software Services Pvt. Ltd.

www.degruyterbrill.com
Questions about General Product Safety Regulation:
productsafety@degruyterbrill.com

Contents

Beyond The Page: One Code, Ongoing Support

You'll notice throughout the book there's a QR code. It's there for those of you who want to go further, readers who also want to watch, listen, download and apply.

It links to the BALANCING ACT Resource Hub, a practical extension of the tools and ideas shared here. Scan it any time to access:
– Extended interviews and real-time insights.
– Downloadable tools, worksheets, and frameworks.
– Visual explainers and coaching prompts.
– Articles and updates on performance, wellbeing and leadership.

Dip in when it's useful. Share it with your team. Use it to take things forward.
www.balancing-act.co.uk

EXPLORE MORE

Access practical tools, expert insights and additional content from BALANCING ACT

Scan the QR code or visit:
www.balancing-act.co.uk

MORE CLARITY. MORE TOOLS. YOUR NEXT STEP.

Acknowledgments

Writing this book has been a balancing act, one I didn't do alone.

To my children, Bailey, Darcie and Brodie, thank you for grounding me, stretching me, and teaching me daily about resilience, joy and perspective. You appear in these pages because your lessons are real and your voices matter.

To the experts and contributors whose voices enrich this book, Floyd, Anne-Sophie, Adam, Alison, John, and Anne, thank you for your expertise, honesty, time, and the trust you placed in this process. You helped shape something far greater than a single perspective.

To those who supported this project in less visible but deeply important ways, through encouragement, flexibility, perspective, or simply the right words when they were needed most, thank you. You made this book possible and one I'm proud to share.

Foreword

We are not defined by our status, money or the roles we have had in life. We are defined by the person we become on the journey. That's not just about climbing higher, it's about *balancing what matters* on the way up. It's about alignment of our inner compass.

Sarah Brennand has written a book that cuts through the noise. *Balancing Act* is not about having it all, it's about *knowing what you need*, building a system that supports it, and having the courage to recalibrate when life shifts beneath your feet.

What I admire most about Sarah's work is its depth and honesty. She combines real-life pressure with sharp tools, lived stories, and science-backed insight. This isn't theory - it's strategy you can live by.

Your compass is in your hands. Let this book help you align it.

Floyd Woodrow MBE DCM
Founder, Compass for Life | Chairman, Quantum Group

The Cast And Context Behind This Book

This book is the result of decades spent working at the intersection of leadership, learning and performance, not from a single lens, but through a wide-angle view of what success really takes and what it really costs.

Over the years, my work has taken me from academic institutions to executive boardrooms, from international sports teams to frontline teams in high-pressure hospitality environments. Early on, when asked to contribute academic research, I gravitated instinctively toward high-performance settings, studying Michelin-starred restaurants and the role of emotional intelligence and language in elite performance. What these environments share is a relentless demand for precision. The margin for error is small and performance must be consistently repeatable, not just occasionally remarkable.

I've always been drawn to the pace of business, the challenge of change and the need to act fast. I feel fortunate to have spent years surrounded by brilliant people, experts in human physiology, nutrition, psychology, commercial acumen, leadership and beyond. Many of them remain voices in my head, part of what I think of as my 'virtual board', mentors, colleagues, clients, and co-creators whose insights I carry and pass on.

This book brings those voices to you, and it brings you new ones too.

Inside these pages, you'll meet Olympic athletes, military leaders, behavioural scientists, financial experts and psychologists, as well as some of the highest performing individuals I've ever worked with, many of whom you won't find on podiums or front pages. You'll also hear from my children. Not often, this isn't a parenting book, but where their experiences reflect a universal truth about performance, growth, resilience or fear, their stories belong here too. I've learned just as much from them as I have from anyone else and if you're a parent, some of those lessons will resonate too.

We all live a balancing act. This book doesn't promise perfection, but it does offer a way to calibrate. It shares a model, a language, and a lens for thinking differently about your personal and professional performance, whether you're aiming to advance your career, pivot direction, protect your energy, or redefine success on your own terms.

So, don't just take my word for it. Listen to the patterns in the stories, the wisdom in the tools and the honesty in the voices of those who have led under load, faced uncertainty, and kept moving forward. Maybe, as you read, you'll start to hear your own voice a little more clearly too. You've heard why I wrote this book. Now let me show you who helped shape it.

Meet The Voices Behind The Book

Each of the individuals featured here represents a distinct pathway to performance, shaped by personal context and season of life. Some are clients I've worked with, others long-time colleagues and a few are friends I deeply admire. You'll hear their voices throughout the book, adding depth, diversity, and truth to the conversation on what it really means to lead a successful life.

To ensure this book reflects not only my own insights but a fuller and richer perspective, I've drawn on interviews and trusted expertise across neuroscience, finance, elite sport, and business leadership. You'll meet those who lead from the front, those who lead from within and those who quietly shape the systems that enable others to thrive.

I also share parts of my own journey, not just as author, coach, educator, or trainer, but as a business leader, mother of three and challenge seeker. Someone who has tested these tools in fast-moving, real-world conditions. You'll meet me not only in the margins of the frameworks, but as a lived example of what it means to recalibrate in real time.

This is the cast and context of the book, the featured voices who bring these ideas to life and demonstrate what it means to master your own balancing act across work, wealth and wellbeing.

Success In Four Dimensions

Success has no single script. While science and strategy can guide us, their power lies in how we apply them, guided by who we are, what matters to us and the moment we're in.

Throughout this book, you'll meet four remarkable individuals, Floyd, Anne-Sophie, Adam, and Alison, each representing a unique and personal journey to high performance and leadership. Their careers span sectors as diverse as elite military, global consultancy, elite sport, energy, engineering, and youth development.

They are not presented as perfect role models, but as real-world case examples. Proof that success is as individual as a fingerprint. They've each leveraged the principles explored in this book differently. What they have in common is self-awareness, resilience, and the ability to translate insight into action.

You may identify more with one story than another. That's the point. The journey to mastering your own balancing act isn't about copying a template, it's about developing and adapting tools to fit your mission and circumstances. These four individuals show us how.

Let me introduce you.

Floyd Woodrow MBE DCM
Elite Military Leader | Founder, Compass for Life | Chairman, Quantum Group

Floyd Woodrow is a decorated former SAS major turned international leadership consultant, fintech executive and social impact champion. Best known for his distinguished 23-year career in the British Army, including service in the elite 22 Special Air Service (SAS), Floyd was one of the youngest soldiers ever selected for the SAS at age 22. He was awarded the Distinguished Conduct Medal (DCM) for bravery in Iraq and later received an MBE for his service in Afghanistan.

Floyd's story doesn't end with the military though. In fact, that was just the first act. Upon leaving the forces, he pivoted into business, law, psychology, and education. Today, he is Chairman of The Quantum Group, a fintech innovation firm, Founder of Compass for Life, a global training, and consultancy advising elite performers and senior leaders across business, sport, government, and education, and he is the Founder of the Compass for Life Foundation helping disadvantaged children build purpose and direction through aspiration and structure.

In this book, Floyd's voice offers a powerful blueprint for what it means to design a life of alignment, lead under pressure, and keep recalibrating towards your mission, even when the route changes. Floyd is a firm believer that success is not bestowed, it's created. His widely used Compass for Life model blends military precision with personal purpose. His leadership philosophy is values-driven, deeply human, and laser-focused on strategic clarity and self-awareness.

Floyd doesn't describe himself as successful, he just gets on with the work. But his life, across extreme environments, shifting sectors and lifelong learning, offers a clear message. You are the architect of your future, but only if you choose to be. Most recently, Floyd has been exploring how artificial intelligence can be used to support human performance. He has developed N-Lighten, a digital AI tool designed to help individuals track behavioural patterns, assess progress, and stay aligned with their goals. The concept reflects Floyd's core mission to equip people with the awareness and systems they need to realise their potential. As with every chapter of his journey, from elite soldier to educator, business strategist to AI innovator, Floyd continues to evolve with purpose and precision.

How I know Floyd: I was introduced to Floyd by a friend who described him as someone every leader should meet. We connected over shared values and mutual respect, and I've since seen his work in action, especially in education. His insights are deep, practical, and unshakably grounded.

Anne-Sophie Amiot
Global Energy Executive | Vice President, Sales & Strategy | Advocate for Women in Engineering

Anne-Sophie Amiot is Vice President of Sales & Strategy at Wood PLC, a global engineering consultancy. A senior international executive with a decade of leadership roles, including Vice President of Growth & Development and Strategic Accounts, she has led complex, cross-regional initiatives across Europe, the Middle East and Africa.

I first met Anne-Sophie in Milan in early 2024 and was immediately struck by her presence, she was thoughtful, engaging and quietly powerful. Anne-Sophie leads without ego, building trust through consistency, curiosity, and calm authority.

With a background in chemistry and engineering, she began in technical roles before quickly transitioning to client-facing work, where she discovered a natural strength in connecting with people and navigating complexity. Today, Anne-Sophie combines technical depth with emotional intelligence to lead global strategy and shape diverse, high-performing teams.

Her leadership philosophy is built on reflection, feedback and staying grounded in her values. *"If there was no fear, it wouldn't be fun,"* she told me. A reminder that courage and growth go hand in hand.

Anne-Sophie is a committed advocate for women in engineering and inclusive leadership. Whether mentoring colleagues, walking to meetings, or protecting time for family dinner, she models a version of success that is ambitious, adaptive, and deeply human. In this book, her voice offers a globally minded, emotionally intelligent view of what it means to lead sustainably, on your own terms and with room to evolve.

How I know Anne-Sophie: I delivered work for Anne-Sophie in Milan. Within hours, I saw she was a leader who created clarity, cohesion and respect across a joint venture team spanning nationalities and organisations. No egos, just direction, energy and integrity. Her story had to be included.

Adam Burgess
Olympic Medallist | Breathwork Educator | Resilient High-Performer

Adam Burgess is an Olympic silver medallist and one of Britain's most accomplished canoe slalom athletes. With a career spanning over 15 years at the elite level, Adam has represented Great Britain at the Tokyo 2020 and Paris 2024 Olympic Games, achieving a historic silver medal in the C1 event in Paris, becoming the first British man to reach the Olympic podium in this category since 2008.

Born in Stoke-on-Trent, Adam's journey into elite sport began almost by accident. After missing the first sign-up window at age 10, he took a last-minute spot at a local canoe club, thanks to another child dropping out. That small twist became a defining turning point. From early morning solo training before school to relocating at 16 to pursue his dreams, Adam's story is one of perseverance, self-leadership, and deep personal investment in his craft. In 2025 Adam was recognised by Nottingham Trent University with an honorary Doctor of Sport degree, reflecting both his sporting achievements and his ability to inspire future students. A graduate of the same institution, his academic and athletic journey remain deeply intertwined.

In recent years, Adam has also emerged as a thought leader in the science of breath and recovery. After overcoming a career-threatening shoulder injury, he developed a passion for breathwork and now runs the Inspired Breath Academy, delivering coaching to athletes, business leaders and wellness professionals. His approach blends science with lived experience, promoting mental clarity and physiological balance.

What makes Adam's path so compelling is his dual identity of an elite athlete and self-driven entrepreneur. His model of high performance is not one of force, but flow. He trains independently, embraces uncertainty, and speaks openly about the psychological load of competitive cycles, the role of emotional regulation and the business side of sport. His philosophy is simple, to adapt constantly, to invest in recovery and to build a life that performs under pressure. In this book, Adam's experiences offer insight into sustainable performance, breath-led emotional regulation and what it takes to navigate a results-driven world while maintaining personal wellbeing.

How I know Adam: Adam was once a student of mine at Nottingham Trent University, where I taught on his Sport Science and Management degree. Even then, his potential was clear. He balanced academic demands with competitive high-level training and has gone on to embody high performance with depth and humility.

Alison Oliver MBE
CEO, Youth Sport Trust | Purpose-Led Leader | Advocate for Youth Wellbeing

Alison Oliver is the Chief Executive Officer of the Youth Sport Trust, one of the UK's most influential charities dedicated to improving young people's lives through the power of sport, physical activity, and play. Since taking on the role in 2015 (after joining the charity in 2004), Ali has led with heart, vision and a deeply held belief in the transformative power of movement for physical, cognitive, emotional, and social development.

Her career began as a PE teacher in Essex, later moving to become Head of PE at Millfield School, followed by a leadership role at the University of Bath where she helped shape the TEAMBath netball franchise and led the Physical Education PGCE programme. Her journey has been mission-led rather than meticulously planned, anchored by three simple values that continue to guide her, these are to work hard, make yourself useful and seize opportunities.

Under Ali's leadership, the Youth Sport Trust has influenced policy and curriculum and led global initiatives such as the International Inspirations Programme, part of the legacy of London 2012, impacting millions of children across 20 countries.

Ali was awarded an MBE in 2020 for services to sport and young people and in the same year was named Best Leader (Not-for-Profit) in The Sunday Times 100 Best Companies Awards. She currently serves on several boards, including the Sport for Development Coalition, Youth United Foundation and The Wave Project.

Her leadership philosophy blends strategic clarity with human compassion. Whether navigating political headwinds or supporting team resilience in the face of uncertainty, she leads from the front with humility, accountability, and unwavering optimism. As she says, *"People don't need extraordinary leaders. They need leaders who help them become extraordinary."*

Ali is featured throughout this book not only as a sector leader but as a case study in sustainable leadership, resilience and balancing personal mission with professional demands.

How I know Ali: I had the privilege of working alongside Ali in my early career at the Youth Sport Trust. It's where I learned the power of values-led leadership and mission-driven culture. Her influence shaped much of what I understand about people and purpose.

Real Stories, Real Respect

Throughout this book, you'll encounter more, and different stories drawn from real coaching conversations, training sessions, leadership transitions and moments of personal recalibration. Many of these examples reflect the lived experiences of clients I've worked with, individuals managing uncertainty, striving for success, and making intentional shifts in their work and their life.

In recognition of the trust placed in these relationships, several of these stories have been anonymised or carefully adapted. Names, roles, sectors, and identifiable details may have been changed, but the core insights and turning points remain true to the original experiences. They are not included to showcase outcomes, but to guide the process of growth and to recognise the courage it takes to make meaningful change and lead with intention.

Meet The Experts In Performance Wellbeing And Wealth

While the voices you've met so far reflect lived experience and leadership in action, they are only part of the picture. Sustainable performance is shaped by mindset and motivation, and also by science and strategy. That's why this book is also grounded in the contributions of technical experts, professionals whose insights bring depth and evidence to the ideas we explore. From neuroscience and performance psychology to financial planning and strategic wellbeing, these voices sharpen the tools and frameworks you'll encounter.

Let me introduce you to John and Anne.

Dr. John Sullivan
Clinical Sport Psychologist | Sport Scientist | Creator of the PROCESS Model

John P. Sullivan is a Clinical Sport Psychologist and Sport Scientist who currently serves as the Head of Psychology at High Performance Sport New Zealand. With over 30 years of clinical, academic, and applied experience, he is internationally recognized for his contributions to the integration of psychology, neuroscience, and human performance.

From 2000 to 2016, Dr. Sullivan served as Director of Sports Science and Clinical Care with the New England Patriots of the National Football League, playing a key role during one of the most successful periods in the team's history. His expertise has also been sought by a range of elite organizations, including the English Premier League, The Football Association, Premier Rugby League, Australian

Football League, and numerous Olympic National Teams. Across his career, he has supported athletes and professionals across 43 different sports—spanning individual, team, combat, and motorsport disciplines.

In addition to his work in sport, Dr. Sullivan has served as a subject matter expert for high-performance environments in the military and aerospace sectors. He has advised U.S. Special Operations Command (USSOCOM), the National Aeronautics and Space Administration (NASA), and Defense Advanced Research Projects Agency (DARPA) on critical topics including neurological resilience, decision-making, concussion, and human performance under pressure.

A committed contributor to the scientific community, Dr. Sullivan has authored peer-reviewed articles and has been featured in leading media outlets such as *The Atlantic, The Guardian, The New York Times, ESPN*, and *Sports Illustrated*. He is the co-author of *The Brain Always Wins*, with a second edition *The Brain Always Wins* 2 released in 2025. He is also currently working on two forthcoming books — one exploring human factors in sport, and the other examining the fundamentals of science and their critical relevance in today's post-truth era.

Dr. Sullivan maintains academic appointments as a Visiting Scholar at Queensland University of Technology and has previously served on faculty at Brown University Medical School and the University of Rhode Island Psychology and Neuroscience departments.

Originally from the United States, Dr. Sullivan previously practiced and taught in Washington, D.C., and Newport, Rhode Island, before relocating to New Zealand to continue his work in supporting athletes, coaches, and systems through a brain-first approach to performance and wellbeing.

How I know John: I was introduced to John in 2012 while exploring research on the role of language in high performance. His ability to bridge clinical insight with real-world application across multiple domains is exceptional. We've stayed in touch ever since and his thinking continues to influence my approach to performance and resilience.

Anne McClean
Partner and Head of Wealth | Chartered Financial Planner and Certified Financial Planner | Specialist in Strategic Financial Planning

Anne McClean is a multi-award-winning wealth strategist with two decades of experience advising high-achieving professionals, business owners and families on how to translate earnings into long-term financial security and purpose-led decision-making. Currently a Partner and Head of Wealth at IPS Capital, Anne previously served as a Partner at Smith & Williamson (now Evelyn Partners) and holds Fellowships with both the Personal Finance Society and the Chartered Institute for Securities and Investment.

Anne's expertise bridges complex financial planning with clarity, empathy, and a deep understanding of human motivation. Whether her clients are scaling businesses, transitioning careers, or preparing for generational legacy, her advice helps demystify financial systems and align capital with life aspirations. She specialises in ensuring that the life being built today is structurally and emotionally supported by the decisions made for tomorrow.

Named a Top-Rated Adviser multiple times by VouchedFor and recognised by the Personal Finance Society and Women in Finance Awards, Anne is trusted for her depth of knowledge, her calm, grounded presence, and her ability to create confidence in moments of uncertainty.

Anne's insights appear throughout the Money-Mission paradigm in this book, enriching topics including wealth strategy, liquidity, legacy planning and building a successful future that reflects what matters most. Her contribution offers a powerful reminder that financial confidence is about more than numbers, it's about proactive planning and making your money work in service of your bigger purpose.

How I know Anne: Anne and I met at baby sensory classes while on maternity leave with our firstborns. Our conversations on work, motherhood and money quickly revealed her as someone who brought sharp intelligence and grounded care to financial strategy.

Science And Research

While the voices and lived experiences in this book offer real-world context, they are underpinned by something equally important: science and research. Sustainable performance and executive success aren't just shaped by experience, they're built on tested tools, repeatable models and rigorous insight drawn from decades of interdisciplinary research.

Throughout the book you'll find principles and practices grounded in neuroscience and brain performance, clinical and sport psychology, emotional and behavioural regulation, strategic planning and financial wellbeing, performance physiology and recovery, and leadership development and organisational design. These ideas have been tested in elite environments, from corporate boardrooms and education systems to Olympic programmes and special forces.

The tools you'll find in this book have been applied and refined over years of coaching, training, consulting, and leading in complex high-pressure contexts.

They work not because they are universal, but because they are adaptable. They meet you where you are and evolve with you as your context changes.

We Are All Living The BALANCING ACT

Myself Included.

The Balancing Act isn't a metaphor. It's the lived reality of modern leadership, juggling strategic ambition with human limits, professional delivery with personal wellbeing and short-term performance with long-term sustainability. I created this book to bring structure to that reality, offering a practical framework for achieving success across work, wealth and wellbeing.

Here's a bit about me, too:

Sarah Brennand
Executive Coach | Strategic Educator | Performance and Leadership Specialist

I'm Sarah Brennand. I'm an executive coach, strategic educator and international trainer and advisor to professionals and businesses operating in high-pressure, high-performance environments. I'm the Founder of L7 Executive Coaching and Co-Founder of Illuminare Executive Education, organisations that deliver leadership and business solutions across the UK, Europe, the Middle East, and Asia.

My work centres on strategy and performance. Practical, commercial, and focused on what works. I support leaders to move with pace, to make better decisions and to operate from a place of focus and alignment. Whether I'm advising a founder, supporting a senior team, or building capability within a business, the goal remains the same, results, led by people.

Over the years, I've worked across diverse sectors including finance, engineering, education, hospitality, energy and elite sport. I've supported organisations through growth and transformation and coached individuals at pivotal moments where leadership, performance and wellbeing needed to shift in sync. In a world shaped by rapid change and evolving technology, I believe human capability is still the ultimate differentiator. The way we think, adapt and lead is what drives meaningful and lasting results.

I've also lived the balancing act this book explores. I'm a proud mum to three amazing children. Balancing career growth with raising a family has been one of the most formative experiences of my life. It's sharpened my priorities, tested my patience, and deepened my understanding of resilience in everyday action. My children inspire me, they keep me grounded and remind me what matters.

Alongside this, I choose challenge, something that's mine alone. I've completed multiple challenge and ultra-endurance events including the Welsh 3000s, and finished the SAS Fan Dance three times in one weekend, with weight fully loaded and first in my category. These moments aren't about proving anything to anyone else. They give me something to train for and act as a reminder that performing under pressure requires mindset, structure and stamina, just like leadership.

This book brings it all together through the strategic models I use with clients, the tools that drive performance and the mindset that sustains it. BALANCING ACT is a formula for mastering work, wealth and wellbeing. A practical toolkit for those serious about achieving sustainable success.

Section One: **Introduction: The Executive Tightrope**

Imagine yourself walking a tightrope stretched between two towering skyscrapers. Below lies the cityscape of modern professional life, a complex environment of opportunity, pressure, and constant decision-making. Each step demands focus, balance, and deliberate movement. One misstep can throw everything off course, yet standing still is not an option. This is the reality of your executive journey.

In today's global, always-on business environment, traditional ideas of success built around titles, status, and conventional measures of wealth, no longer tell the full story. While these markers may be visible, they often fail to reflect what really matters. Many professionals find themselves exhausted at the summit of a mountain they never meant to climb, questioning whether the rewards justify the cost.

Sustainable success now requires something more. It demands focus, alignment, and the ability to manage the interdependencies between professional ambition, personal wellbeing, and meaningful purpose. At the core of such ability lies a mindset shaped by connection and calibration. Yet these skills are rarely taught in traditional leadership development or business education programmes.

Over the past two decades, I've worked as an international executive coach and leadership specialist, partnering with CEOs, founders and senior leaders across industries and global markets. My work focuses on the strategy and performance of businesses and their people, helping individuals lead with intent, organisations grow with purpose and leadership teams perform under pressure. This experience, combined with research and science revealed a recurring theme. The most effective leaders aren't the ones always pushing harder; they're the ones thinking more deliberately about how all parts of their life and leadership interact.

This book brings together these insights, offering a structured, practical methodology that has been developed and tested in high-performance environments. At the heart of this approach is the Calibration Model. A framework I created to help leaders recalibrate in real time, across three essential, interconnected paradigms:

Money-Mission: Aligning financial reward with meaningful contribution. Redefining what it means to be wealthy.

Mental-Physical: Integrating psychological resilience and physical vitality.

Work-Life: Successfully integrating professional ambition with personal fulfilment.

These paradigms don't operate in isolation, they're interdependent and dynamic, shaping how leaders make decisions and sustain performance over time. The Calibration Model was developed to reflect this complexity. Grounded in executive practice and informed by science, it offers a practical system leaders can apply directly to real-world challenges.

Throughout this book, you'll be introduced to tools, models, scientific insights, and real-world examples, from expert contributors to anonymised client experiences, demonstrating how this approach works in practice. Their stories, combined with structured exercises and reflective prompts, provide a clear lens through which to assess your own direction, priorities, and performance.

This book will show you how to lead with greater clarity, using your resources wisely and directing your energy where it counts. When you operate with strategic alignment, you gain momentum, make smarter decisions, and minimise unnecessary effort. In short, you become more effective and more likely to achieve meaningful sustainable success.

In Chapter 1: Success Re-Imagined, we begin by challenging outdated definitions and asking the question at the heart of modern professional life. What does success and wealth really mean for you now, and in the future you're building?

Chapter 1
Success Re-Imagined

Have You Been Aiming At The Wrong Target?

What if everything you thought you knew about success was incomplete, or even misleading?

Is success just about money? Is wealth only measured in financial terms?

Do you really and fully understand what you're striving for, down to the absolute details of it, so that when you get there, you really do recognise it, celebrate it, and enjoy it?

Too often, we chase success based on vague aspirations or external markers, assuming more money, a bigger title or prestige will bring fulfilment. But without a clear, deeply considered definition of what success means to us, we risk years of effort leading to a destination that feels hollow.

Real success comes from alignment, not accumulation.

What Does Wealth Really Mean To YOU?

Is it financial security, freedom, influence, or something else entirely? How does your work contribute to your long-term vision of success? Where does wellbeing fit into the equation, ensuring that achievement doesn't come at the cost of your health, relationships, or happiness?

In today's ever-moving world, where work, wealth and wellbeing are deeply interconnected, the traditional view of success no longer serves us. This section challenges conventional thinking and introduces a fundamentally different perspective, one where success is no longer a rigid goalpost but a dynamic balance of multiple dimensions.

Through this book we'll draw from science, research and real-world experience with global leaders and elite performers to explore three essential paradigms that shape sustainable success, along with the tools to calibrate your balance and maintain momentum as you walk the executive tightrope.

The insights shared will open new possibilities for professional excellence, laying the foundation for a more nuanced, strategic, and fulfilling approach to achievement. One that empowers you to master the delicate balancing act of work, wealth and wellbeing, ensuring that success is not just attained, but sustained.

The Illusion Of Linear Success

For generations, success has been portrayed as a linear journey, a clear path leading to a singular destination. We've been conditioned to view it through narrow lenses, the size of our salary, or the prestige of our title. Yet, as we stand at the threshold of a new era in professional excellence, this conventional wisdom is increasingly proving not just incomplete, but potentially harmful.

Consider for a moment, how many executives have you encountered who reached their supposed 'peak', only to find themselves grappling with burnout, strained relationships, or a disconnected sense of achievement. Is this really what they envisaged or hoped for?

Studies indicate that one in four professionals struggle with mental health challenges, with many feeling disconnected from their sense of purpose despite achieving their financial goals. The evidence is clear, it's no longer just a question of ambition, but of alignment, and that changes everything.

The Paradigm Shift: Success As A Dynamic Balance

The reality is that success in the real-world of modern leadership demands a fundamental reconceptualisation. Rather than a destination (although this is important too and we'll come back to it shortly), success must be understood also as a state of dynamic equilibrium. A continuous balancing act across multiple dimensions of professional and personal life.

Before you begin applying this framework, I want to invite you to consider something fundamental . . . Have you genuinely defined what success is and means? What it looks and feels like for 'you'? Not just in outcomes, but in how you want to feel, live and lead. Both on your journey towards it and also when you arrive.

Many of us start our careers aiming for 'more', more income, more responsibility, more respect. We often want what we've seen . . . just slightly 'more', but everyone starts from a different place. We're shaped by different models of what's 'normal' or 'acceptable'. If your parents worked for others, starting your own business may feel bold. If success in your world was measured by titles or security, flexibility may feel risky.

That's why your definition matters. If success is to be sustainable, it has to be designed with intention. The journey and the destination.

Through my work I've observed time and time again that sustainable success emerges from the masterful orchestration of three critical paradigms:

1. **The Money-Mission Paradigm**
2. **The Mental-Physical Paradigm**
3. **The Work-Life Paradigm**

When even one of these is out of sync, it shows, in your energy, your focus, your leadership, or your relationships.

The problem isn't lack of effort. It's aiming at a version of success that was never fully your own, or never fully complete.

That's what BALANCING ACT is all about, learning, reflecting and redefining what success really means and how to achieve it in a way that's genuinely fulfilling, not just outwardly impressive.

Let's now explore what is meant by each paradigm.

1 The Money-Mission Paradigm

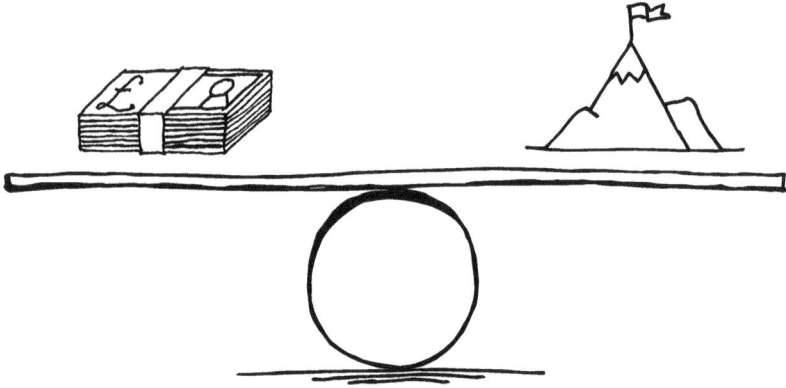

Finding the balance between financial stability and purposeful impact.

Money provides the foundation, it funds your focus, fuels your freedom, and enables the mission that motivates you. When financial clarity is paired with a strong sense of mission, it becomes easier to make aligned decisions and invest your energy with purpose.

High-performing professionals thrive when money and mission work in tandem from the start, not as separate milestones, but as interconnected levers. Financial strength creates options and mission brings meaning. Together, they form a strategy for sustainable, purpose-driven success.

Throughout my career, I've returned to this alignment time and again, for myself and for others. Early on, my drive to develop others pushed me into executive coaching and education. I was motivated to make an impact, urgently, but I soon realised that without a solid personal and financial foundation, I couldn't lead sustainably or at scale.

At the time, I resisted advice to 'secure your own foundation first'. Slowing down felt like stepping back. With experience though came insight. That foundation, emotional, logistical, and financial, didn't hold me back, it gave me the stability and momentum to do meaningful work that lasts.

It's a lesson I share often. It's not always comfortable to hear, but it's essential to understand. If you're serious about sustainable success, you need more than passion, you need a plan.

The well-known aviation safety rule makes it clear. Secure your own oxygen mask before helping others. It's not selfish and it doesn't mean delaying your mission, it means being equipped to deliver it. Investing in your own stability creates the platform you need to lead and achieve at pace and with impact. Financial readiness isn't the opposite of purpose, it's what enables it.

Both research and lived experience confirm this. Studies found that mission-driven leaders who planned for financial stability early reported significantly higher life satisfaction and more resilient decision-making over time. Another found that social entrepreneurs who established sound financial models before scaling were more likely to achieve lasting impact. More than just data, this is about real people making real choices.

Take Floyd Woodrow DCM MBE, who, while still on active military duty, studied law and psychology to prepare for a future beyond the uniform. His goal wasn't to jump ship, but to ensure that his next mission would be just as meaningful as those that came before and that he'd be ready for it.

Or Anne-Sophie Amiot, who continued working after relocating to the UK and giving birth to her third child, even though the cost of a full-time nanny and work-related travel meant her salary barely covered the expense. Why? Because her career mattered. Her purpose mattered. Staying connected to that purpose, even at a financial cost, kept her identity and long-term trajectory intact, and that mattered.

Or Adam Burgess, who juggled elite sport with his academic studies and launched his breathwork academy alongside it. He wasn't waiting for retirement or injury to start planning his future. He was creating options, laying down stepping stones toward impact that would outlast his sporting career.

And Alison Oliver MBE, who leads in the children's health charity sector, always keeps one eye on the financials, not just to sustain the charity's current work, but to secure its future. She often describes this stage of her life as entering her 'third age', not yet ready to step away, but already aware of the ripple affect her eventual departure could cause. She's planning ahead, not only for herself, but for the mission she has stewarded so carefully. She understands that lasting impact is about both the work being done now and leaving behind strong structures for others to build on.

Each of these stories shows what strategic alignment looks like in practice. Rather than choosing one path over another, it's about building both tracks at the same time, so they reinforce each other, not compete.

I've known many other professionals who've made similar choices, choosing to scale back in one area in order to scale up more sustainably later. Like a leader who reduced her pro bono work while building a business that now funds a charitable foundation, or a CEO who focused on profitability first and then built a development programme for his team.

What they all share is a mindset that sees financial strength as more than an endgame, it became the enabler of meaningful work. Money and mission don't need to be pursued in sequence; they should evolve in parallel. Each strengthens the other.

Think of it like climbing a mountain. Your energy, supplies and financial resources all need careful management, and so does your mission and sense of direction. Without both, you won't reach the summit. If you do, you won't stay there for long.

That balance often reflects deeply personal motivations. For some, it's about securing safety for their family. For others, it's the freedom to build, create, lead, or serve. Whatever the driver, the secret lies in understanding it, owning it, and making sure it's built into your professional strategy, not bolted on later.

Maslow's hierarchy offers useful perspective here. Foundational needs, security, stability, and health, make space for purpose and contribution. When those foundations are respected rather than ignored, the path forward becomes clearer and more rewarding.

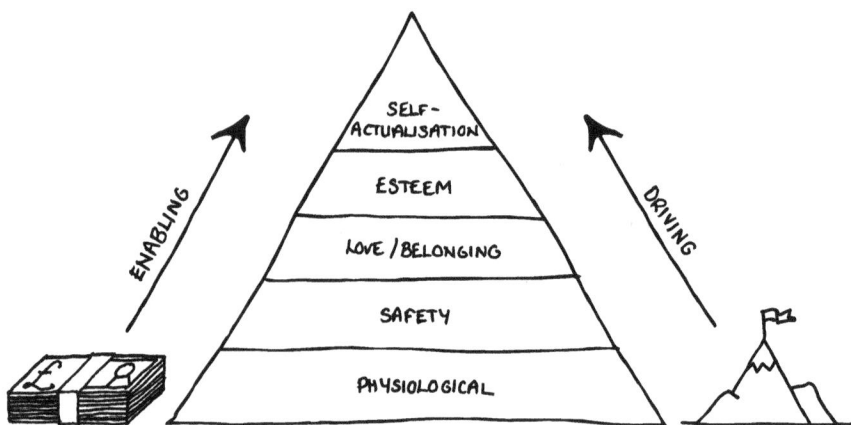

2 The Mental-Physical Paradigm

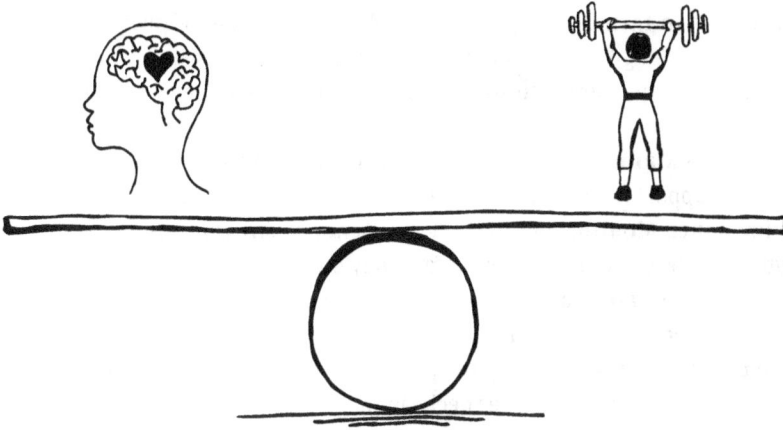

The myth of the sacrificial executive, trading health for high performance, no longer holds.

Today's most effective leaders are those who deliberately invest in the systems that sustain them, not the ones who push through at all costs. High-performance leadership rests on often-invisible foundations like recovery rhythms and psychological strength. When mental and physical health are working in sync, leaders make better decisions, maintain energy, and are better positioned to sustain momentum without burning out.

Health underpins every aspect of performance. When your body and mind are in sync, you're more focused, more present, and more adaptable. Resilience is often positioned as a mindset, but in practice, it's the integration of mindset and physiology that drives sustainable performance. You can't lead well if your nervous system is constantly in survival mode, or if your energy is being depleted faster than it's restored.

The evidence is strong. Integrated routines that include movement, rest, sleep, nutrition, and recovery lead to improved and more consistent performance under pressure, including sharper decisions and quicker emotional resets. This connection isn't abstract, it's visible in the daily rhythms of leaders like Anne-Sophie, Alison, Floyd, and Adam. Whether it's walking meetings, outdoor thinking time, structured recovery blocks, baking, music or breathwork, each have found ways to build energy and balance into their system. The details differ, but the principle holds, sustained performance starts with integration. Whether you're an athlete or an executive, consistent rhythmic integration builds consistent results.

Four Foundations Of Integrated Performance

When it comes to mental and physical wellbeing, sustainable progress comes from intentional design, not just habit. Structure supports consistency and consistency builds capacity. These four foundations help leaders embed integration into the everyday:

1. **Preventive Maintenance:** Regular movement, quality sleep and recovery routines support the nervous system and build long-term resilience.
2. **Performance Monitoring:** Tracking your energy, stress levels and recovery rhythms helps catch imbalances before they escalate.
3. **Recovery Programming:** Planned recovery, before it's needed, sustains performance, and reduces the risk of burnout.
4. **Environmental Design:** Designing physical and digital spaces to reduce friction and protect focus enhances decision-making and emotional clarity.

Leaders who embed these principles feel better and work smarter, reporting an increase in strategic effectiveness, a rise in team engagement and a decrease in burnout. These principles provide the foundation for successful performance.

Designing For Energy And Clarity

INSIGHT

While we often focus on goals and outcomes, performance is also shaped by the spaces we move through every day. Environment influences attention, energy, and recovery far more than we realise. For leaders under pressure, even subtle design shifts can make a meaningful difference.

When workspaces are thoughtfully designed for calm and focus, they act as quiet reinforcements of our intentions. The lighting, acoustics, movement flow and sensory cues in a space can reduce decision fatigue and help regulate our cognitive load. The same is true for digital environments, structure your online world to create breathing space, rather than more noise.

Strategic recovery becomes easier when it's supported by the space around you. That might mean scheduling protected blocks in your calendar for active recovery, designing quiet corners in your workspace, or setting digital boundaries that protect attention.

Leaders who adopt this thinking don't wait for rest to be earned; they embed it into the system.

Co-Drivers Of Performance

Mental and physical health aren't add-ons. They work in tandem to support high performance, just like strength and mobility, or focus and rest.

Just as elite athletes train for output and recovery, leaders who structure their days around both capacity and restoration unlock a more powerful and sustainable rhythm. It's this alignment that creates the focussed energy and impact that leadership demands over time.

As Dr. John Sullivan highlights, nutrition helped shape the evolution of the human brain, fuelling not only cognition but emotional resilience and adaptability. We didn't evolve on thought alone; we evolved by learning how to fuel and regulate the systems that allow us to connect, lead and thrive.

That remains true today. Integrated wellbeing isn't a side project, it's part of how effective leadership gets done.

3 The Work-Life Paradigm

The traditional concept of 'work-life balance' suggests two forces in constant competition. But for today's leaders, that separation feels outdated. The line between work and life isn't fixed, it's fluid.

When approached with intention, that fluidity becomes a strength. What's needed now is not compartmentalisation, but integrated harmony, a dynamic rhythm where professional ambition and personal wellbeing move together, reinforcing rather than undermining one another.

How you spend your time shapes how you experience your life. Balancing work and life doesn't mean you have to always compromise. More often, it means learning to design a day-to-day rhythm that reflects what matters most. Success includes the people you love and the moments that matter. High performance is most powerful when it's part of a life you actually enjoy.

Integration doesn't mean working constantly. It means designing your life so that your work supports your values, your home life fuels your energy, and your daily rhythm reflects who you are, not just what you do.

Our bodies aren't built for constant output. As Dr. John Sullivan explains, even our breath mirrors this truth. Inhale to energise, exhale to reset. This natural rhythm, the 'cosine wave' of energy in motion, is the body's built-in reminder to peak, rest, repeat.

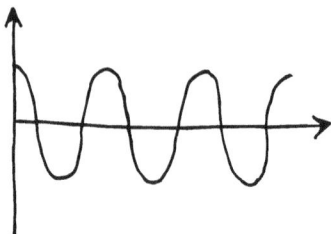

When leaders design their days around focused effort followed by intentional recovery, they work with their biology, not against it.

Rhythm, Not Rigidity

Resilient brains are built, not born. Everyday behaviours, how you sleep, move, breathe, eat, and pause, shape your neurological capacity for brain regulation and decision-making. Sullivan's PROCESS Model reinforces that the brain thrives on cycles of stimulation and recovery.

Integration happens when your day reflects those cycles. That might look like structuring your calendar to honour business demands and family milestones, or it might mean moving a key meeting to protect your midday run because that's when you do your best thinking. Business wide, you can apply this approach to the development of a team culture that supports flexibility without sacrificing outcomes. Organisations that support this sort of integrated flexibility see the results. Research links flexible working cultures to increased engagement, higher retention, and stronger wellbeing outcomes. Individuals report greater satisfaction when work aligns with their values and when boundaries are respected on both sides. Technology when used intentionally, can enhance focus, rather than fragment it.

However, you don't need research to recognise when integration is working, you feel it. You feel it when you leave a challenging workday and still have the energy to be fully present at home; when your calendar reflects your priorities, not just meetings but milestones that matter, and you feel it when your work aligns with your values, making it easier to stay motivated and harder to burn out.

Living It Personally

For me, integration isn't a theory, it's how I've built my life. I avoid scheduling meetings before 9am whenever possible so I can see my children off to school and do some exercise. Being present in those moments matters to me and starting the day with fresh air or exercise gives me focus and energy. I'll often work some weekends, not out of pressure, but by choice, because it means I can be there for school shows, sports days, or a midweek dog walk with my mum.

My children see me work. They see that I enjoy what I do, and they also see that work fits around life, not the other way around. That normalises a different rhythm, one that works for us. It supports both my energy and my priorities. It's not perfect, but it fits. That's the point.

Principles That Support Integration

Work-life harmony takes more than intention. There are four core principles that underpin sustainable integration:
1. **Customisation:** Integration looks different for everyone.
2. **Flexibility:** Because life evolves, and leadership must evolve with it.
3. **Communication:** Clarity builds connection and reduces friction.
4. **Support Systems:** No one sustains success alone.

The goal is not perfection. It's rhythm. The ability to stay attuned to what matters most, even as life, work and leadership demands change around you.

Balance, Connection And Calibration

When your Money-Mission alignment is strong, you're energised by what you do.

When your Mental-Physical health is integrated, you can perform well and live well.

And when your Work-Life Paradigm is in harmony, life feels like it fits, not just functions.

As Dr. John Sullivan reminds us: *"You can't take population research and use that as a direct guide to help elite individuals, because individuals are all so unique. Human beings are varied, that's the rule, not the exception."* This insight speaks to the need for personalised leadership strategies. The Calibration Model, which I'll introduce you to shortly, honours this individuality, offering you the tools to align performance with your own values, rhythms, and roles.

All three paradigms are interwoven. When one shifts, the others feel it. But when they align, when your mission fuels your work, your work supports your life and your life sustains your wellbeing, that's when momentum builds.

So, ask yourself:

Where in your world could you shift from compartmentalisation to integration?

What small changes could create ripple effects across the systems that matter most?

Because the real shift, and one today's high performers are already making is toward greater alignment. Where energy, purpose, performance, and personal priorities reinforce one another.

When it comes to sustainable success, insight alone isn't enough.You have to live it, in how you work, lead and live.

Four Very Different Beginnings

Before we explore the Calibration Model and the science of sustained success, let's revisit four individuals who demonstrate how diverse, personal, and nonlinear real success journeys can be. These four, now all highly accomplished, Adam, Ali, Floyd, and Anne-Sophie, come from vastly different backgrounds, sectors and stages of life. Yet they share something powerful in common, each of them pursued success on their own terms.

Their beginnings weren't mapped out with rigid long-term plans (though plans do feature along the way). Instead, their journeys evolved through pivotal moments, bold decisions, and a willingness to trust themselves, often before the path was totally clear.

You've already encountered their voices across the Money-Mission, Mental-Physical and Work-Life paradigms. Now, here's a little more about where those stories began. You'll continue to see how they've each calibrated, adapted, and grown through different choices and how they apply the principles in this book to their own lives and leadership.

Adam Burgess: Olympic Canoeist & Breathwork Educator

Adam's journey began at age 10, not with a polished plan but with a forgotten permission slip. *"I only got the place at the local canoe club because someone else dropped out,"* he says. *"That one decision changed everything."* What followed was a decade of grit, early morning solo training and eventually, moving away from home at 16 to train with the national team. His path is one of emotional connection to performance, personal independence, and the power of rituals. *"At the start gate, I'm not making new decisions, I'm trusting my instincts to know how to respond to anything new"*

Alison Oliver MBE: CEO, Youth Sport Trust

Ali never set out to become a CEO. Her journey began with a deep love of sport and movement, a values-driven work ethic and an openness to opportunity. *"Work hard, make yourself useful and seize opportunities,"* this simple mantra shaped her path from PE teacher to national leader. *"I never had a long-term plan,"* she says. *"But when I met people on a mission, I knew I wanted to be part of it."*

Floyd Woodrow MBE DCM: Former SAS Major, Founder of Compass for Life

At age 12, Floyd declared he would join the Parachute Regiment and the SAS, and that's exactly what he did, joining one of the world's most elite military units by 22. But his success didn't stop there. From law school to psychology, fintech to elite education, Floyd's journey has been about growth, contribution, and human potential. *"I don't see success,"* he says. *"I just do the work, and I follow my Super North Star."*

Anne-Sophie Amiot: Global Energy Executive & Advocate for Women in Engineering

Anne-Sophie studied chemistry and engineering before starting her career in technical roles. Her strength with people however, soon moved her into client-facing and strategic leadership. Today, she leads international energy projects while championing inclusive leadership across her sector. *"Almost every step came from someone saying, 'you'd be good at this',"* she says. That openness to challenge and trust in others' belief has shaped her journey. When she needs to reset, she bakes. *"I do it to bring joy to others."* That same intention runs through her leadership in her thoughtful, calm, and quietly powerful approach.

These profiles serve as living examples that success doesn't follow a formula; it follows alignment. Their stories will accompany us throughout the book as we examine how to live and perform successfully and in balance.

Chapter 2
The Power Of Purpose And Balance

Having explored the three critical paradigms underpinning sustainable success, we now turn to how these interact with your ultimate destination. This synergy between journey and destination becomes the foundation for meaningful achievement, where high performance doesn't happen in a moment, but becomes a way of living.

Achieving success requires us to embrace two essential truths:

1. The indispensable role of a clear and compelling destination (we're all familiar with the saying 'how can you reach a goal if you don't know where you're headed?').
2. The importance of maintaining balance across our three core paradigms while in pursuit of success.

PURPOSE: Your Vision Of Success, Your North Star

Your vision of success, your 'North Star', is more than a motivational slogan, when strategically aligned with your purpose it becomes your internal compass, a personal destination that shapes how you make decisions, focus your energy, and maintain momentum. It doesn't have to be dramatic or world-changing (though it might be). What matters is that it's deeply meaningful to you. Something you 'own'.

One of the clearest examples of purpose I've encountered came from Floyd Woodrow. At the age of 12, he set his sights on joining the Parachute Regiment. He didn't fully understand why at the time, he just felt drawn to it. What he followed was what he calls his Super North Star, an intuitive, non-linear pull that aligned with his values, goals, and sense of meaning. He didn't have a rigid plan he just trusted the direction of travel. For many high performers, purpose isn't always rationalised from the start. It's felt. It's often tested over time too. The key is to listen to what consistently draws your attention and make space for that instinct to inform your choices.

Floyd expresses this now through his Compass for Life model and his concept of the Super North Star, a clearly defined purpose that acts as both compass and catalyst. From his military and leadership experience, Floyd reinforces what science now confirms, our goals don't just give us direction, they shape how we think and behave and therefore the choices we make and the path we follow.

Neuroscience supports this. Setting meaningful goals activates areas of the brain involved in motivation and executive control, particularly the prefrontal cortex and the mesolimbic dopamine system, regions critical for planning, attention, and drive. Clear goals help to keep you on track and improve how your brain functions. Goal clarity, it turns out, enhances both motivation and cognitive performance.

Yet, this isn't just about brain scans and productivity hacks. Humans are naturally wired for goal-directed behaviour. Goals help us prioritise and take ownership, without them, we're more likely to drift, or default to the expectations of others.

But there's a catch. When goals become too narrow, when we chase one outcome at the expense of everything else, we risk developing tunnel vision. We miss the wider picture, often shown through fluctuations in our health, relationships, or our sense of purpose. That's why your North Star must be multidimensional and balanced across all paradigms, not just a single, siloed goal.

This book won't offer a one-size-fits-all goal-setting worksheet. Instead, it invites you to define a vision that spans work, wealth and wellbeing. A holistic approach, so you don't achieve one thing at the cost of everything else.

Later, we'll explore how fear, of both failure and success, can distort what we believe we're 'allowed' to want. Many people hide or downplay ambitions to avoid judgement or disappointment. I've done it too.

So, here's your invitation:

Define ambition on your own terms. Whether bold and visible or quiet and personal, what matters is that your direction is authentic and strategically aligned.

Floyd Woodrow calls this your Super North Star, a guiding purpose that fuels action, provides clarity in chaos and evolves as you grow. His military and business achievements weren't the result of a rigid plan, but a journey led by clarity and adaptability. As he puts it, *"Everything we do toward a goal teaches us something. Even if we pivot, it isn't wasted. There's no failure, only feedback."*

For Ali Oliver, purpose has always been her anchor. Her path wasn't defined by long-term goals but by recognising when a mission resonated. *"I've never had a fixed plan,"* she says. *"But I've always known when I've heard something worth chasing."* That deep resonance became her compass in charity leadership. In ambiguity and change, her purpose acts as a decision filter. Her mantra, *"Work hard, make yourself useful and seize opportunities,"* reflects a grounded, purposeful approach that has sustained her through complexity without needing a rigid map.

Adam Burgess mirrors this in elite sport. *"At the start gate, I'm not trying to decide. I've already decided. I'm just trusting my system."* His clarity of purpose allows him to enter high-pressure moments with composure and flow. He's already made the critical decisions in training, on race day, he lets them unfold. This alignment between purpose and process drives performance and calm under pressure.

Anne-Sophie's experience reflects another vital dimension of purposeful action, through trusting others to help shape a vision when it isn't immediately clear. Her journey hasn't followed a perfectly linear path, there have been moments of uncertainty where the goal felt out of reach or undefined. Rather than force progressive decisions prematurely, she allowed enjoyment and challenge to guide her forward and invited others into the process. Through conversation, collaboration and staying open to feedback, she shaped a purpose that felt right. Her North Star wasn't forged in isolation, but through curiosity and trust. That trust, in herself and others, has allowed her vision to evolve with confidence.

Your North Star becomes your 'why', your fuel when energy dips, your anchor in uncertainty and your filter when making hard choices. Having purpose is powerful, its where sustainable success begins.

BALANCE: Calibration Is Key

Sustainable success begins with clarity, not a vague wish, but a vivid, strategic, and balanced vision. This is where the **Defining Your North Star** and **WHY-Mapping** exercises come in. They are active frameworks for translating intention into real-world impact. You can complete them on your own or involve trusted voices to focus your direction.

You'll find the full versions of both exercises and templates at the end of this chapter. What follows here is a brief overview of each exercise to help you understand their position, purpose, and power.

- **Exercise 1. Defining Your North Star: Calibration Exercise**

A strategic visualisation and planning tool that turns aspiration into architecture.

You'll map out a vivid five-year vision across the three Calibration Paradigms of Money-Mission, Mental-Physical and Work-Life. The exercise guides you to:
- Define personal markers of success.
- Anticipate barriers and balance breakers.
- Create a roadmap grounded in both ambition and sustainability.

The result? A practical blueprint for a life and career that stretch and inspire you, without tipping you into overload.

– **Exercise 2. WHY-Mapping** WHY?

Inspired by the original 5 Whys method developed by Sakichi Toyoda, this adapted version goes beyond analysis to fuel action.

Through a structured dive into your emotional drivers, you'll:
– Uncover the real reasons your goals matter.
– Identify imbalances in your motivation.
– Reconnect with a purpose that fuels progress, even when pressure builds.

This is your resilience-in-action tool. It makes your goals matter and stick.

Introducing The Calibration Model

Defining your North Star provides direction. Staying on course, however, calls for something more. It takes balance, connection, and continuous calibration to sustain the path toward it.

Most success models offer expertise in isolation, productivity here, financial planning there, but rarely account for the full human system you're managing. They may help you master specific skills, from personal efficiency to strategic leadership, yet often ignore how these parts interact or conflict in real life.

Fitness programmes might help you improve your physical health whilst overlooking the pressures of raising a family. Career advancement models can lead to the boardroom but neglect the impact on mental wellbeing. Financial systems may build wealth yet miss fulfilment and purpose. Success in one domain can all too easily come at the cost of another.

This is the very gap the Calibration Model is designed to close.

Why Calibration?

The Calibration Model recognises that sustainable success comes from integration across all areas, rather than intensity in just one. It provides a dynamic framework that helps you:
– Balance professional, personal and mission-driven goals.
– Stay alert to hidden trade-offs.
– Adapt intentionally when your priorities shift.

If you push for impact without making space for recovery, your resilience suffers. If you win professionally but lose your health, joy, or connection, what kind of success is that? There's no perfect symmetry, what matters is knowing what balance looks and feels like for you, and how to adjust as your life and professional roles evolve.

Visual Frameworks For Sustainable Success

The Calibration Model brings together six interconnected life segments across the three crucial paradigms:

Money
Evaluate and improve
financial stability

Work
Analyse and enhance
job fulfilment

Mental Health
Focus on improving
mental health

Physical Health
Work on maintaining
physical fitness

Life
Strive for a balanced
and fulfilling life

Mission
Connect actions with
personal mission

Money, Mission, Mental, Physical, Work and Life are not isolated parts of your identity, they're fluid systems. When one is overextended or undernourished, the others respond. You'll learn to track this interdependence and recognise when it's time to recalibrate.

The Calibration Tools: Inner Capabilities For Outer Balance

To stay aligned across these six segments, you need strong inner capability. That's where the three Calibration Tools come in, the drivers that help you stay grounded, adaptable, and clear-headed when life gets complex:
- **Emotional Intelligence (EQ):** Your ability to recognise, regulate and use emotion constructively, in yourself and with others.
- **Skilled Communication:** The ability to express clearly, influence effectively and connect meaningfully across roles and relationships.
- **The Resilience Advantage:** Your capacity to recover quickly, adapt under pressure and sustain performance over time.

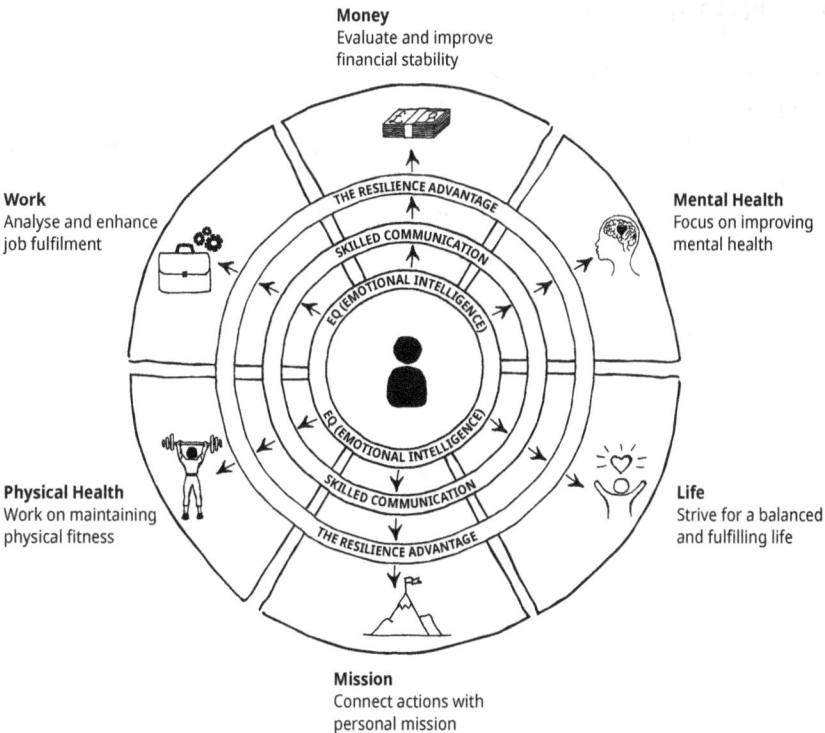

Money
Evaluate and improve financial stability

Work
Analyse and enhance job fulfilment

Mental Health
Focus on improving mental health

THE RESILIENCE ADVANTAGE
SKILLED COMMUNICATION
EQ (EMOTIONAL INTELLIGENCE)
EQ (EMOTIONAL INTELLIGENCE)
SKILLED COMMUNICATION
THE RESILIENCE ADVANTAGE

Physical Health
Work on maintaining physical fitness

Life
Strive for a balanced and fulfilling life

Mission
Connect actions with personal mission

These aren't soft skills. They're stability anchors. Without them, balance breaks. With them, you're equipped to lead not just a full and successful life, but one that's worth sustaining.

Leading Into Action

Now it's time to shift gear, from insight to action and from reflection to deliberate practice. Begin your journey with the two guided exercises at the end of this chapter:

– **Exercise 1: Defining Your North Star** to create a vivid, multi-dimensional five-year vision.
– **Exercise 2: WHY-Mapping** to connect that vision to deep personal purpose.

These tools are your foundation for applying the Calibration Model. Use them now and return to them whenever your clarity wavers or your environment changes.

Coming Up: Sharpening Your Tools

Next, we'll explore the Calibration Tools in depth, first Emotional Intelligence, followed by Skilled Communication and The Resilience Advantage. These are the capabilities that allow you to regulate pressure, lead with clarity and adapt sustainably over time.

This is where success becomes lived experience.

Implementation Exercises For Chapter 2

– **Exercise 1: Defining Your North Star**
– **Exercise 2: WHY-Mapping** (ideally complete within 48 hours of exercise 1)

Defining Your North Star

INTRODUCTION TO THE EXERCISE
Your North Star is the destination that illuminates your path, fuels your actions, and gives meaning to your progress.

This exercise is designed to help you shape a vivid five-year vision of success, one that's both aspirational and actionable. You'll also clarify the milestones that will mark your journey along the way, and reflect on how your vision aligns with what matters most to you.

These shorter milestones act as markers of success, offering opportunities to celebrate and reaffirm your progress. You'll also explore how this vision fits into a broader context, recognising that this is just one of many possible destinations in your life's journey.

For now, focus deeply on making this destination meaningful to you. The aim is to activate both emotional and cognitive commitment, the inner focus that drives consistent, purpose-led action.

Part 1: Vision Crystallisation

Suggested Time: 30 Minutes

1. **Future Success Visualisation**
   – Find a quiet space where you can focus without distractions.
   – Close your eyes and project yourself five years into the future, visualising the success you plan to achieve.
   – Visualise a day where everything aligns, where you feel successful, purposeful, and balanced.
2. **Vision Mapping Across Paradigms**
   Write detailed responses for each paradigm:
   a) **Money-Mission**
      1. What financial achievements will define this success for you?
      2. How are you creating meaningful impact?
   b) **Mental-Physical**
      3. What mental state characterises your success?
      4. How does your peak health feel?
   c) **Work-Life**
      5. What does your ideal day look like?
      6. Who shares in your success?

Part 2: Mapping Markers Of Success

Suggested Time:
20 Minutes

Now that you've envisioned your destination, let's translate that into measurable steps. These are your calibration points, indicators that keep you aligned.

1. **Markers Of Success**
   - **For Each Paradigm (Money-Mission, Mental-Physical, Work-Life), Identify:**
     - What must you achieve to reach your vision?
     - What are the shorter milestones along the way?
     - How will you know you're on the right track?

   Here are a few milestone examples to guide your thinking:
   - **A Financial Milestone** (e.g., reaching a specific income or funding goal within 2 years).
   - **A Health Improvement Milestone** (e.g., being able to run 10k or reducing stress).
   - **A Work-Life Balance Milestone** (e.g., committing to regular family time or vacations).

2. **Celebration And Recognition**
   - **For Each Milestone, Decide:**
     - How will you celebrate this achievement?
     - What will you do to recognise yourself and others involved in the success?
   - **For Your North Star Destination:** Plan a special celebration or event to honour your hard work and commitment.

Part 3: North Star Alignment

Suggested Time:
10 Minutes

1. **Congruence Check**
   Use the checklist below to assess how strongly your vision aligns with your values and energy. Rate each statement from 1 (strongly disagree) to 5 (strongly agree).
   - This vision energises me.
   - The goals stretch yet inspire me.
   - Success includes meaningful impact.
   - The vision balances all paradigms.
   - I can clearly articulate why this matters to me.

2. **Impact Analysis**
   Purposeful goals often create ripple effects. Let's explore the broader impact of what you're working toward.
   For Each Major Goal, Answer:
   - Who benefits besides me?
   - What broader impact does it create?
   - How does it align with my values?

Part 4: From Vision To Execution: Planning Your Milestones

Suggested Time:
20 Minutes

1. **Milestone Mapping**
   Create a timeline for achieving your vision:
   - 90-day action steps.
   - 1-year milestones.
   - 3-year achievements.
   - 5-year vision realisation.

2. **Balance Integration**
   For each milestone, reflect on how to maintain balance across your life domains. Consider time, energy, health, and support. For each milestone, identify:
   - Required resources.
   - Potential challenges.
   - Support needed.
   - Balance maintenance strategies.

Part 5: Broader Vision Reflection

Suggested Time:
15 Minutes

1. **Recognising The Bigger Picture**
   - Reflect on how this vision is one of many potential destinations in your life.
   - Consider that there may be other, longer-term goals that stretch beyond five years.

2. **Why This Vision, Now?**
   - Write a short paragraph on why this particular destination is the most important to you right now.
   - How does it energise and inspire you to take action?

3. **Commitment**
   - Describe how focusing on this vision will spark your motivation and guide your decision-making.
   - Write a short commitment statement to reinforce your intent. For example:
     "I commit to pursuing this vision because it reflects what matters most to me right now [insert reason]."

You're on your way!

By defining your North Star and identifying the milestones that lead to it, you've created both a compelling vision and a practical roadmap. Along the way, don't forget to celebrate your successes, recognise your progress, and recalibrate as needed.

Your North Star isn't fixed. It evolves as you grow. Today though, it gives you direction, a purpose-driven map for the next stretch of your journey.

Need inspiration or extra support? Scan the QR code or visit www.balancing-act.co.uk to access completed examples, downloadable templates and additional guidance to help you bring your North Star to life.

WHY-Mapping: Motivation in Motion

Reframing The Power Of WHY: From Problem-Solving To Purpose-Finding

INNOVATION INSIGHT

While Toyota's famous 5 Whys model has been used globally for decades to investigate problems, I've reimagined this powerful technique into something equally transformative, a proactive tool for purpose discovery and sustained motivation.

The original model, developed by Sakichi Toyoda in the 1930s, became foundational to Lean Thinking and Six Sigma methodology, asking *"Why?"* five times to reach the root cause of a problem.

WHY-Mapping Inverts That Logic.

Instead of looking backwards to uncover what went wrong, it looks forward strengthening what's right. It helps you:
- Discover your deeper motivations.
- Strengthen commitment to your vision.
- Ensure balanced energy allocation.
- Maintain forward momentum.

Where the original fixed what's broken, this version fuels what moves you.

INTRODUCTION TO THE EXERCISE

Suggested Time:
15 Minutes

Knowing your destination is powerful, but it's your WHY that keeps you moving. WHY-Mapping is a calibration tool designed to strengthen your emotional connection to your goals and sustain your motivation over time.

Use It To:
- Validate your direction.
- Strengthen and reconnect with your purpose when motivation dips.
- Spot imbalance across life paradigms.
- Recalibrate energy and commitment as needed.

HOW TO MAP YOUR WHY

1. Place your North Star vision in the centre of a blank page.
2. Draw 3–5 major goal branches radiating outward. Use the three paradigms to guide you (Money-Mission, Mental-Physical, Work-Life).
3. For each goal branch, ask:
   - *"Why is this important to me?"*
   - Then take that answer and ask *"Why?"* again.
   - Continue until you've asked *"Why?"* five times.
4. Circle the answers that resonate most deeply.
5. Reflect on your answers:
   - Does this WHY genuinely energise you?
   - Will it help you stay committed and balanced?
   - If not, what needs to change? your goal, your approach, or your allocation of time and energy?

RECOMMENDED

CALIBRATION TIP: Use colour-coding for each paradigm (e.g. gold = Money-Mission, Blue = Mental-Physical, green = Work-Life). This will help you spot imbalance or over-concentration.

IMPLEMENTATION SCHEDULE:

- Initial use: Right after defining your North Star.
- Monthly check-ins: Use for reflection and course correction.
- Quarterly reviews: Ensure ongoing strategic alignment.
- During major transitions: Career shifts, personal life changes, burnout, or recalibration periods.

INSIGHT

This five-layer questioning method activates deeper motivation centres in the brain, strengthening the link between daily action and core purpose. The more you revisit your WHY, the stronger the neural connections and the easier it becomes to stay aligned and engaged.

————

Section Two: **The Art Of Integrated Performance –
The Three Essential Tools
Of Calibration**

Sustainable success requires more than technical skill or ambition, it calls for the ability to stay grounded, connected, and adaptable in the face of ongoing demands. Over years of working with high-performing professionals and drawing on evidence-based practice, I've identified three essential calibration tools that underpin effective leadership and integrated performance:

1. **Emotional Intelligence:** The foundation for self-awareness, relational effectiveness, and calm, considered decision-making.
2. **Skilled Communication:** The bridge to clarity, influence, and meaningful connection across all areas of life and leadership.
3. **The Resilience Advantage:** The capacity to respond under pressure and consistently positively engage.

These tools work in combination, helping you calibrate how you think, communicate and respond, especially under pressure. Together, they support alignment between what you aim for and how you operate, linking your values to your actions and your energy to your impact.

As we move into this next section, you'll notice a slight shift in tone. We'll be drawing more directly from the research, theory, and science behind these tools, not to overload but to deepen your understanding. This part of the book is designed to equip you with evidence-based insights that reinforce the strategies and exercises we've already explored, giving you both the why and the how behind integrated performance.

In the chapters that follow, we'll begin with Emotional Intelligence, often described as the 'hidden architecture' of success. Then we'll turn to Skilled Communication, where insight meets influence. Finally, we'll explore The Resilience Advantage, not just the ability to bounce back, but to stay well and lead well under load.

Together, these tools form the internal infrastructure of integrated performance, supporting how you lead and live and how you move forward toward what matters.

Chapter 3
Emotional Intelligence – The Hidden Architecture Of Success

Picture two professionals standing at the same career crossroads. Both graduated from respected universities with the same expertise, impressive degrees, outstanding references, and high level technical skills. Yet their professional trajectories couldn't be more different.

Person A rapidly ascends through their organisation, leading complex global projects, managing challenging team dynamics with ease and consistently delivering exceptional results. Their ability to develop strong relationships has earned them a reputation for being highly trusted and respected. Colleagues frequently refer to them as a go-to leader, known for their approachability and collaboration across departments.

In contrast, Person B, despite technical brilliance, struggles to gain traction, finding themselves repeatedly overlooked for promotions and facing interpersonal challenges that hinder their visibility and the trust needed to progress.

The critical difference? **Emotional Intelligence.**

I have witnessed this scenario play out countless times. Technical skills are the price of entry, however emotional intelligence is the key that unlocks extraordinary professional success.

We know we need it, we know we can develop it, but exactly what is 'emotional intelligence'?

Defining Emotional Intelligence

Emotional intelligence is the hidden superpower of high-performing professionals, a complex capability that shapes how we approach, interpret, and respond to challenges, connect with others and lead under pressure. At its core, emotional intelligence is the ability to recognise, understand, manage, and effectively use emotions, both our own and those of others.

Viktor E. Frankl captures its essence perfectly:

"Between stimulus and response there is a space. In that space is our power to choose our response. In our response lies our growth and our freedom."

Emotional intelligence reminds us that we have choice for all of our responses and reactions.

The Language Of Emotional Intelligence

You may have heard people use 'EI' and 'EQ' interchangeably? If so, that's perfectly fine. However, to clear up any confusion, it's helpful to understand the subtle difference:

- **EI (Emotional Intelligence):** The broader concept describing our emotional capabilities.
- **EQ (Emotional Quotient):** The specific measure of these capabilities, much like how IQ measures cognitive intelligence.

Think of it like this, EI is the skill set and EQ is how we measure that skill set. Just as you can improve your physical fitness, you can develop and enhance your emotional intelligence.

Emotional Intelligence And The Brain: A Unified Framework

Recent neuroscience has revolutionised our understanding of emotional intelligence, moving it from an abstract concept to a tangible set of brain-based capabilities. Rather than thinking of different emotional functions in isolation, we now understand emotional intelligence as a highly integrated process, involving perception, processing, regulation and response.

To help make this more relatable, think of your brain as a high-performing team or organisation. Each region has a role to play, like departments in a business or players in a sports team. Emotional intelligence acts as the head coach or strategic lead, ensuring all parts work together seamlessly.

Let's explore how this works:

Emotional Intelligence In Action: Your Brain As A Team

- **Perceive** (Reading emotional cues): Your fusiform gyrus and superior temporal sulcus act like your scanning and reception department, constantly reading faces, tone, and body language, helping you notice subtle emotional signals that others might miss.

- **Process** (Making sense of emotion): The ventromedial and dorsolateral prefrontal cortex are your analytical and strategy teams. They integrate emotional data with logic, creating 'emotionally enhanced thinking', judgment that's enriched, not impaired, by emotion.
- **Regulate** (Managing emotional response): The anterior cingulate cortex and prefrontal regions act like your HR and governance team, helping you pause, weigh options, and choose the best course of action, especially under pressure.
- **Connect** (Relating to others effectively): The insula and mirror neuron systems function like your culture and relationships department, helping you feel what others feel, manage social dynamics well and build trust through emotional resonance.

This integrated leadership system enables exceptional professionals not just to experience emotion, but to use it as strategic data, enhancing self-regulation, building trust, and informing better decisions.

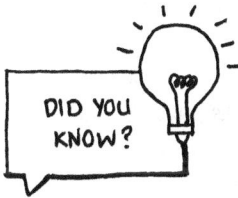

DID YOU KNOW?

Research suggests that leaders with highly developed emotional intelligence demonstrate stronger neural connectivity between emotion and decision-making centres, more efficient emotion regulation pathways and better integration of emotional and cognitive processing.

Perhaps the most exciting discovery in modern neuroscience is that emotional intelligence, unlike IQ, isn't fixed, it's highly malleable. Through what neuroscientists call neuroplasticity, your brain can literally rewire itself to enhance emotional intelligence capabilities.

Understanding this has reshaped how we approach leadership development. We no longer treat emotional intelligence as a vague soft skill, but something we can deliberately train and strengthen through repeatable, targeted practices that reshape the brain's emotional architecture.

Building Leadership-Ready Neural Networks

There are two primary mechanisms that drive emotional intelligence development:

- **Structural Enhancement** (like strength training for your brain): Targeted emotional intelligence practices reinforce neural pathways in key brain regions, building emotional processing highways that make responses quicker and more effective.
- **Functional Optimisation** (like musical improvisation): Through consistent practice, the brain fine-tunes how it processes emotion, making responses more fluid, contextual and adaptive in real time.

Consider Clare, a senior leader in financial investment. Despite her technical expertise, she struggled with composure during high-pressure presentations. Her amygdala, the brain's emotional early-warning system, was triggering an oversized stress response, undermining her performance. Through targeted coaching, Clare created her 'reset process', a structured breathing and reflection routine that activated her parasympathetic nervous system. By applying this technique regularly, she not only improved her delivery but also reconnected with her enjoyment of public speaking.

During our interview, Olympic canoeist Adam Burgess explained that his ability to regulate emotion wasn't just about mental toughness, it was physical, emotional, and cognitive. *"Breath became my reset. When I learned how to recognise early signals and downregulate, everything changed."* This insight reflects how elite individuals can use embodied emotional awareness to maintain peak performance.

Dr. John Sullivan adds that *"Breath is one of the few systems we can consciously control that directly influences both psychological and physiological state."* In high-performance environments, breath becomes a frontline tool for managing stress and stabilising decision-making under pressure.

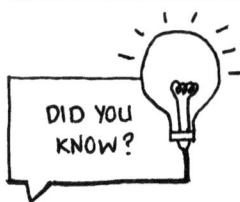

DID YOU KNOW?

Leaders who develop emotional regulation capacity demonstrate better stress management in crisis situations, more effective stakeholder relationships and stronger team engagement scores.

Enhancing Social Intelligence: Strengthening The Brain's 'Social WIFI'

Emotional intelligence isn't just about understanding yourself, it's also the foundation for connecting with and influencing others. This capacity is supported by neural systems responsible for empathy, trust-building and relational awareness.

One key system here is the mirror neuron network, which helps us perceive and synchronise with others' emotional states. The more we consciously engage in emotional perspective-taking, the more finely tuned this system becomes. Think of it as upgrading your brain's social Wi-Fi for a faster, clearer, and more accurate emotional connection. Like boosting bandwidth for human connection.

Structured practices such as active listening and deliberate reflection enhance this system's efficiency, creating more responsive, trustworthy leadership. These advancements offer a clear, evidence-backed roadmap to building the emotional agility, composure and connection that define high-impact leadership.

INSIGHT

Structured emotional intelligence practice has shown to lead to improved neural efficiency in emotion regulation, increased social signal processing capacity and stronger integration between emotion and cognition.

Social intelligence is often about reading between the lines, what's unsaid, unseen, or underestimated. It's about meeting people where they are, not where you expect them to be.

I've seen this from both sides.

I remember going to buy a car recently, not a cheap one either. I'd already done all the research online and knew the exact model, colour, and spec I wanted. But I turned up deliberately dressed for comfort, more gym-ready than purchase-ready.

I walked around the vehicle of the model I'd come to see, clearly interested, clearly focused. Yet, for 37 minutes, no one approached me. A few staff looked over from their desks, but no one got up. I wasn't asked if I needed help, despite being the only person seriously engaging with a particular car. When someone eventually did speak to me, the interaction was casual, pleasant but low energy. I stayed for nearly two hours before we finalised the paperwork so I could buy the car, rushed in the end due to the time it had taken to move to contract.

A few days later, I returned to collect the car, this time in my 'going out for dinner' clothes (I genuinely was going out for dinner after). I was greeted within 10 minutes, not by someone who knew my name, or because they knew I was there to collect, but simply (and I'm assuming here) because of how I looked. Same me, but entirely different treatment. It was a quiet but powerful reminder that many judgments happen before a word is spoken.

When I first entered leadership, I was told that how you present yourself affects how others treat you. One of my early bosses was so fixed on appearance that he judged people by the pattern of their socks. Ties had to be done up to the top and straight. You wouldn't get away with that now in most sectors, and thank goodness we've moved on. My husband, for example, delights in defying the boring sock norm. But the principle still lingers in different forms. These biases still exist. It takes social intelligence to see beyond them and not replicate them.

I once met the director of a racecourse, laid-back, informal, and wonderfully approachable. I'd invited him to guest speak for students. Many relaxed around him so much that one even referred to him as 'his mate'. It didn't go down particularly well, but it showed the power of presence and presentation in shaping perceptions and boundaries.

At the other end of the spectrum, I've interviewed and worked with some of the most prestigious Michelin-starred directors and head chefs in the world. One of the most memorable is Diego Masciaga, a legendary figure in international hospitality. Diego spent over 30 years managing The Waterside Inn, the first restaurant outside France to hold three Michelin stars for 40 consecutive years, an unbroken record that remains a symbol of excellence in service and cuisine. During that time, he welcomed royalty, heads of state, celebrities, and global leaders, earning his own accolades along the way, including the Cavaliere Ordine al Merito della Repubblica Italiana (the Italian equivalent of a knighthood) and the Grand Prix de l'Art de la Salle.

Diego once told me a story that has always stayed with me. A guest arrived at The Waterside Inn wearing torn jeans and a very casual top, a stark contrast to the restaurant's elegant setting and subtle dress code. Rather than make assumptions or respond with discomfort, Diego quietly asked the team to check the guest's name. It turned out they were a figure of great international influence and regard. Had the team judged solely by appearance, they could have made a serious misstep.

That moment wasn't luck, it was leadership through social intelligence. Diego has mastered the ability to meet people at their level, whoever they are, wherever they come from. During the times we met, he told me how he used to rise early each day to read the news, so he could connect with guests from any background on their terms. He never talked up or down, always at or just below the level of alignment. That ability to tune in, to create comfort without hierarchy, is what makes him exceptional.

These lessons aren't limited to fine dining. They apply to boardrooms, coaching rooms, classrooms, and dealerships. Social intelligence means staying aware of context while refusing to default to assumption. It means being curious enough to discover who someone really is before you decide how to treat them.

As a coach and trainer, I bring that same mindset into every session. Of course, a lot can be planned, frameworks, exercises, objectives, but the ability to flex is just as important. Real impact comes from tuning in to individual needs, the energy in the room and the topics that matter most on the day. I never assume I know where we'll begin. I meet the person, or the team, who walks in the door or logs in online that day, not the version I spoke to last week.

Social intelligence means staying curious, staying present and staying open. It's about being ready to adapt, to listen before leading and to engage without assumption. In fast-paced, high-pressure environments, that ability to respond in real time is not a soft skill, it's a strategic one.

Turning Science Into Strategy

Understanding the neuroscience behind emotional intelligence is just the first step. To apply this knowledge in real leadership settings, we need frameworks that translate theory into meaningful action.

Among the many models that have emerged, Daniel Goleman's is arguably the most widely recognised and practically applicable. His research connects emotional intelligence with measurable leadership performance, drawing from longitudinal studies across more than 500 global organisations. Goleman's findings are striking. Emotional intelligence accounts for up to 90% of what distinguishes exceptional leaders from their peers, while technical skills often serve as baseline requirements. At the heart of Goleman's model are five interconnected domains that underpin leadership effectiveness and sustainable high performance.

Let's take a look at this model:

The Five Domains Of Goleman's Emotional Intelligence Model

1. **Self-Awareness:** This is your internal compass. It involves recognising your emotions, strengths, limitations, values, and motivations. Neuroscientifically, it engages the insula and anterior cingulate cortex. High self-awareness leads to stronger decisions and more authentic team relationships.
2. **Self-Regulation:** Respond, don't react. Building on self-awareness, self-regulation is the ability to manage emotional responses, especially under pressure. It involves activating the prefrontal cortex, enabling what neuroscientists describe as emotional brake patterns, moments of conscious pause

between stimulus and response. This skill is foundational to composure, particularly in high-pressure environments. Leaders with strong self-regulation often perform at their best in times of crisis or rapid change. They remain steady when others stall and adaptable when the path ahead shifts.

The lesson here is around feeling and moving. Before a major selection race, Olympic canoeist Adam Burgess found himself sitting still, but with his heart racing. *"It was crazy,"* he said. *"I wasn't even moving."* Instead of trying to suppress the stress, Adam recognised the mismatch between his physical state and his environment. *"I just needed to move,"* he said. *"I left the session and went for a walk."* By tuning in and taking physical action, he closed the loop on stress, rather than letting it linger. Sometimes, regulation doesn't mean calming down, it means responding with intention, not reaction.

3. **Motivation:** This domain taps into internal drive, the energy to pursue goals beyond external rewards. It activates the brain's dopaminergic and prefrontal systems, creating alignment between purpose and persistence. Motivation fuels sustainable achievement without burnout and that motivation often begins with emotional connection. As Ali Oliver, puts it: *"People just need to feel valued, inspired, have a sense of purpose and they'll do extraordinary things."* When leaders understand what really drives those around them, not just performance metrics, but emotional resonance, they create commitment, a force which is far more powerful than compliance. The result is sustained effort anchored in meaning, not pressure. Motivation, in this way, becomes less about pushing and more about connecting people to purpose.

4. **Empathy:** Empathy involves understanding others' perspectives and emotions. It's more than kindness, it's strategy. Mirror neurons and mentalising networks support this capacity, which is critical for inclusive leadership and global team dynamics.

5. **Social Skills:** This final domain brings all others together. It shapes how leaders influence, connect and collaborate. Through the activation of social cognition networks, it supports trust-building within teams and alignment across stakeholders and cultures.

These five domains don't work in silos. The power lies in integration.

Consider Catherine, a senior leader in education navigating a major organisational transformation. Her self-awareness revealed how her own anxiety could affect team morale. With self-regulation, she remained calm and clear. Her empathy helped her understand resistance and her social skills enabled her to build the alliances that made the change possible. Motivation kept her and her team focused on the bigger mission.

Together, these five domains build emotional agility, the capacity to stay grounded and responsive, even in moments of pressure or change.

As former SAS officer Floyd Woodrow explains, *"In special operations, it wasn't the toughest people who thrived. It was the ones who could stay emotionally agile . . . we trained for that deliberately."* This emotional duality, he notes, is what makes the difference in moments that matter.

EQ For High Performance

Recent research confirms that emotional intelligence is not a fixed trait, it's a dynamic capability. Goleman's five domains can be developed intentionally through a cycle of Awareness, Practice, and Integration:
- **Awareness:** Recognising your own emotional triggers and patterns and how they influence decisions and relationships.
- **Practice:** Applying strategies that reshape neural pathways, such as regulation techniques, active listening, or empathy mapping.
- **Integration:** Embedding these behaviours consistently into daily leadership practice, until they become instinctive.

This is where the science meets strategy. Neuroscience shows that targeted emotional intelligence development rewires the brain for better stress regulation, emotional processing and relational acuity. Leaders who invest in this development see measurable improvement in three critical areas:
1. **Decision-Making:** Emotional-cognitive integration enables leaders to think with both logic and empathy, enhancing judgment under pressure.
2. **Relationship Management:** By reading emotional signals and adjusting their approach, emotionally intelligent leaders foster stronger trust, collaboration and influence.
3. **Organisational Culture:** High-EQ leaders create cultures of psychological safety, where people feel seen, heard and valued, unlocking a higher level of performance and innovation.

Emotional intelligence transforms reactivity into presence and pressure into performance.

Rather than viewing emotions as obstacles to be overcome, this model shows how properly managed emotions become catalysts for high performance. The key lies in the achievement of emotional-cognitive integration, the sophisticated interplay between emotional awareness and rational thinking that characterises peak professional performance.

This integration manifests particularly clearly in high-pressure situations. Leaders with developed emotional intelligence maintain pressure equilibrium, the ability to stay 'balanced' and effective even under intense stress. This capability emerges from the interaction of all five domains. Self-awareness monitors stress levels, self-regulation manages responses, motivation maintains focus, empathy guides team support and social skills enable effective communication.

Dr. Sullivan adds nuance to this by introducing the concept of attention oscillation. In high-pressure moments, knowing when to zoom in (associate) or zoom out (dissociate) is critical. *"Even elite athletes don't stay locked in 100% of the time,"* he says. *"Our brain needs moments of deliberate disconnection to manage energy and emotion effectively."* Leaders can adopt the same strategy to sustain performance under load.

Measuring And Developing EQ: The Power Of EQ-i 2.0

To improve what you can't yet see, you need the right lens. That's where tools like the EQ-i 2.0 assessment come in. Based on decades of validated research, it translates emotional intelligence from theory into tangible insight.

I've worked with many different profiling tools over the years, and I've found the EQ-i 2.0 to be particularly powerful. Think of it as a high-resolution scan of your emotional performance landscape, highlighting your current strengths and development priorities.

What sets this tool apart is its ability to reflect the full multidimensional nature of emotional intelligence, while also offering clear and actionable development paths. This makes it ideal not just for self-awareness, but for strategic growth and performance calibration at all levels of leadership.

How the EQ-i 2.0 Works

The model organises emotional intelligence into five composite areas, each underpinned by three core competencies. Together, they form an interconnected system of 15 skills, offering a personalised profile of how you engage with yourself, others, and challenges.

1. **Self-Perception:** Your internal lens, how well you know, accept, and develop yourself.
   - Self-Regard: Your ability to see and accept your strengths and limitations.
   - Self-Actualisation: Your drive to pursue meaningful goals and realise potential.

- Emotional Self-Awareness: Your capacity to recognise and understand your own emotions.
2. **Self-Expression:** Your external projection, how authentically and assertively you communicate.
   - Emotional Expression: How effectively you express feelings in a constructive way.
   - Assertiveness: Your ability to communicate opinions, needs and boundaries respectfully.
   - Independence: Your capacity to act autonomously, while staying emotionally grounded.
3. **Interpersonal:** Your relational toolkit, how you build trust, demonstrate empathy, and collaborate.
   - Interpersonal Relationships: The depth and quality of your connections with others.
   - Empathy: The ability to understand and relate to others' perspectives and emotions.
   - Social Responsibility: Your orientation toward collaboration, contribution, and community.
4. **Decision Making:** Your cognitive-emotional integration, how you process information under pressure.
   - Problem Solving: Using emotional data to make effective decisions.
   - Reality Testing: Staying objective and grounded, especially when emotions are high.
   - Impulse Control: Managing emotional impulses to respond rather than react.
5. **Stress Management:** Your resilience architecture, how well you adapt and sustain performance.
   - Flexibility: Your ability to adjust thoughts, behaviours, and emotions in real time.
   - Stress Tolerance: Your capacity to stay calm and effective in demanding situations.
   - Optimism: Your ability to maintain a constructive mindset, even during setbacks.

Each component is assessed on a continuum, meaning there's no pass or fail, only insight into how well-developed (or over-relied upon) a capability might be. It creates developmental readiness, helping individuals see not just how they're perceived, but how they operate under pressure, in relationships and in complex environments. This makes it particularly useful during career transitions, organisational change, team realignment and role expansion.

One executive I worked with shared how their EQ-i 2.0 results revealed an unexpected disconnect. They scored highly on empathy, yet significantly lower on emotional expression. As they reflected, they noted: *"I cared deeply about my team, but I wasn't showing it. I assumed they knew, but in reality, they couldn't."* By focusing their development on expressing emotion, they transformed how they connected across their teams and wider business. The shift was tangible, feedback improved, trust deepened and collaboration flourished.

In high-performance environments, technical competence is rarely the limiting factor. It's emotional undercurrents, miscommunication, unmanaged stress and unmet needs that derail progress. Emotional intelligence gives leaders the internal tools to stay calibrated, connected and clear. The EQ-i 2.0 provides the scaffolding for that development, a structured, evidence-based personal roadmap that moves emotional intelligence from something abstract into something measurable and trainable.

This is what it means to calibrate emotional intelligence, to surface blind spots, strengthen capability and sustain performance.

If you'd like to find out more about emotional intelligence profiling, or to request one for yourself or your team, you'll be able to find further information at: www.balancing-act.co.uk

The Bridge To Enhanced Communication And Resilience

As we transition into the next chapters on communication and resilience, one thing becomes clear, emotional intelligence is not just relevant, it's foundational. The capabilities of skilled communication and resilience don't sit on top of emotional intelligence, they grow out of it.

Research consistently shows that leaders with high emotional intelligence communicate more effectively across all channels, from one-to-one conversations to high-pressure boardroom settings. This isn't coincidental, the neural networks that underpin emotional intelligence also enable sophisticated signal sending and receiving, allowing us to tune into others and express ourselves with greater clarity. Consider for a moment, self-awareness. Leaders who understand their emotional patterns are better equipped to communicate with authenticity and adapt their style in real time. Having empathy sharpens their ability to read the room, and self-regulation keeps messaging measured.

As Ali Oliver, CEO of the Youth Sport Trust, explains: *"We're emotionally connected leaders and that connection creates a culture where you can lead with empathy without feeling like you're giving up authority. It's not an either/or."*

The connection between emotional intelligence and resilience is equally profound. Studies show that emotional intelligence is the strongest predictor of leadership resilience under pressure. This of course makes sense, because it's our ability to process and regulate emotion that directly shapes how we handle disruption and ongoing demands. When developed intentionally, emotional intelligence creates a resilient response architecture, an internal wiring that allows leaders to stay agile and effective under load.

Ali's approach offers a compelling case study in how emotional intelligence can be embedded at the cultural level. At the Youth Sport Trust, she replaced a once-a-year pulse survey with a triannual rhythm of listening, strategically spaced across the academic year to capture different emotional climates. *"If there's a rhythm of listening across the year, you can tell when something's wrong,"* she explains. The shift was to enable them to gather more meaningful data, creating a culture that responded to context, not just metrics.

Beyond the numbers, Ali anchors her leadership in candid team conversations and proactive wellbeing check-ins. In every board meeting, staff wellbeing is a standing item, not simply to monitor burnout or performance, but to ask who's struggling, who might need support and who deserves recognition or celebration? That's emotional intelligence at scale, not as a soft add-on, but as a strategic lever for team strength and long-term performance.

As we move into communication, remember that the strongest leaders aren't those who avoid emotion, they're the ones who understand it, manage and express themselves with intention. That's where skilled communication comes in, and that's the next vital capability we're about to explore.

Chapter 4
Skilled Communication – The Bridge To Success

Words Create Worlds

Have you ever walked away from a conversation absolutely certain you were clear, only to discover later that your message was completely misunderstood? Or found yourself frustrated by a colleague who seems to speak an entirely different language, despite using the same words?

These moments of disconnection, these communication gaps, can make the difference between success and setback.

In important negotiations, three carefully chosen words can transform conflict into collaboration. During organisational change, the right metaphor can turn resistance into enthusiasm. In crucial conversations, a moment of genuine connection can build trust that lasts years. Yet these same situations, handled without skilled communication, can erode trust, create resistance, and derail careers.

In our hyper-connected age, where messages travel across continents in an instant and meetings span time zones with a click, a paradox has emerged. Although there are more ways to communicate than ever before, the art of meaningful connection that builds trust, inspires action, and drives sustainable success remains elusive for many leaders.

As we explored in previous chapters, sustainable success demands mastery of certain fundamental tools. We've examined Emotional Intelligence as one such essential instrument, now we turn to another crucial calibration tool, Skilled Communication. Far more than just conveying information, communication serves as the vital bridge between intention and impact, and between potential and achievement.

The Three Paradigms Of Success And The Role Of Communication

The impact of communication on professional success can't be overstated. Even the most brilliant ideas remain unrealised if they're not conveyed effectively.

Think about your own journey. How many opportunities have hinged not just on what you knew, but on how well you could communicate that knowledge? How often has your success across all three paradigms of Money-Mission, Mental-Physical and Work-Life depended on your ability to translate insights into clear, compelling messages?

In every aspect of professional life, communication acts as a bridge, connecting knowledge to action, ideas to execution and people to shared understanding. When communication is clear, strategic, and calibrated to its audience, it has the power to amplify success.

Each paradigm presents distinct communication challenges and opportunities. Mastering communication in each of these areas removes friction, enhances influence, and accelerates outcomes.

Here are a few examples:

Paradigm	Examples Of Success-Driven Communication	Communication Risks When Misaligned
Money-Mission	– Winning a competitive bid by articulating value convincingly. – Building high-trust relationships through effective networking. – Negotiating contracts with precision. – Pitching new initiatives persuasively to stakeholders. – Securing investor buy-in by translating complex data into compelling narratives. – Enhancing leadership presence through confident communication.	– Losing deals due to unclear value propositions. – Struggling to gain executive buy-in because of data-heavy, uninspiring pitches. – Networking efforts falling flat due to lack of authentic connection. – Misdirected communication in sales, leading to lost revenue opportunities.
Mental-Physical	– Effectively articulating boundaries in high-stress environments. – Communicating needs and expectations clearly to reduce burnout. – Using constructive dialogue to manage conflicts with emotional intelligence. – Expressing stress or challenges to gain support rather than internalising them. – Advocating for wellbeing initiatives within an organisation.	– Increased stress due to unclear delegation or unrealistic workload distribution. – Workplace conflicts escalating due to reactive or emotionally charged responses. – Poor mental health outcomes from an inability to express challenges effectively. – Misalignment between personal wellbeing and professional demands, leading to disengagement.
Work-Life	– Setting clear expectations with colleagues and clients to maintain work-life balance. – Managing remote/hybrid work relationships with thoughtful, transparent communication.	– Work-life boundaries eroding due to lack of assertiveness in communication. – Professional relationships suffering from poor follow-through or mismanaged expectations.

(continued)

Paradigm	Examples Of Success-Driven Communication	Communication Risks When Misaligned
	– Ensuring alignment with leadership on long-term career goals. – Strengthening personal relationships through better listening and presence. – Leveraging storytelling to create shared understanding at home and at work.	– Feeling disconnected from purpose due to ineffective conversations about career growth. – Increased personal stress due to unclear communication in relationships.

If we look at professionals who excel across all three paradigms, one key factor stands out, they communicate clearly and with purpose. Whether they're negotiating multimillion-pound deals, developing team trust, or advocating for their own wellbeing, they know that success isn't just about what they say, it's about how it's received.

When you learn to fine-tune your communication, you bridge the gap between potential and performance. In turn, this creates momentum, drives results and ensures long-term fulfilment and success.

An Example Of How A Simple Communication Shift Created Executive Buy-In

Sarah, a brilliant marketing director I worked with, faced a critical moment in her career. Her team had developed an innovative market expansion plan, backed by data and analysis, but she struggled to gain client buy-in.

During an important presentation, she noticed the client's subtle shift in body language, they leaned back, developed a slight frown, as she detailed the financial projections. She could have continued pushing data, but instead, she paused and adjusted.

"Let me share a story about how this strategy would transform customer experience."

The shift was immediate. The client leaned forward, engaged. By the end of the meeting, Sarah had full support for the initiative.

What changed? Not the strategy itself, but how Sarah communicated it. She recognised that while data speaks to the mind, stories engage both mind and emotion, creating a 'whole-brain engagement'.

The Three Bridges Of Professional Communication

After years of working with, listening to, and learning from top executives, business owners and high-performing teams, I've come to recognise three critical communication bridges that every professional must master to achieve sustainable success:

1. **The Clarity Bridge:** Ensuring your message is understood as intended.
2. **The Trust Bridge:** Building and maintaining strong professional relationships.
3. **The Impact Bridge:** Moving from ideas to action.

Let's now explore how each bridge contributes to your professional success:

1 Building The CLARITY Bridge: Adding Context, Precision And Action

THE CLARITY BRIDGE
ENSURING YOUR MESSAGE IS
UNDERSTOOD AS INTENDED

Clear communication isn't just about speaking or writing well, it's about ensuring that your message is received as intended. The ability to convey ideas with precision is the foundation of effective leadership, collaboration, and decision-making. Without clarity, even the most well-meaning messages can cause confusion, inefficiency, or inaction.

In professional settings, a lack of clarity often leads to unnecessary back-and-forth communication, slowing progress, misinterpretation of priorities, leading to misalignment and decision-making delays, as teams struggle to decipher intent.

To see this in action, let's consider Michael, a technical expert recently promoted to lead a global team. His deep expertise made him a valuable leader, but his communication style created friction. A typical email from him looked like this: *"Project metrics indicate suboptimal performance. We need to implement enhanced protocols immediately."*

Clear to him, perhaps, but his team was left wondering which metrics specifically? What counts as 'suboptimal'? Which protocols need enhancement? What does 'immediately' mean in practice?

Michael's message lacked communication clarity, a common issue, especially in written form, where context and intent are not visually or audibly reinforced.

With some simple but powerful tweaks, he added four key elements:
1. **Context:** Set the stage, explain what's happening.
2. **Specifics:** Provide concrete details, what exactly needs attention?
3. **Impact:** Explain why it matters, who or what is affected?
4. **Action:** Clarify next steps, what should be done, by whom and when?

Here's how Michael refined his message:
(Revised email:)

"Our customer response time has increased to 48 hours this quarter (Context), double our target of 24 hours (Specifics). This impacts both customer satisfaction and our service level agreements (Impact). I'd like to meet with each team lead tomorrow to identify and implement specific process improvements (Action)."

The result? Immediate clarity, faster team response and improved performance.

The written word lacks the natural cues of face-to-face interaction, making clarity and context non-negotiable. Without them, messages risk misinterpretation, delays, or resistance, even when intentions are good.

To ensure communication clarity, always ask yourself:
Does my message provide enough context?
Have I been specific enough to avoid ambiguity?
Have I explained why this matters to my audience?
Are next steps clear and actionable?

Floyd shares how deep internal awareness supports clear external communication: *"I'm aware the thoughts I have in my head are not necessarily what I believe. I can move behind my thoughts. That's how I manage my emotions. Once I'm aware of them, I can choose how to think, respond, and perform."* Floyd describes how learning to pause and observe his internal dialogue gave him control over how he leads, speaks, and connects. He explains that this awareness affects not just language, but emotional state, performance, and presence.

More than self-awareness, this is a powerful communication skill. When you can move behind your thoughts, not live inside them, you can speak with greater intention, manage your responses under pressure and lead conversations with greater emotional precision.

When communication is calibrated for clarity, it strengthens relationships and accelerates professional success.

2 Building The TRUST Bridge: The Art Of Connection

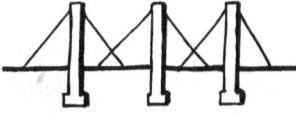

THE TRUST BRIDGE
BUILDING AND MAINTAINING
STRONG PROFESSIONAL RELATIONSHIPS

The Trust Bridge is perhaps the most nuanced yet crucial of the three communication bridges.

Teams with high trust levels are more productive and more engaged, yet building this bridge requires more than just clear messaging. It demands an understanding of both the visible and invisible elements of communication and connection.

PART ONE: Understanding Communication Styles

The mystery of why we instantly click with some people while struggling to connect with others often comes down to something far more systematic than chemistry or chance. These immediate connections, or disconnections, frequently stem from what neuroscientists and neuro linguistic programming (NLP) experts call 'representational systems', our preferred ways of processing and expressing information.

Lisa's story perfectly illustrates this principle. A retail executive with exceptional creative vision, Lisa couldn't understand why her relationship with her new boss felt so strained. Their meetings, despite shared goals and aligned values, often left them both feeling frustrated and misunderstood. Through our work together, we discovered something fascinating, Lisa naturally communicated in highly visual language, painting pictures with her words and literally showing her vision. Her boss, in contrast, processed information primarily through kinaesthetic (feeling-based) language, needing to grasp concepts and get a handle on situations.

This mismatch created subtle but persistent tension in their interactions. A typical exchange might go like this:

Lisa: *"I can see where we need to focus. Let me show you the picture I'm envisioning for Q3."*

Lisa's Boss: *"Something doesn't feel right about this approach. I need to get a grip on how this connects with our core values."*

Neither was wrong, they were simply speaking different sensory languages, creating a neural processing mismatch. This triggered subtle but significant stress responses in both parties, making their interactions feel unnecessarily difficult.

This contrast becomes even clearer when we compare Lisa's experience to Sarah's executive presentation challenge (which we explored earlier).

Sarah's client disengaged when confronted with too much data and responded better to storytelling. Lisa's boss, in contrast, needed more structure, more detail and a clear tie to core business values.

This highlights some fundamental truths about communication. People process information differently, we all have unique sensory and cognitive preferences, and emotional intelligence allows us to recognise, adapt to, and align with these differences.

I've seen this dynamic play out in a very personal way with my daughter, Darcie, a 10-year-old competitive gymnast. Like many athletes, Darcie has moments where mental blocks appear, especially after a growth spurt or when re-learning a skill, she's previously been injured doing. On bars, her spatial alignment can shift overnight. On floor, she's sometimes paused mid-sequence, hesitating during a flick that includes a move where she once broke her arm.

As her parent and therefore her coach-by-proxy at home, only when she asks and only with her coach's knowledge, I've learned to tune into the subtleties, the way she speaks about a move, the rhythm of her practice, the cues in her body language. Sometimes she needs to walk away from the skill for weeks. Other times, it's about breaking it down or injecting a bit of positive pressure or urgency. For Darcie, what consistently helps is decomposing the movement into smaller parts, re-establishing rhythm, and building trust, step by step.

One breakthrough came during her back flick to handspring. She had a mental block, she would pause halfway, lose momentum and stall. Together (after many and different attempts to help) we added an auditory cue, "Now", that I would call out at the exact moment she needed to commit to the second jump (her idea). It mattered that it was me saying it. We rehearsed it with long pauses, then gradually shortened them, to three seconds . . . then two . . . one . . . half . . . until there was no pause left. We closed the gap and suddenly she was flying (quite literally through the air), my voice playing in her head even when I no longer said the word aloud.

It was a reminder that skilled communication isn't just about having the right words, it's about using the right words, at the right time, delivered by the right person, in the right way for the person receiving them. Not for the comfort or rhythm of the person delivering them. In pressured moments, timing, tone, and trust matter just as much as the message itself.

By developing self-awareness and awareness of others, we gain sensory acuity, the ability to perceive, interpret and adjust to the processing styles and emotional states of those around us. This is the foundation of skilled communication. To achieve 'flexible fluency' we must master the three primary communication representation systems of visual, auditory, and kinaesthetic.

Here are some examples of how they differ:

The Three Main Languages Of Business Communication

Representation System (Communication Style)	How They Process Information	What Works Best for Them	Common Pitfalls
Visual Communicators	Think in images and patterns.	– Diagrams, charts, and visual aids. – Vivid descriptions that 'paint a picture'. – Conceptual overviews before details.	– May overlook details and execution. – Can lose audience if they rely only on visuals without structure.
Auditory Communicators	Process best through sound and rhythm.	– Discussions and verbal explanations. – Podcasts or structured verbal debriefs. – Tone of voice and word choice matter.	– May struggle with detail in written communication. – Can disengage with overly complex visuals.
Kinaesthetic Communicators	Need to 'feel' ideas emotionally or physically.	– Real-world examples and hands-on learning. – Storytelling that evokes real emotions and connections. – Relatable, values-driven discussions.	– Can feel disconnected from abstract concepts. – May struggle to stay engaged with just facts and data.

Beyond Style: The Role Of Culture And Context

While communication preferences often stem from individual processing styles, they're also deeply shaped by broader influences, cultural frameworks, social norms, and ingrained traditions. These unseen forces affect not just how we communicate, but who is heard, when, and how meaning is made.

In global or diverse teams, emotionally intelligent communication requires cultural awareness, the ability to read the room, honour different dynamics and adapt with respect. In this way, cultural intelligence becomes a natural extension of emotional intelligence, enhancing both our message and its impact.

Anne-Sophie, with her experience working across international markets, offered a powerful reflection on this from her early career: *"I remember going on site in India very early in my career. I'd be in a meeting with a male colleague and even if I said something, the client wouldn't acknowledge it until he repeated it. You can either fight that behaviour or choose your battles. I decided to focus my energy where I could make the most impact. That taught me a lot about how to read the room and respect cultural context."*

It's important to note, this wasn't a critique of any one culture, but an honest reflection on how power dynamics and social norms can present differently across contexts.

I've experienced this myself. In the Middle East, I once led a senior meeting where my male colleague received the first handshake and follow-up questions, yet in other leadership settings within the same region, I was welcomed with great respect and authority. These aren't contradictions. They're cultural calibrations, shaped not just by tradition, but by role, timing, environment, and relational nuance.

We see these patterns in our own lives too. At my son's football games, dads and male relatives often crowd the side-lines. At my daughter's gymnastics or dance events, it's mums and women who show up in greater numbers. These aren't hard rules, just social echoes. Culture mixes with choice, interest, habit and opportunity.

The most skilled communicators stay curious. They observe, adjust, and ask questions. Where is my voice most useful here? Sometimes the moment calls for leading, sometimes it means supporting someone else to lead, and occasionally, it means stepping back and recognising the moment isn't yours to own. That's not weakness, it's wisdom.

Anne-Sophie now leads multicultural teams across regions, and she brings that same awareness to her leadership: *"It's not about forcing people to behave the same. Not everyone wants the same amount of speaking time around the table. It's about noticing what matters to them and creating space for that, so they can bring what's important to them forward."*

Her story is a reminder that skilled communication means more than delivering the right words, it depends on knowing and understanding how they'll be received and felt. Trust grows when leaders communicate with genuine awareness of their audience.

PART TWO: Building Trust Through Communication Congruence

Understanding communication styles lays the groundwork, but building lasting trust demands more. It requires communication congruence, the alignment between what we say, how we say it, and what we do.

When our language, tone and behaviours reinforce one another, trust becomes more than possible, it becomes sustainable. Congruence transforms communication from a transactional act into a relationship-building force.

By combining fluency across the primary communication representation systems with congruent action, we begin to build trust that lasts, even under pressure or change. Trust tends to deepen when four qualities consistently show in how we communicate and behave, these are consistency, transparency, receptivity and follow-through.

Trust builds when our communication stays steady and aligned, when what we say, how we say it, and how we act all matches. That's consistency in action. Transparency matters too. Leaders who share not only decisions but the reasons behind them, who speak openly about challenges as well as progress, tend to create far deeper trust across their teams.

Receptivity, the willingness to truly listen, to take feedback seriously and to create space for differing perspectives often makes the difference between surface-level trust, and genuine rapport and follow-through. It's where trust becomes durable and it's built when people see that what was promised is actually delivered, again and again, in small ways as well as big ones.

Ali Oliver models this mindset of transparency in how she reviews performance: *"When we look at impact reports and end-of-year reviews, I don't just want to see the shiny achievements. I always ask to see the things we didn't achieve too. That's part of the story. That's part of the feedback."*

She reminds us that skilled communication includes celebrating progress and also acknowledging what didn't deliver as planned. Often, what we leave unsaid holds just as much insight as what we do share. Ali's approach highlights the value of full visibility, where honesty and feedback create the conditions for real progress.

Trust is the foundation of all effective communication. When it's paired with intention and follow-through, communication can drive genuine action. A leader who's relatable and clear builds connection, a leader who matches that with purposeful delivery builds momentum.

This is where the Impact Bridge comes into play.

Once communication is understood (Clarity Bridge) and trusted (Trust Bridge), the next step is translating it into meaningful outcomes. Leaders who create the greatest impact are those who move ideas into motion, turning vision into execution, and strategy into measurable results.

In the next section, we'll look at how to bridge the space between trust and action, so your communication not only informs and connects, but also activates change and delivers tangible progress.

3 Building The IMPACT Bridge: From Words To Results

THE IMPACT BRIDGE
MOVING FROM IDEAS
TO ACTION

The Impact Bridge is where understanding and trust translate into meaningful outcomes. It's the final piece of the communication ecosystem, where clarity becomes momentum, and connection leads to action.

Creating a strong impact bridge means designing communication with intention, so ideas turn into progress and people feel both clear and committed.

There are four communication shifts that consistently help ideas become action. These principles are simple to apply and offer a practical way to close the gap between vision and results:

Four Elements That Strengthen Communication For Impact

Element	What It Does	How to Apply It
1. Actionable Direction	Turns vision into specific, measurable action.	Set clear success criteria, timelines, and responsibilities. Keep outcomes tangible and trackable. Example: Rather than saying *"We need to digitise,"* try: *"Each team will identify 3 key processes for digitisation this quarter, with plans due by 15 March."*
2. Momentum Builders	Keeps things moving and energy high.	Celebrate early wins, track visible progress, and address blocks quickly. Example: Use fortnightly 'Progress Showcases' where teams present small but meaningful updates.
3. Engagement Design	Encourages ownership and alignment across stakeholders.	Adapt the message to each audience, invite contribution, and foster co-creation. Example: Don't just announce a big initiative, hold role-specific conversations so people understand their role in it.
4. Results Visibility	Strengthens commitment through feedback and recognition.	Share what's working, highlight the difference being made, and adjust based on data. Example: *"Since launch, response time is 32% faster and client satisfaction is up 19%."*

To apply these principles, start by anchoring them to something real. A challenge or opportunity already on your desk. You might be rolling out a new initiative or looking to strengthen engagement and accountability within your team.

The Impact Bridge can serve as a tool to help you shape communication that informs and drives action and alignment.

Here are four simple steps:

1. **Clarify the Goal:** Define what success looks like, in practical, measurable terms that everyone can understand.
2. **Create Momentum:** Identify early markers of progress. Small wins build confidence and keep energy moving.
3. **Engage Stakeholders:** Adapt your message to suit different audiences, ensuring relevance and buy-in at every level.
4. **Reinforce Results:** Track and share progress. When people can see impact, commitment deepens.

Quick Reflection:

Think of a current initiative you're leading.

Revisit your last communication about it, was it clear, actionable, and engaging?

Choose one of the elements above and identify a simple improvement you could make right now.

Small shifts in how we communicate can dramatically shift what gets done and how people feel while doing it.

The Three Bridges In Action

While each bridge, Clarity, Trust, and Impact, plays a distinct role, their true power comes from integration. Leaders who seamlessly combine these elements see exponential improvements in execution, engagement and results.

When all three bridges work together, you'll experience faster execution, stronger stakeholder buy-in, higher engagement and more sustainable success, all vital to maintain your success momentum.

The Emotional Interpretation Of Language

While we often think of communication as logic and structure, the emotional interpretation of language plays an equally powerful role. A simple shift in phrasing can instantly reduce anxiety, build trust, or defuse defensiveness.

THE CLARITY BRIDGE
ENSURING YOUR MESSAGE IS
UNDERSTOOD AS INTENDED

THE TRUST BRIDGE
BUILDING AND MAINTAINING
STRONG PROFESSIONAL RELATIONSHIPS

THE IMPACT BRIDGE
MOVING FROM IDEAS
TO ACTION

- **Clarity** ———▶ Creates the path.
- **Trust** ———▶ Provides the motivation to walk it.
- **Impact** ———▶ Ensures the journey leads to meaningful results.

Anne McClean, a Chartered and Certified Financial Planner, describes this vividly: *"Some clients get visibly anxious when they see their money balance going down, even if it's just market movement (or planned retirement spending!). I've learned to reframe how I talk about it, instead of 'spending' or 'loss', I talk about reallocating or investing toward future value."*

Olympic canoeist Adam Burgess described how his awareness of language evolved through working with sport psychologists. For him, the shift in communication was not just technical, but emotional and strategic: *"My awareness of the power of language really started with a sport psych perspective. I learned that the brain doesn't process negatives in the way we think it does, if I tell myself not to touch the pole when I race, I usually will. So, the shift is to focus on what space do I need to be in, rather than the thing I want to avoid."*

He explains how this awareness has become second nature: *"I'm so aware of it now. If I say something like 'don't do this' or 'I don't want to be here', I catch it straight away. Even if it's difficult to reframe things positively, it forces me to ask, what do I actually mean? What's my intention here?"*

Anne-Sophie offered a similarly powerful insight about the common ground between science and relationships, this being the desire to learn. *"Being curious,"* she explains, *"is what takes you far, in science, yes, because it gets very technical very fast. But human relationships are vast. You never stop learning. There's no single rule that always works, it's a constant process of reassessing."*

For her, skilled communication is more than a technical skillset, it's a mindset of curiosity. It's rooted in openness, learning in motion, and bringing the best of yourself to each interaction. She reminds us that communication, like science, is a discipline of ongoing discovery.

Whether discussing finance, feedback, or failure, the language you choose becomes a lever for confidence or concern.

Mastering Digital Communication: Building Connection And Influence Online

We've touched on digital communication, but now it's time to take a closer look.

In an age where virtual meetings, messaging platforms and online visibility shape how we lead and influence, digital communication is no longer optional. The modern leader must be able to connect, engage and build trust in environments where tone can be misread, body language is limited, and distractions are constant.

Research suggests the majority of professionals still view remote communication as less effective than in-person, often due to reduced non-verbal cues, engagement difficulties and ambiguity in tone. But here lies the opportunity, because when you learn to communicate with presence and intentionality in virtual spaces, you bridge the gap and you set yourself apart. Leaders who master digital communication can strengthen their influence and build trust across wider networks.

Virtual Meetings: The Art Of Digital Presence

In a world where video conferencing and hybrid work has replaced boardroom discussions, a strong digital presence has become essential for effective leadership. Virtual meetings come with unique challenges though. Attention spans are shorter and studies show we retain less from online interactions than from in-person discussions. Without the full cues of eye contact, body language, and shared space, it's harder to build trust and hold attention. Engagement takes more conscious effort. Add in screen fatigue and the increased cognitive load of virtual environments, where multitasking and digital distractions are constant, and the communication landscape becomes even more complex.

RECOMMENDED

Here Are A Few Useful Strategies You Can Use To Improve Digital Presence And Engagement

- **The 60/20/20 Rule:** Structure meetings with 60% discussion, 20% direct engagement and 20% interaction (polls, Q&A, or reflections) to combat passive listening.
- **Strategic Pauses:** Silence in virtual settings often feels uncomfortable, leading to rushed conversations. Adding a 3-second pause after key points will allow for absorption and response.
- **The Digital Presence:** The most effective leaders adopt a deliberate screen presence:

  - Eye Contact: Position your camera at eye level and maintain engagement as if speaking in person.
  - Vocal Precision: Use intonation shifts to emphasise key messages and maintain attention.
  - Hand Gestures with intent: Subtle hand movements within frame reinforces key points.

Email Effectiveness: The Science Of Written Precision

Email remains one of the most widely used, and often misused, communication tools in executive life. Despite its speed and convenience, it can easily become a source of misinterpretation, inefficiency, and unnecessary friction. Common issues include unclear tone, buried key points, and extended back-and-forth threads that slow down decision-making. For some, these challenges spill over into WhatsApp, LinkedIn messages, meeting chats, and the ever-growing mix of written channels we now rely on. Without a clear approach, communication quickly becomes cluttered, and clarity, the one thing we need most, gets lost in the noise.

So, what's the solution? While email and other written platforms are essential to modern work, they're rarely used to full effect. Improving email effectiveness, and written communication more broadly, starts with a clear, structured approach. The **CLEAR Framework** is simple to apply and will help ensure your messages are concise, actionable, and well-received, increasing engagement and reducing the risk of misinterpretation.

C – Context First: Start with 'why' the email matters to provide immediate clarity.

L – Logical Flow: Structure sentences so the email is easy to scan and absorb.

E – Emphasis on Action: Specify the next steps required from the recipient.

A – Adaptive Tone: Adjust formality based on the recipient and context.

R – Responsive Design: Use formatting tools such as bullet points and bolding to highlight key takeaways.

Example: Applying The CLEAR Framework
Consider the following before-and-after example demonstrating how an email can be refined for clarity and impact.

Before (Ineffective Email)
"Hi team, I wanted to check in on the report. It's important we get it done ASAP. Let me know where we are."

This message lacks context, structure, and clear next steps. Without specifics, team members may be uncertain about expectations, leading to delays and misalignment.

After (CLEAR Framework Applied)
Subject: Status Update Required – Q3 Market Report

*"Hi team,
We need to finalise the Q3 Market Report by Friday to meet the executive review deadline.
Current Progress: Please share updates on outstanding sections.
Next Steps: Assign final edits and review formatting by Thursday.
Thanks for your input, I look forward to finalising this."*

This revised version applies the CLEAR Framework by:
- Providing immediate context on the deadline.
- Structuring the message for easy scanning.
- Outlining specific actions required.
- Using a professional yet approachable tone.

By making these small adjustments, the sender ensures faster responses, reduced confusion, and greater accountability.

Through this chapter we've explored communication as more than just a professional skill, it's a critical bridge between ideas and action, between potential and performance.

Across the three core paradigms of sustainable success, communication plays a defining role, it supports Money-Mission alignment by helping leaders clearly articulate value and purpose, it underpins Mental-Physical wellbeing through boundary-setting, self-expression and emotionally intelligent dialogue and it shapes Work-Life integration by fostering empathy and clear meaningful connection.

From the Clarity Bridge, which focuses on precision and context, to the Trust Bridge, built on congruence and connection and finally the Impact Bridge, which transforms insight into action, this chapter lays a framework for developing skilled communication as a strategic leadership tool. We've also explored how digital communication has redefined how leaders engage and influence, highlighting practical ways to strengthen virtual presence and improve written communication, building trust in online spaces.

Even the most powerful communication relies on something deeper to be fully sustainable. That's where our next calibration tool comes in. If communication is the bridge between what you know and what others understand, resilience is the foundation that keeps that bridge steady under pressure. In high-level leadership, clarity, and energy matter, but it's resilience that allows you to carry them forward consistently, especially when the demands rise.

So now, let's explore the final core calibration tool, The Resilience Advantage, and how it enables high performers to stay strong and maintain momentum . . . especially during the times when it matters most.

Explore More:

To continue developing your communication precision and emotional fluency, visit www.balancing-act.co.uk or scan the QR code here. You'll find practical frameworks, exercises, and scripts to enhance your leadership communication across contexts.

EXPLORE MORE

MORE CLARITY. MORE TOOLS. YOUR NEXT STEP.

Chapter 5
Building Your Resilience Advantage

Resilience is more than recovery from challenge, trauma, or failure, it's the ability to recalibrate and move forward with intention. In the high-wire act of modern leadership, sustainable success relies not on relentless endurance, or big bounce backs, but on responsive adaptation. Resilient leaders are those who can meet pressure with clear a mind, reset quickly, and stay fully present in the moments that matter most.

While skill and balance are essential, even the most accomplished performers rely on systems of support and recovery to sustain long-term success.

Traditionally, resilience research has been shaped by powerful narratives of recovery from trauma, stories of individuals overcoming profound adversity to achieve remarkable success. These accounts, while deeply inspiring, represent only one dimension of resilience. Thankfully, resilience isn't solely forged through hardship. While extreme challenges can accelerate its development, it can also build incrementally, through daily tests of perseverance, adaptability, and emotional regulation. Whether it's handling professional setbacks, managing high-pressure situations, or maintaining personal commitments, every experience strengthens your capacity to withstand and grow from challenges.

Resilience As A Learned Skill

Like emotional intelligence and skilled communication, resilience is a trainable capability that you can actively develop.

When you build it with intention, you create internal architecture that supports you through every kind of challenge, from significant life disruptions to the quieter, everyday pressures that gradually drain energy and focus.

Resilience gives you the ability to stay grounded, responsive, and effective across changing demands. It strengthens focus, adaptability, confidence and composure, the very qualities that drive long-term, high-performance leadership.

Think about a time when staying balanced felt almost impossible. Perhaps it was during a major career move, a personal setback, or one of those high-pressure periods where everything seemed to land at once. Staying centred in those moments doesn't happen by accident, it draws on the habits and mental foundations you've already built and the neural strength you've trained over time.

Resilience isn't simply a reaction; it's deeply connected to how the brain is wired. The great news here is that this wiring is adaptable.

People who actively develop and strengthen resilience show increased activity in the prefrontal cortex, the part of the brain that manages emotion, clarity of thought and strategic decision-making. These benefits aren't limited to moments of crisis, they present themselves daily, in how we lead, how we adapt and how we maintain focus and energy through the inevitable ups and downs of life and leadership.

Olympic canoeist Adam Burgess offers a powerful metaphor for resilience under pressure, on reviewing performance he notes: *"We always strip it back to what was the intention that led to that outcome? Not the technique in the moment, because in the next race I might be in a different position, or the river might be different. It's about going in with the same intention but staying open. If you cling too tightly to a specific process, you can shut yourself down, you miss better ways of doing things, or you don't see the threat coming."*

This insight highlights something essential about resilient leadership. Success comes not from sticking to a fixed proven approach, but from knowing how to recalibrate as the conditions change.

The Three Dimensions Of Professional Resilience

The modern workplace demands different types of resilience depending on the challenges faced. Think of these as balancing techniques, each essential for staying steady on your executive tightrope.

There are three distinct categories of resilience necessary for long-term success:

1. **Daily Operational Resilience:** (Sustaining Performance Across Routine Demands). This is your foundation for managing ongoing pressures while maintaining effectiveness. More and more professionals are experiencing burnout, not due to major crises, but from the cumulative impact of daily stressors. Like a tightrope walker's constant micro-adjustments, your ability to stay steady in daily operations is crucial for long-term success.

2. **Transitional Resilience:** (Managing Change And Career Evolution). This is the stabilising force that allows you to adapt during periods of transition, whether it's a career shift, change of leadership, or major organisational transformation. Leaders who practice preventative resilience, actively managing their energy and boundaries during transitions, tend to demonstrate higher long-term effectiveness than those who operate through pure reactivity.

3. **High-Performance Resilience:** (Thriving Under Peak Demands). This form of resilience is what sustains elite performance under extreme pressure. Studies of military leaders and elite athletes highlight that high-stakes environments require specialised resilience capabilities. Just as a tightrope walker must develop

different skills for a more treacherous crossing, high-performance resilience enables leaders to sustain peak output without compromising wellbeing.

When you practise proactive resilience strategies, such as strategic rest, boundary setting and recovery planning, you help regulate cortisol levels and reduce the risk of stress-related burnout. Resilience is about recognising early warning signals in both body and mind and responding before they escalate. When properly calibrated, these cues allow you to course-correct, reset and sustain high performance. Knowing when to pause, seek support, or shift your approach is as critical as knowing when to push forward.

Developing Your Resilience Architecture

As we explore each type of resilience, it's essential to recognise that building resilience means constructing both defence and direction, a sphere for sustainable success. Imagine this sphere as a protective yet permeable boundary surrounding you. It functions as an intelligent filter, allowing you to engage productively with obstacles while maintaining balance and enjoyment.

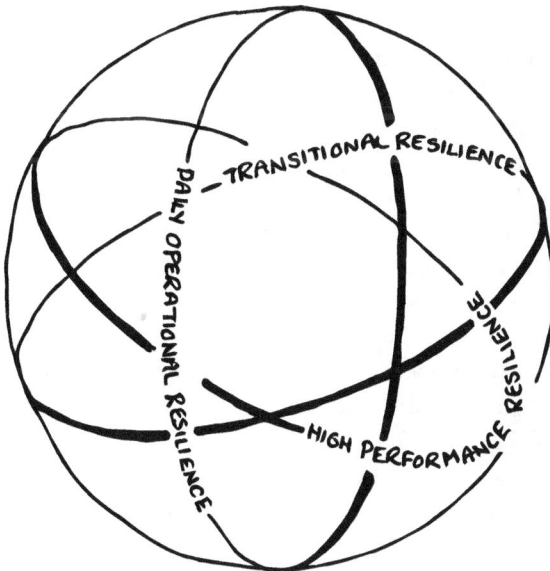

Developing this kind of three-tier resilience architecture equips you to recover from setbacks with greater speed and composure. It builds the wisdom to minimise unnecessary strain, the discernment to know when to lean in or step back, and the capacity to align your everyday actions with your longer-term vision.

When this architecture is integrated with the three paradigms that shape lasting success, its impact deepens. It supports sustained momentum while balancing financial achievement with purposeful contribution. It enables you to improve stamina, strengthen recovery, and stay emotionally regulated under pressure, and it empowers you to set healthy boundaries and protect alignment between your professional goals and personal wellbeing.

Mastering resilience across these areas is what enables you to thrive consistently, not just push through. After all, reaching your destination is important, but sustainable success should also allow you to enjoy the journey.

In the following pages, we'll take a closer look at how resilience functions in daily operations, during transitions, and in high-performance environments. You'll also discover practical tools and strategies for strengthening resilience in ways that align with both your personal and professional ambitions.

1 Daily Operational Resilience: Your Foundation For Success

Daily Operational Resilience is where sustainability begins. Think of it as your baseline balance on the tightrope, the steady state that helps you stay grounded and energised through everyday demands. It's the kind of resilience that supports consistent performance, even when the pressure is subtle but persistent.

Ali leads a charity without core funding yet maintains a tone of optimism across her team. *"There's no point in translating financial uncertainty into organisational anxiety,"* she explains. *"People need to feel possibility."* Her resilience strategy is deeply human, protecting culture while navigating tough terrain.

What's fascinating is that this form of resilience operates both at the conscious level and within the body's deeper systems. Leaders who develop this steady-state capacity often report higher job satisfaction, better work-life integration, and even physiological benefits. Their bodies begin to process stress differently, entering what neuroscientists call adaptive equilibrium, a state of dynamic balance that enables sustained high performance without tipping into burnout.

The Science Of Daily Operational Resilience

While mindset and strategy are critical, Daily Operational Resilience is also grounded in biology. At its core, this form of resilience is physiological. Your body keeps the score.

One of the key scientific concepts here is allostatic load, the cumulative impact of ongoing stress on your system. Unlike acute stress from a major event, allostatic load builds slowly, shaped by the everyday demands and pressures that gradually wear down your capacity over time.

Tools like the Resilience Quotient Inventory (RQi) help measure how individuals respond to and recover from stress. This framework assesses beliefs, behaviours, and environmental factors that act as buffers against burnout. Individuals with a high resilience quotient tend to share some notable physiological markers:
- They show more stable cortisol rhythms throughout the day (less hormonal volatility).
- They have healthier heart rate variability, indicating greater physical adaptability.
- They demonstrate stronger neural connectivity between emotional and rational brain centres, helping them stay composed and clear-headed under pressure.

These biological patterns reinforce what resilient leaders often report, that consistent performance isn't just a mindset, it's a state the body can be trained to support.

INSIGHT

Common Traits Of Individuals With High Operational Resilience:

Mental Strength
- Optimism: A positive outlook and belief that challenges can be overcome successfully.
- Self-Efficacy: Confidence in their own ability to solve problems and achieve goals.
- Personal Control: Belief in having control over their own circumstances rather than attributing outcomes to external factors like fate.

Purpose
- A strong sense of meaning or purpose in life, with clear goals aligned with personal values and strengths.
- Belief that their setbacks are less likely to derail them because they are committed to their long-term objectives.

Emotional Intelligence
–   High self-awareness and self-esteem, allowing effective management of emotions during stress-
    ful situations.
–   Self-compassion, which prevents excessive self-criticism and fosters emotional recovery.

Physical Stamina
–   Healthy lifestyle habits such as regular exercise, balanced nutrition, quality sleep and maintain-
    ing a work-life balance.

Social Network
–   Strong social support systems, including family, friends, colleagues, or mentors to confide in
    during challenging times.

Additional Traits:
–   Humour: Ability to laugh at misfortunes, which helps alleviate stress.
–   Facing Fear: Willingness to confront fears and step out of comfort zones for personal growth.
–   Faith or Spirituality: Finding strength through spiritual beliefs or practices (though not univer-
    sally required).

This all offers an interesting insight into the development of Daily Operational Resilience. The goal then, is not to eliminate stress completely (that's not realistic), it's to improve your response to it, physically, mentally, and emotionally.

That starts with understanding your 'Energy Calibration System', the way you manage, protect, and can recharge your energy so that resilience becomes part of how you live and succeed each day.

Building Your Energy Calibration System

Whilst traditional time management techniques teach us to squeeze more into each day, if you've ever hit 3pm feeling drained, with hours left to go, you already know that time isn't the real issue, it's energy.

Managing your energy (in alignment with time) is the key to sustainable success. Your energy is not one-dimensional, it comes from four interconnected sources, these are physical stamina, emotional state, mental clarity, and a sense of purpose. This is the foundation of your Energy Calibration System, a practical tool to help you build capacity, not just cope.

So, how do you create a system that works for you? Let's break down the three essential steps that will help you structure your routines, environments and recovery practices in a way that matches the real demands of your life and leadership.

STEP 1: Energy Mapping

The first step is understanding your natural energy pattern across the four performance energies:

1. **PHYSICAL ENERGY:** Your biological capacity for movement, recovery, and stamina. This includes sleep, hydration, nutrition, and physical fitness.
2. **EMOTIONAL ENERGY:** The quality and regulation of your inner emotional world. This influences how you respond to pressure, how quickly you recover from emotional setbacks and your ability to lead with empathy.
3. **MENTAL ENERGY:** Your cognitive bandwidth, your attention span, decision-making, problem-solving and focus. This fluctuates depending on fatigue, distraction, and cognitive load.
4. **PURPOSE ENERGY:** Your sense of alignment with what matters. This includes meaning, motivation and clarity of direction, the fuel that makes hard work feel worthwhile.

Each day, your energy fluctuates across these dimensions. Learning to notice and adjust them, like dials on a soundboard, is how you'll build resilience and prevent burnout.

Start by observing your chronotype, your natural internal rhythm that governs when you feel most focused, energised, and creative. Then layer in the four energy dimensions to identify how they rise and fall throughout your day. We usually have a clear preference for one of four chronotypes and this often shows in the way we talk, work, and plan our lives. Some people are wired to rise early and hit the gym before sunrise, while others get their best ideas after 10pm. I often find myself in conversations with clients and colleagues about their preferred time of day to train, work, or travel and yet, when we look at their diaries, their work schedules often don't reflect these preferences.

In my own team, we've built this insight into our systems. We run regular 'Pulse' meetings at 10am, a deliberate choice that respects everyone's rhythm. It gives early risers time to train or work, late-night thinkers time to come online gradually and everyone a shared window to connect with focus.

Understanding your own rhythm means you can align your most demanding work with the times you naturally have the most energy.

These are the most common daily energy patterns:
- **Early Peak:** High energy and focus in the morning.
- **Late Peak:** Higher performance in the afternoon or evening.
- **Dual Peak:** Two clear bursts of energy, often mid-morning, and early evening.
- **Steady State:** Consistent energy throughout the day with fewer spikes or crashes.

Once you understand your rhythm, start noticing when each energy domain is at its best and when it needs attention.

DID YOU KNOW?

Just as tightrope walkers rely on rhythm for balance, research shows that during peak performance, our neural networks synchronise with heart rate, creating what's called psychophysiological coherence, a resilient brain-body rhythm.

STEP 2: Task-Energy Alignment

Think of your day like a performance on a tightrope, every step needs to be intentional. Just as a performer wouldn't attempt their hardest move when fatigued, neither should you tackle your most demanding tasks when your energy dips. Yet, according to research, professionals spend more than 30% of their peak energy time on low-value tasks, simply due to poor planning and misaligned scheduling.

This is where you have an opportunity to create better Task-Energy Alignment. Use your mental energy peaks for strategy, problem-solving and key decisions, apply your emotional energy to conversations, stakeholder engagement and conflict resolution, use your purpose energy for visioning, team building and values-based leadership and schedule tasks like admin, emails, or structured work during lower physical or cognitive energy periods. When you align what you're doing with how your energy naturally flows, everything feels more fluid and less forced.

When I coach high performers, we regularly walk through a calendar recalibration/energy mapping exercise, aligning their task types to their energy peaks. Without fail, even small changes produce significant results. For example, an education leader rescheduled team meetings to mid-afternoon to free up her most focused hours for strategy and saw her decision-making speed and clarity improve significantly.

In another case, a client leading a fitness and wellbeing company noticed their in-person meetings were becoming long and stagnant. He surprised his team by removing the chairs from the meeting room one week, instantly transforming the format into energised, focused 'stand-up huddles' (as he newly named them). The meetings were shorter, more dynamic, and naturally incorporated movement, not only boosting focus, but reinforcing the company's values around physical energy and flow.

The lessons here? Task-Energy alignment doesn't need to be rigid or prescriptive. It can be creative, cultural and deeply personal.

Ask yourself: How can you bring movement into strategy? Focus into collaboration? Purpose into your calendar?

For those of you starting to think big, what changes might allow you to align your energy with your task output and intentionally map across all paradigms of success? This is how small shifts become sustainable systems and increase your chance of success.

STEP 3: The Recovery Rhythm

Finally, great performers don't only focus on output, they master the art of renewal. They have learnt when and how to pause.

Just as tightrope walkers make micro-adjustments to stay balanced, top performers build in micro-recoveries to sustain their output. These aren't hour-long breaks, but short, strategic pauses that reset the nervous system and boost focus.

These small shifts restore psychophysiological coherence, a state scientists refer to when your brain and heart rhythms sync, promoting focus, calm and improved decision-making. Research shows that regular micro-breaks reduce cortisol spikes and can improve prefrontal cortex function, leading to better judgment. They also regulate autonomic nervous system balance, helping you shift from stress to stability faster.

Micro-recovery includes physical rest and also nutritional reset, small intentional acts that replenish the body and recalibrate the mind. As Dr. John Sullivan explains, *"Taking breaks, fuelling, hydrating, or moving, is a signal to your nervous system that you're supporting recovery."* Leaders who intentionally incorporate these strategic fuelling points into their day are enhancing their potential for a higher level of performance.

For Anne-Sophie, breaks are more than recovery, they form part of cultural rituals. She explains: *"It's important for me to step away from my desk, especially over lunch. When I'm in the office, I always try to make time to eat with colleagues. Sharing the moment helps us switch off mentally and restart fresh."*

She notes that even at home this reset is essential, though sometimes harder to structure. Her approach? Movement, novelty, and joy: *"If I'm working remotely, I walk around, look for something different to do, maybe baking, maybe reading. It helps switch my brain into a different mode. I love baking because it's manual, the brain goes into off mode and joy comes not just from doing it, but from sharing it."*

This type of emotionally intelligent recovery, blending physical, cognitive, and cultural signals, is exactly the type of rhythm that sustains performance over time. These micro-recovery opportunities, tiny yet powerful moments, provide space to reset your mind and body. The signs you need one are often subtle, they include symptoms such as foggy thinking, slower processing, or a lack of creativity (mental), frustration or dips in motivation (emotional), shallow breathing, rest-lessness (physical) or procrastination and detachment (purpose-driven).

Even 3–5 minutes of intentional reset, stepping outside, deep breathing or simply switching contexts has shown to restore coherence across all four energy systems. Just as elite tightrope walkers use pauses to regain balance, high-performing leaders can use these micro-moments to maintain focus and resilience across their day.

Adam likes to talk about breathing as a form of behaviour, explaining that *"the guy who's breathing through his nose has a lot more composure than the one who's panting."* He uses a simple acronym 'NGSE' to check in with his breathing throughout the day, this stands for Nasal, Gentle, Slow, Expansive. These four cues help him reset, regulate, and maintain composure under pressure. *"Control of breath,"* he said, *"is control of state."*

When you consciously design your day around recovery, you protect your energy, and you expand your capacity. Your Energy Calibration System becomes a sustainable rhythm that supports both performance and wellbeing. The beauty of this intentional design? You don't have to worry about avoiding burnout, it simply becomes a natural by-product. The focus stays on what energises you and that's what keeps you resilient.

Each step becomes steadier, more intentional, and more energised.

And like the tightrope walker, it all starts to flow.

From Daily Mastery To Transitional Strength

When you integrate energy mapping with recovery rhythms, you begin to build your Daily Operational Resilience. This becomes your internal compass, helping you sustain focus and energy in the moments that matter. However, it's real value is revealed not in ease, but in pressure. Next, we'll explore Transitional Resilience, carrying your daily rhythm into seasons of uncertainty or reinvention.

It's your mastery of the everyday that prepares you for the extraordinary, strengthening your response when the landscape shifts.

2 Transitional Resilience: Strengthening Stability Through Change And Evolution

If Daily Operational Resilience is what keeps you balanced during everyday pressures, then Transitional Resilience is your ability to stay steady when the environment shifts, when the wind picks up or the wire beneath your feet begins to sway.

In today's world, change isn't something that happens occasionally, it's a constant.

According to McKinsey, over 70% of leaders are responsible for managing major organisational transitions every 18 to 24 months, often while also managing changes in their own roles, goals, and identities.

What makes this form of resilience so powerful is how it works at the neurological level.

Research reveals that leaders who handle transitions well have distinct brain patterns. They process uncertainty and disruption differently than those who find change destabilising. Their ability to adapt is reflected in how their brains are wired to anticipate and respond.

This changes the way we think about managing change. Transitional Resilience requires us to read the environment early, adjust with agility and maintain internal steadiness in the midst of external movement. Significant change, whether personal or professional, triggers a complex mix of physical and emotional responses. While we often talk about resilience in broad terms, science is beginning to show us exactly what's happening beneath the surface.

Individuals with high levels of Transitional Resilience tend to share three core traits:

1. **Adaptive Flexibility:** Their stress response systems recover quickly after the initial shock of change, allowing them to return to a steady state more efficiently.
2. **Cognitive Agility:** Even in the face of uncertainty, they maintain the ability to focus, plan and make decisions, all of which are core functions of executive thinking that often become compromised under pressure.
3. **Emotional Stability:** They regulate their emotional responses consistently, helping them remain calm and steady during disruption.

Rather than trying to eliminate discomfort or unpredictability, which simply isn't realistic, the goal is to build a Change Calibration System: a proactive, intentional approach to strengthening both body and mind, so they can adapt without losing focus or direction.

Transitional Resilience is about learning to meet change with confidence, composure, and flexibility, not once, but repeatedly, and sustainably.

Floyd Woodrow reflected on this directly when discussing his own transitions. *"I wasn't skilled, so I was coming into a place where I was a novice,"* he shared, speaking about the challenge of stepping into new, unfamiliar environments. *"But I could rely on some of the skills that I had . . . life has been a journey, and I had so many great tools that I could now transfer into any area, and they stood up under pressure."* His ability to lead, communicate, make decisions and pivot quickly didn't disappear just because the context changed. Those core skills, developed under intense conditions, became anchors. They travelled with him, reinforcing the idea that building Transitional Resilience is focussed on knowing how to apply what you already know and have, in new ways.

Building Your Change Calibration System

Leaders who handle transitions well survive change and use it as a springboard for growth.

In a wide-ranging review of resilience strategy and performance, studies found that resilient organisations consistently outperform their peers, especially during periods of uncertainty and change. They recover, they innovate, they adapt and maintain high engagement and operational effectiveness. The takeaway? Resilience, especially through transitions, is your new competitive advantage.

Here's how to build your own Change Calibration System, step by step:

STEP 1: Change Sensing

Just as a tightrope walker must feel even the subtlest shift in the wire, resilient leaders learn to sense change before it fully arrives. This early awareness gives them a powerful edge.

There are three areas of change awareness:
1. **Environmental Scanning:** Paying attention to shifts in your external context (markets, industry trends, political or economic movement).
2. **Organisational Pulse-Taking:** Tuning in to internal signals, cultural shifts, new pressures, or emerging tensions.
3. **Personal Calibration:** Checking in with your own readiness, emotional signals, mindset shifts, or intuitive resistance.

STEP 2: Change Integration

Think of this as your internal structure for adapting when the wind suddenly picks up. When change hits, your response needs to be both quick and considered, reactive, yet stable.

There are three key components that will help you to build your ability to integrate change:
1. **Cognitive Processing:** Mentally rehearsing change scenarios, reframing challenges as opportunities and strategising how to adapt effectively.

2. **Emotional Management:** Recognising and naming emotional responses, expressing emotion constructively and intentionally and building networks that offer emotional support.
3. **Behavioural Adaptation:** Responding with flexibility, building new skillsets, and learning through action and reflection.

STEP 3: Transition Support Framework

Even the best tightrope walker needs anchors, whether it's a counterbalance pole or a safety net. In the same way, successful leaders build a robust support system to stay grounded during uncertainty. Leaders with well-developed support frameworks are more likely to maintain consistent high level performance during change, be better at managing stress and be more successful when leading new initiatives.

Your Transition Support Framework should include three types of anchors:
1. **Professional Anchors:** Trusted mentors, peer networks and access to growth and development tools.
2. **Personal Stabilisers:** Family and friends, health and wellness practices and routines that promote recovery.
3. **Strategic Resources:** Tools and templates for change management, coaching or expert support, learning opportunities that keep you agile.

STEP 4: The Recovery-Growth Cycle

Change, when approached properly, can make us stronger. The adaptation paradox describes how stress, when followed by intentional recovery, leads to growth. Much like muscle development:

strain + recovery = strength.

This Recovery-Growth Cycle includes three interconnected phases:
1. **Active Engagement:** Consciously participating in the change process, managing your energy with intention, and developing the specific skills needed for the new landscape.
2. **Intentional Recovery:** Taking time to reflect, building in moments for rest and reset and allowing space for your brain and body to consolidate learning.
3. **Growth Integration:** Capturing what you've learned, embedding new capabilities into your leadership style, and building confidence through small wins and visible progress.

When these phases are acknowledged and integrated, change becomes less of a disruption and a platform for transformation.

The Power Of Forward Motion

By building your Change Calibration System, through sensing, integration, support, and recovery, you create the ability to stay balanced in turbulence and to grow stronger because of it. The science confirms what many high-performing leaders already know through experience; when transitional resilience is intentional, change becomes more than a challenge, it becomes a turning point.

But there's one more subtle, powerful ingredient to this kind of growth, it's something I call the 'Power of Forward Motion'.

I first discovered this concept while preparing for university presentations. In those moments before I had to speak, full of nerves, often dreading what was ahead (ironic, considering the work I do now!), I realised something surprisingly helpful.

Time doesn't stop.

It moves forward, no matter how ready we feel, no matter how much we want the moment to last, or to end. I remember thinking: *"No matter how this goes, in an hour, it will be over. By tonight, I'll be looking back, either proud or with something to learn."*

That shift in mindset became one of the earliest resilience tools I used. It turned panic into perspective. When you realise that every moment is temporary, you gain power, not just to endure it, but to choose how you'll reflect on it later.

So now, when a challenge presents itself, I ask:
– Will I look back and see a moment I handled with focus and integrity?
– Will I use it as a lesson that strengthens me?
– Will I prove to myself, again, that I'm more capable than I, or others thought?

This is where resilience moves beyond survival. It becomes strategy. It connects back to your North Star, your long-term vision, reminding you that every difficult moment is part of the path.

You're not just moving through change. You're moving toward something better. Even if you don't like the change, even if it wasn't part of the plan, it's happening. Your only power lies in how you respond.

As we now turn toward High-Performance Resilience, you'll see how everything we've explored, from daily energy management to transitional strength and forward momentum, sets the foundation for something more. This is where you move from reacting to change, to choosing your path, more challenging, more meaningful, and more fully aligned with the resilience architecture you've built.

3 High-Performance Resilience: Excellence Under Pressure

High-Performance Resilience is not just your ability to handle pressure, it's your capacity to deliver when the pressure peaks. When the wire is high, when the margin for error is small, when the stakes are great, you still deliver. Not once. Consistently.

This goes beyond managing stress. It's learning how to sustain energy, focus and wellbeing while producing exceptional results. It's about performing at your best without sacrificing yourself to do it.

What separates the highest-performing leaders is rarely experience alone, more often it's the ability to maintain peak focus and composure in the most challenging circumstances. These are the people making high-pressure decisions, steering through uncertainty, leading critical change, all whilst doing so with unshakable steadiness. They've mastered pressure-enhanced performance.

This pattern mirrors what we see in elite sports and other high-pressure domains. Olympic athletes, military commanders, and trauma surgeons all train for their 'moment under fire'. Their performance systems are built for skill and for sustainable, repeatable excellence under pressure. A key concept uniting these worlds? The flow state.

Under pressure, high performers do more than cope, they shift into a different operating mode. The brain becomes more energy efficient. It processes faster, filters and sharpens focus. It's a neurological sweet spot, where instinct, precision and adaptability merge.

This is where performance psychology and neuroscience converge, not to help us push harder, but to help us perform smarter. As Dr. John Sullivan describes, the goal is *"health in motion,"* creating a performance system that aligns with how the brain works under pressure. This includes building systems that support recovery, regulate stress, and enable strategic focus. One of the most powerful tools he's developed to support this is the PROCESS Model, a practical framework to align your physiology, psychology, and performance in real time.

When resilience is viewed as a trainable system, it opens the door to structured improvement. It allows us to upgrade the operating system we lead from, moment by moment, day by day.

Dr. Sullivan's insights remind us: *"The brain performs better under pressure when conditions align with how it actually works."* When we're fatigued, emotionally overloaded, or under-recovered, our performance narrows. But when our internal systems are aligned, we gain range, flexibility, and speed. The PROCESS Model provides a roadmap for doing exactly that.

Introducing The PROCESS Model

The PROCESS Model is a neuroscience-informed framework designed to strengthen high-performance resilience. It brings together seven interconnected domains that shape how your brain and body perform under pressure:

P - **PHYSICAL ACTIVITY**
R - **REST AND RECOVERY**
O - **OPTIMAL NUTRITION**
C - **COGNITIVE LOAD**
E - **EMOTIONAL MANAGEMENT**
S - **SOCIALISATION**
S - **SYNERGY**

Together, these domains create the internal architecture for resilience. Each one plays a critical role in stabilising and enhancing your energy, focus, adaptability, and emotional regulation. But their real power lies in how they integrate.

This model isn't rigid. It's designed for the realities of modern leadership, where unpredictability is the norm and consistent performance is expected. Rather than offering a one-size-fits-all solution, PROCESS provides a flexible, practical system to help you adapt and lead from the inside out. Dr John Sullivan reminds us: *"We have control over nothing in our lives. It's absolutely an illusion . . . But the cool part is that we have influence and management over everything."*

Adam learnt this on the water. He talks about the importance of letting the water lead.

"I used to plan every stroke," Adam said, recalling his early training years. *"Now I just plan the spaces."* This shift in mindset, away from rigid control and towards flow, transformed his consistency. *"It's about intention, not technique."*

That mindset shift, from control to influence, is key for lasting high performance. The PROCESS Model doesn't impose discipline from the outside; it enhances adaptability from within. It equips you with the tools to manage your energy, decision-making, emotions and recovery with focus and precision.

You'll notice how each PROCESS domain links back to earlier concepts in this book, particularly the Mental-Physical Paradigm. When we enhance how the brain functions, everything else follows. Our cognitive performance becomes more stable, our decisions become sharper, and our leadership becomes more consistent, even when the pressures on.

Let's now explore each element of the PROCESS Model through a closer lens. What follows is more than just explanation, it's an invitation to align your daily habits, leadership behaviours and recovery strategies with how your brain and body are designed to function at their best. Each section unpacks the science and connects theory to real-world resilience.

PHYSICAL ACTIVITY

Physical activity is often associated with fitness or stress relief. But in high-performance resilience, it plays a deeper role, it's a neurological intervention. Movement is physical, and it's also cognitive, emotional and systemic. Every time we move with purpose, we engage the brain in a recalibration process that sharpens focus, regulates emotion and boosts adaptability under pressure. Strategic movement activates a powerful conversation between brain and body, influencing everything from clarity and motivation to our ability to stay composed through challenge.

One of the most effective ways to enhance neuroplasticity, the brain's capacity to rewire and grow, is through regular physical activity. Movement stimulates the release of Brain-Derived Neurotrophic Factor (BDNF), often called Miracle-Gro for the brain. BDNF strengthens neural networks and enhances learning and adaptation.

As Dr. John Sullivan reminds us: *"More is not better. Better is better."*

Sustainable performance starts with movement that fits your rhythm, not someone else's plan. Think in terms of intentional patterns that align with your energy, your leadership demands and your daily flow (rather than packing your training plan with high volume and intensity). Whether it's a walk, a short strength session, or simply taking the stairs, consistency is what creates real impact.

Building Biological Resilience

Resilience has a physiological footprint. Each time you move with focus, you stimulate a neurochemical cascade:
- Dopamine fuels motivation.
- Serotonin stabilises emotional tone.
- Norepinephrine sharpens attention and alertness.

These chemicals regulate your mood and actively enhance your brain's readiness for pressure, decision-making and adaptation. This is especially critical in the current leadership landscape.

Today's executive faces an unprecedented cognitive load, constant information, career-changing decisions and ongoing emotional demand. Over time, this creates neural fatigue, reduced adaptability, and heightened stress reactivity. Physical activity acts as a form of neural maintenance and upgrade. It supports mitochondrial health (the brain's energy system), increases energy availability at the cellular level and improves overall metabolic function. The result? Sharper thinking, more sustainable focus and better decision-making capacity, even when demands are high.

Not All Movement Is Equal

Activities that challenge coordination, learning and emotional presence, such as dance, martial arts, or racquet sports, offer deeper cognitive benefits than repetitive routines alone. These dynamic movements strengthen executive function, spatial awareness and resilience under variable conditions.

As Sullivan puts it: *"We're not just training muscles. We're training the nervous system for performance."*

It's this kind of movement that's strategic, varied and mentally engaging, that builds biological resilience.

RECOMMENDED

Simple Ways To Integrate Movement Into High-Performance Life

1. **Cognitive-Physical Fusion**
   - Take walking calls or pace while reviewing reports.
   - Pair movement with memory tasks. e.g., learning lines while cycling on a static bike.
   - Join an activity that demands decision-making in motion (e.g., dance or martial arts).
   - Use movement to rehearse, walk through your keynote or negotiation preparation aloud.

2. **Strategic Movement Windows**
   - Morning: A 15-minute walk outside boosts dopamine and primes the brain for focused work.
   - Midday: Take short movement breaks, stretching, bodyweight drills, or walking between meetings to reset.
   - Evening: Engage in decompression movement, yoga, strength work, or a brisk walk to support recovery.

3. **Neurological Movement Diversity**
   - Cardio (run, swim, cycle) for oxygenation and stamina.
   - Strength training for resilience and neuroendocrine health.
   - Coordination-based activities (Pilates, drumming, racquet sports) for neural complexity.
   - Novel challenges like climbing or paddleboarding to stimulate new learning pathways.

4. **Workplace Integration**
   - Use standing desks or movement-enabled work zones.
   - Schedule short micro-breaks every 50–60 minutes to prevent focus fatigue.
   - Introduce team-based movement challenges to promote culture and connection.
   - Reframe movement as a cognitive enhancer, not a time cost.

5. **Purposeful Recovery**
    – Practice walking meditation after lunch to reduce stress.
    – Stretch while listening to a podcast or review notes in motion.
    – Use breath-led mobility work to support parasympathetic recovery.
    – Prioritise quality of movement over intensity, posture and breath, and rhythm over brute force.

Movement should be thought of as something that helps you do your work better, rather than just something you do for fun (or not!) before or after it. Regular, well-timed physical activity fuels attention, regulates emotion and will sharpen your leadership focus and presence.

High-performance resilience isn't just built in the boardroom. It's built in motion.

REST AND RECOVERY

In high-performance environments, rest is often misunderstood, seen as a pause, a luxury, or something that happens only when everything else is done. But in reality, rest is not passive. It is an active neurological process, essential for resilience, focus, and sustained performance.

Think of your brain as a high-functioning system. Like any elite machine, it requires intentional maintenance, and rest is its most powerful reset mechanism. We often assume resilience is forged in moments of stress or challenge, but biologically, resilience is built during deliberate recovery.

As Dr. John Sullivan explains, *"Everything is a poison . . . it just depends on the dose. Build it up and we build tolerance and resilience."* This insight reframes how we understand stress, not as something to avoid, but as a tool for adaptation. Just as physical resistance builds muscle, structured exposure to challenge followed by intentional recovery is what strengthens the brain's resilience over time. It's the rhythm between effort and rest that makes high performance sustainable.

Every time you rest, your brain initiates a series of essential recalibration processes. It consolidates learning, processes emotional experiences, and reorganises and strengthens neural networks. Rest is a form of performance engineering, a critical stage in the resilience cycle that prepares the brain to meet tomorrows demands.

Sullivan emphasises that these rest cycles are essential. He advises leaders to build their day around ultradian rhythms, such as 45–90-minute focus blocks followed by short breaks. These micro-recovery cycles protect against cognitive overload and support sharper executive functioning. Technology even exists to track and train these rhythms in real time; a tool Sullivan uses with Olympic athletes and high-pressure professionals alike.

The Rhythm Of Renewal

Your brain operates on natural cycles, most notably, ultradian rhythms, which run in 90-minute intervals throughout the day. Within these cycles, your brain moves through peaks and troughs of alertness and energy. One particularly important recovery window typically falls between 2:00pm and 3:30pm, a time when cognitive and physiological systems benefit most from a strategic pause.

By understanding and working with these natural rhythms (think back to what you learnt about energy patterns and rhythms in Transitional Resilience), rest becomes a performance enhancement tool.

The Science Of Sleep

Sleep is a biological necessity and it's also a neurological reconstruction process. During deep sleep stages your brain undergoes vital operations, it performs memory consolidation, emotional processing, and strategic reorganisation of neural pathways. These are important foundations of creativity, decision-making and emotional stability.

At a chemical level, sleep supports the brain's self-repair, cortisol levels normalise, calming the stress response; melatonin supports cellular recovery and growth hormone aids neuroplasticity, helping the brain rewire and adapt. Chronic sleep deprivation, by contrast, has a measurable impact by impairing decision-making and compromising emotional regulation. In short, poor sleep goes far beyond fatigue, it actively undermines your brain's ability to function and perform under pressure. It's neural sabotage.

Meditation And Intentional Reset

Meditation and mindful relaxation are more than stress relievers, they're powerful tools for retraining the brain and enhancing performance under pressure. They activate the parasympathetic nervous system, which supports recovery and calm, they reduce inflammation markers linked to stress and cognitive fatigue, and they promote neuroplasticity, enabling the brain to stay agile under pressure.

Whether you call it meditation, intentional rest, or simply calming the mind, this practice should be part of your performance strategy. In today's world, the edge doesn't come from doing more, it comes from learning to strategically oscillate between periods of high-intensity output and deep, deliberate recovery.

RECOMMENDED

Simple Ways To Integrate Rest And Recovery Into High-Performance Life

1. **Scheduled Recovery Techniques**
   - Work in 90-minute focus cycles with 15-minute breaks, syncing with your own energy rhythm for optimal brain recovery.
   - Taking structured power naps (20–26 minutes) after lunch can restore alertness and boost cognitive speed.
   - Maintain a consistent sleep schedule: Aim to go to bed and wake up at the same time daily, even on weekends.
   - Track your sleep to spot trends in recovery quality.
   - Have a wind-down routine. For example, no screens after 9pm, a hot shower, chamomile tea and 5 minutes of breathwork or journaling.

2. **Circadian Rhythm Optimisation**
   - Use blue light blockers or enable night mode on devices post-sunset to protect melatonin production.
   - Design your sleep space: Blackout blinds, set a cool room temperature (16–18°C), no digital clutter, calming scents like lavender.
   - Use daylight lamps in the morning and lower lighting in the evening to help reinforce your natural sleep cues.

3. **Active Recovery Techniques**
   - Engage in daily meditation (12–20 minutes).
   - Practice deliberate relaxation and breathwork: Use progressive muscle relaxation techniques before bed or mid-afternoon to decompress.
   - Use heart rate variability training to track recovery and stress responses over time.
   - Integrate micro-mindfulness moments, for example a deep breath and reset before your next meeting or during coffee breaks.

4. **Workplace Recovery Integration**
   - Create dedicated recharge zones, even a quiet corner with calming visuals and a comfortable chair.
   - Build recovery periods into meeting and workday structures, for example 10-minute silent thinking time or a quick walk before key decision points.
   - Foster a culture that values rest as part of performance: Encourage teams to take breaks and role-model recovery openly as a leader.
   - Use data and feedback tools to encourage recovery behaviours.

5. **Holistic Recovery Approach**
   - Combine physical, cognitive, and emotional recovery practices.
   - Tailor recovery strategies to individual needs: Introverts may need solitude; extroverts may reset better with connection.
   - Review energy logs or team productivity rhythms monthly to adapt recovery plans for yourself or your teams.
   - Treat recovery as a core leadership habit, not an afterthought.

The most resilient leaders don't wait for exhaustion to rest, they design recovery into their lives before the crash.

Rest is a strategy, recovery is performance insurance and resilience starts in the recalibration, not the sprint.

OPTIMAL NUTRITION

While movement primes the brain, it must be sustained with quality inputs. As Dr. John Sullivan explains, *"We only eat for two reasons, to produce neurological transmission, neurochemicals and to produce some vitamins and minerals that go alongside them."*

Food, in this model, means fuelling for cognitive clarity, stable mood and leadership resilience. Nutrition becomes a form of internal performance strategy. As Sullivan puts it: *"Food is medicine."*

The choices you make at the table directly impact your ability to perform throughout the day. Nutrition is food, its fuel and it's a molecular performance strategy, it's the foundation upon which your brain's operating system is built and enhanced. Every bite you consume initiates a biochemical conversation. The nutrients you choose become messengers, sending signals that either support or compromise your brain's ability to perform, adapt and recover.

Although it makes up only 3% of our overall weight, the brain consumes approximately 30% of our calories and 50% of our overall daily oxygen intake. This metabolic demand means that a general approach to eating is not sufficient, not if you want to maintain balance and perform at the highest levels. High performance requires a targeted nutritional strategy, one that supports resilience and brain function at a cellular level.

Food For Thought

Each nutrient plays a distinct role in shaping how your brain functions. Omega-3 fatty acids act as maintenance workers, preserving the myelin sheath that allows rapid, accurate communication between neurons; antioxidants defend your cells from oxidative stress, protecting the brain's delicate structures and B-complex vitamins support mitochondrial energy production, ensuring the brain has the resources to sustain focus.

The diversity of your diet directly influences neuroplasticity, the brain's ability to form new pathways, reorganise itself and adapt to challenges. A varied, nutrient-rich diet becomes a daily upgrade, improving everything from cognitive flexibility to emotional regulation. Neurotransmitter production, for example, is significantly influenced by what we eat. Tryptophan-rich foods support serotonin, enhancing mood stability and stress regulation and tyrosine-rich foods promote dopamine, supporting motivation, alertness, and sustained attention; In effect, your diet is writing the chemical language of your performance.

Feeling better is only the beginning, optimal nutrition fuels the biochemical infrastructure that supports resilience and sustained cognitive performance.

The Gut-Brain Axis

Nutrition's influence doesn't stop at the brain. It extends to the gut-brain axis, where the microbiome plays a direct role in mood, cognition and overall neural function. Far beyond digestion, your gut microbiota form part of a sophisticated system that supports cognitive clarity and emotional balance. Probiotic-rich foods promote microbial diversity and a diet rich in whole, unprocessed foods helps regulate inflammation and mood.

The more diverse your nutritional intake, the more resilient your neural ecosystem becomes.

RECOMMENDED

Simple Ways To Improve Nutrition In High-Performance Life

Every meal is a performance intervention:
1. **Molecular Nutrition Management**
   - Boost neurotransmitters with foods like eggs (choline), salmon (omega-3s), turkey (tryptophan) and leafy greens (folate).
   - Implement micronutrient cycling for systemic balance, for example, rotate sources of magnesium (pumpkin seeds, spinach, dark chocolate) and zinc (cashews, chickpeas).

- Intentional meal design: A breakfast of oats, berries and protein supports morning focus; lighter lunches prevent afternoon crashes.
- Eat whole, unprocessed foods, aim for 'real over refined', like choosing sweet potatoes over white bread.

2. **Cognitive Fuel Approach**
   - Hydration target: 2–3 litres of water daily, plus electrolytes after exercise or travel.
   - 30-plant challenge: Track how many different fruits, veg, herbs, grains, legumes and nuts you eat weekly using an app or checklist.
   - Supplement strategically, for example vitamin D in winter, B-complex for stress, omega-3s for focus, based on blood work or guidance.
   - Personalise your fuel: One executive I coach performs better with high-protein breakfasts; another with intermittent fasting. It's important to know your pattern.

3. **Gut-Brain Performance Approach**
   - Probiotic-rich foods: Include kefir, yoghurt, kimchi, sauerkraut, and miso in your weekly meals.
   - Prebiotics: Add garlic, onions, bananas, leeks and oats to support your gut microbiome.
   - Mood-stabilising nutrition: Combine complex carbs (quinoa, lentils) with healthy fats (avocados, nuts) for even energy and emotional regulation.
   - Track your gut response: If dairy or gluten affects focus or energy, adjust accordingly, and explore food sensitivity testing if needed.

4. **Performance Nutrition Tracking**
   - Track nutrition effects: Journal your meals alongside mood and focus levels or use an app for trend analysis.
   - Technology tip: Wearables can sync with your food logs to show energy trends.
   - Create a feedback loop: For example, log high-carb vs. high-fat lunches and compare your afternoon productivity.
   - Review and refine monthly: Update your go-to meals, snacks, or hydration plan based on how your body performs.

5. **Holistic Nutritional Approach**
   - Sync nutrition with sleep: Avoid caffeine after 2pm and heavy meals 2 hours before bed to improve sleep depth.
   - Fuel resilience under pressure: Add magnesium (e.g., spinach, almonds) and adaptogens like ashwagandha during high-stress periods.
   - Build integrated protocols, for example, a 3pm smoothie + 10-minute walk + 2-minute breathwork = powerful midday recalibration.
   - Think ecosystem, not silos: What you eat affects how you move, sleep, lead and communicate. It's all connected.

Nutrition should focus on choice and purpose. A high-performance leader doesn't eat for convenience; they eat with intention. Every choice either supports your cognition or clouds it.

Food is your biochemical advantage.

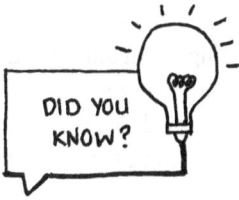

Adam Burgess on Nutritional Principles and Practice:

Adam's approach to nutrition is rooted in simplicity, science and consistency. As an elite athlete, Adam focuses on *"easy wins"* that support long-term health, daily energy and performance under pressure. His philosophy is not about rigid rules, but about informed, refined habits.

– Hydration: Adam uses filtered water, even while travelling (taking his water filter machine with him!).
– Whole Foods: He avoids processed food; focuses on eating real, minimally refined ingredients.
– Adam's chosen supplements (He focuses only what moves the performance needle):
    – Whey Protein: Healthspan brand (chosen for quality and feel).
    – Creatine: Based on bodyweight (0.1g/kg daily).
    – Beta-Alanine: Loaded over time.
    – Concentrated Beetroot Shot: Taken for six days before competition.
    – Multivitamin & Omega-3: Supports immune system and recovery.

"I don't take loads," he says, *"just what has strong evidence behind it and helps me feel good."*

COGNITIVE LOAD

The human brain is not designed for non-stop performance. It is a sophisticated, adaptive system with finite cognitive resources and it thrives under conditions of purposeful engagement, strategic challenge and timely recovery. In a world that rewards constant activity and uninterrupted output, we must learn to balance and manage our cognitive load with intention. Without balance, performance suffers, not from lack of effort, but from a misalignment between capacity and demand.

Managing cognitive load is the practice of understanding, protecting, and enhancing your brain's processing capacity. It is both an art and a science, a way of working with your mind's natural rhythms rather than against them. Think of your cognitive capacity as a high-functioning operating system, responsive, deeply intelligent, but not infinite. Traditional productivity models assume that more input equals more output. In truth, your brain operates in cycles of focus and reset. Overextending those cycles leads to diminished clarity and reduced performance.

In our interview, Dr. Sullivan explains, *"Elite runners are not focussing 100% of their attention on the task 100% of the time."* In leadership, learning when to defocus, or when to disassociate is just as important as learning when and how to apply deep focus. Resting your 'attention' can strategically sustain your performance. This idea of rhythm isn't just mental either, it's physiological. Dr. John Sullivan draws on this principle through the lens of breath. Inhalation pushes energy through the brain, while exhalation is when the body relaxes. Together, they form a cosine curve. This micro-cycling of work, rest, work, rest, is essential for managing cognitive load. When we ignore these rhythms and push linearly through our day, we tire ourselves and we undermine the brain's resilience and energy efficiency.

Each moment of focused attention actively reshapes your brain. You're absorbing information, constructing new neural pathways, and reinforcing the ones that matter. Research suggests most adults can maintain deep focus for around 20 minutes at a time. Your brain is signalling its optimal rhythm for learning and integration. Multitasking may feel productive, but neurologically, it fragments attention and compromises memory encoding. The most effective performers create clear, single-task windows for deep work, followed by structured intervals for processing and recovery. This pattern mirrors how the brain is built to function, with focused effort followed by renewal.

Learning And Adaptation

Each time you recall or apply a piece of knowledge, your brain is reconstructing it, slightly altering the neural pathway it travels. This means learning is a dynamic process, a continuous reshaping of your internal architecture. This reshaping is most effective when matched with rhythm, recovery and challenge, not endless input.

Cognitive performance and resilience go hand in hand. Sustained cognitive strain increases cortisol, which can reduce neuroplasticity and impair your brain's ability to adapt. Managing cognitive load, then, becomes a strategic intervention, one that protects your most valuable performance asset, your mind.

RECOMMENDED

Simple Ways To Manage Cognitive Load In High-Performance Life

1. **Cognitive Engagement Techniques**
   - Use 52-minute focused work blocks: Set a timer, work with full focus for 52 minutes, then take a deliberate 8-minute break, similar to a high-performance sprint. Where you need peak focus, reduce this window down to 20-minutes.
   - Apply active recall and retrieval-based learning: Instead of just re-reading, test yourself. Example: after a meeting or course, write down what you remember without checking your notes.
   - Deliberate practice for complex skills: Break down big skills (like public speaking or data analysis) into smaller parts and practise each with full focus. For example, rehearse just the opening for a presentation until it's polished, then move on to the next part.
   - Design tasks that challenge different parts of the brain: Switch between creative tasks (e.g., brainstorming ideas) and analytical ones (e.g., budgeting or reviewing data) to stimulate different cognitive pathways.

2. **Strategic Recovery Integration**
   - Schedule brain resets throughout the day: Take a 10-minute walk, stare out the window, have a no-phone lunch, or do 5 minutes of box breathing (inhale 4, hold 4, exhale 4, hold 4).
   - Use mindfulness or breathwork to reduce mental strain: If this is a new area for you, there are many different Apps available offering short, guided practices that are great to use between tasks.
   - Build external memory systems: Use a whiteboard, notebook, sticky notes, or even a digital voice note app to store ideas, so your brain doesn't have to hold everything at once.
   - Reflect at the end of your day and ask: What worked today? What drained me? A 3-minute journal helps build metacognitive awareness.

3. **Expand Your Neural Network**
   - Learn new skills that stretch your brain: Have a go at something outside your usual comfort zone or regular activities, for example, learn a new language, instrument, or event coding.
   - Rotate tasks during the day: Don't spend 4 hours in a row on email. Instead, do 45 minutes of email, then switch to something visual or strategic to stimulate different parts of the brain.
   - Track your focus: Use simple apps or good old-fashioned notebooks to rate yourself 1–5 after each work block to build awareness over time.

4. **Stress-Cognition Management**
   - Use breathing to reset your brain under pressure: Have a go at 2 minutes of deep belly breathing before a big meeting or after a frustrating call.
   - Create distraction-free zones: Turn off notifications, put your phone out of reach and use tools like 'Do Not Disturb' or focus music playlists.

– Unplug daily: Schedule screen-free time, even 20 minutes during lunch, while commuting, or before bed.
– Remember to align your work with your energy rhythms: If you're most focused at 9am, don't waste it on admin. Use your highs for your hardest work.

5. **Commit To Continuous Learning**
    – Treat learning as a performance habit: Read 10 pages of a book each morning or listen to an insightful podcast on your walk.
    – Challenge your default thinking: Ask yourself, *"What if the opposite were true?"* or *"How would someone else see this?"*
    – Use real feedback to grow. After a presentation, ask: *"What's one thing I could do better next time?"* (and listen to and take onboard the feedback!).

Remember, learning changes your brain. Every new insight builds new neural connections. Your brain is literally evolving. Cognitive load management does not mean finding ways to squeeze more into your schedule, it requires you to learn how to work in alignment with how your brain performs best, finding your rhythm and your balance.

When you understand your brain's architecture, you can protect it, challenge it, and stretch it, without compromising its long-term capacity. Your mind is your most valuable asset in the pursuit of sustained, high-performance leadership. Think Smarter, Perform Better.

EMOTIONAL MANAGEMENT

Emotions are not passive feelings or distractions from logic, they are neurochemical signals carrying valuable information about your internal state and external environment. When understood and channelled effectively, emotions become a strategic advantage in performance, leadership and resilience.

Emotional management is the practice of recognising, interpreting, and optimising these signals. It involves tuning into the brain's emotional systems, not to override them, but to work with them, strengthening adaptability and enhancing decision-making. The brain is an emotionally intelligent organ, one where emotion and cognition constantly interact. Every emotional response sets off a neurochemical chain reaction, it can enhance clarity, motivation and problem-solving, or it can impair focus and increase reactivity. Performance is not compromised by emotion itself, it's affected by how well emotion is managed.

Reflect back to Chapter 3 to remind yourself that understanding emotional intelligence means understanding the brain systems that shape how we experience, interpret and respond to emotion. These systems don't work in isolation, they operate as an integrated emotional network, influencing how we lead and make better decisions under pressure.

Thanks to neuroplasticity, we can rewire the emotional response system. Mindfulness builds awareness and calm; cognitive reframing strengthens adaptive interpretation; and emotional literacy creates a broader vocabulary for internal experience. The prefrontal cortex, responsible for regulation, judgment and strategic thinking plays a central role. Training this region through reflective focused emotional work enables better leadership and a stronger capacity to recover and recalibrate under pressure.

Your emotional system is data. Learn to read it, work with it, and enhance it.

RECOMMENDED

Simple Ways To Better Manage Your Emotions In High-Performance Life

1. **Neurochemical Self-Regulation**
    - Practise heart rate variability (HRV) training to build nervous system balance (if this is a new area for you, then there are apps or trainers that can guide and support you).
    - Create reset rituals, for example, a walk after intense meetings or cold-water therapy to reset your baseline.
    - Use breathwork in the moment, like box breathing as mentioned earlier, before a pitch or before committing to an important decision.
    - Track your emotional states with mood journaling or utilise colour-coded planners for trends and triggers.

2. **Cognitive-Emotional Integration**
    - Apply mindfulness by pausing and naming the emotion: *"I'm feeling overwhelmed,"* rather than reacting.
    - Use cognitive reframing, shift from *"I'm failing"* to *"I'm learning how to handle pressure better."*
    - Set a development plan, for example, journaling after conflict to review how you handled it and what to adjust.
    - Map patterns, notice, for example, that frustration might commonly follow task-switching without a break.

3. **Stress Response Engineering**
    - Build a system, schedule 3–5-minute breaks into your diary with the same commitment you do your meetings.
    - Stimulate your vagus nerve through humming, cold exposure, or yoga to reduce anxiety fast.

  - Shape your space, natural light, music, scent, and greenery are all known to reduce emotional friction.
  - Use rituals, for example, wind-down routines after work could include journaling or no screens after 9pm.

4. **Enhance Emotional Intelligence**
  - Practice under pressure, for example, rehearse feedback conversations in high-stress simulations.
  - Use reflection prompts: *"What emotion did I lead with today?"* or *"What did I miss emotionally?"*
  - Link outcomes to signals: Notice, perhaps, how avoiding a difficult conversation increased anxiety later.
  - Coach yourself, ask *"What is this emotion telling me?"* and *"How can I respond with intention?"*

5. **Holistic Emotional Management**
  - Blend physical and emotional tools: Train, meditate and reflect in the same daily rhythm.
  - Align with your resilience plan: Anchor emotions to your energy, recovery and mindset systems.
  - Personalise tools, for example use music for emotional reset, therapy dogs, humour playlists, or creative outlets.
  - View emotions as powerful performance enhancers: Treat emotions as internal signals, not noise. They're your performance dashboard.

Emotional mastery is learning to manage your full range of emotion, with agility and purpose.

SOCIALISATION

The human brain is, at its core, a social organ. It evolves through connection, learning, adapting and growing in response to the dynamic interplay of human interaction.

Socialisation is far more than a form of communication. It is a neural expansion process, one in which each meaningful exchange reshapes our cognitive architecture. When we engage with others, we do more than trade ideas, we activate a rich neurochemical and electromagnetic dialogue that enhances learning and resilience.

Each meaningful conversation enables you to absorb new perspectives and model unfamiliar behaviour. You learn to refine your understanding through reflection and feedback. This adaptive process is made possible by mirror neurons, specialised networks in the brain that activate both when we act and when we observe others doing the same. These neurons allow us to learn through observation, develop empathy and build complex social understanding, expanding our cognitive capacity beyond what we could achieve alone.

Social connection also triggers critical neurochemical shifts. Oxytocin, often known as the connection hormone, plays a key role in emotional bonding, but it also enhances performance. It reduces stress, strengthens trust and collaboration, and supports the formation of neural pathways associated with learning and adaptability. Our ability to interpret emotional cues, manage complexity and build trust-rich environments directly influences how we perform under pressure.

The Cost Of Disconnection

Prolonged isolation doesn't just affect mood, it alters how our brain functions.

Research shows that chronic lack of meaningful connection can lead to increased stress and accelerated cognitive decline. Your brain depends on regular, varied and meaningful interaction with others to stay resilient and high functioning. Social interaction, therefore, is a neural necessity.

RECOMMENDED

Simple Ways To Enhance Socialisation For High-Performance Life

1. **Expand Your Neural Network**
   - Seek out diverse social experiences: For example, attend industry-adjacent events or director / manager forums that represent a variety of sectors.
   - Seek opportunities for cross-discipline engagement.
   - Interdisciplinary dialogue: Host informal 'idea swaps' over lunch with people from different departments or sectors, or more formal group coaching sessions.
   - Use conversation to grow: Instead of small talk, ask questions that encourage reflection and provide insight like: *"What's one idea that's changed how you work this year?"*

2. **Make Meaningful Connection**
   - Quality over quantity: Instead of attending every networking event, focus on strengthening 2–3 existing relationships each month.
   - Active listening practice: Practice a '3-second pause' before replying in conversations to encourage better engagement (and to politely check they have finished).
   - Structured networking: Schedule a monthly 'coffee chat' calendar; even just 20-minute calls can build connection.
   - Social learning goals: For each key interaction (a mentor lunch, a client pitch), set a goal, for example: learn one new insight or strengthen alignment.

3. **Develop Collaborative Intelligence**
    –   Cross-cultural networks: Join international masterminds or multicultural peer groups.
    –   Empathy as skill: Before difficult meetings, reflect on the other person's likely mindset and needs, then adjust your tone accordingly.
    –   Social problem-solving: Use 10-minute 'huddles' to brainstorm in pairs before bringing ideas to the larger team.
    –   Smart tech for collaboration: Utilise technology to foster asynchronous teamwork with richer communication than email alone.

4. **Architect Social Resilience**
    –   Mutual support ecosystems: Pair up with a colleague for weekly 'pulse checks' to share success, barriers and energy levels.
    –   Team-based learning: Host reverse mentoring sessions where junior and senior team members swap insights.
    –   Psychological safety practices: Encourage phrases like *"I might be wrong, however . . . "* or *"Here's my early thinking . . . "* in meetings.
    –   Identify relationships you can use as a buffer: During stress, identify 1–2 'resilience allies' you can vent to or bounce ideas off without judgment.

5. **Continuous Social Learning**
    –   Micro-learning moments: After a key conversation, ask yourself: *"What did I learn about them, or myself?"*
    –   Social self-awareness: Notice when your energy dips in social settings, is it content, environment, or timing?
    –   Feedback from interactions: If your team disengages in meetings, reflect, and ask, *"Was my delivery clear? Did I invite input?"*
    –   Train social intelligence: Practice adapting your communication style, for example have a go at using visual examples for creatives, or data-led logic for analysts.

Your network is not just who you know, it's how you grow.

SYNERGY

Where High-Performance Becomes Whole

This final element of the PROCESS Model is where everything comes together. It's the integrative force that transforms isolated habits into a sustainable high-performance system.

Synergy is more than the sum of its parts. It's the alignment of body, brain and behaviour, the convergence of physical, mental, emotional, and social systems into one cohesive rhythm. It's where movement supports cognition, recovery strengthens creativity and emotional intelligence fuels better decision-making. In neuroscience, this is known as cross-domain coherence, the state where multiple brain systems work in harmony to enhance output.

Synergy turns scattered effort into integrated excellence.

When you apply the PROCESS Model synergistically, your nutrition supports your emotional regulation, your recovery fuels your cognitive clarity, your movement sharpens your decision-making, your social connection becomes a source of resilience, and your emotional mastery stabilises your leadership presence. This integration is what separates those who perform well occasionally from those who sustain excellence and elite performance over time. Synergy across performance makes you adaptable, sustainable and whole.

When all parts of your life align with your performance rhythm, the work feels lighter, decisions become clearer, and your impact expands without draining your capacity. More than resilience, it's your Resilience Advantage.

From Preparation To High Performance In Action

High-performance resilience isn't luck. It's design. It emerges from intentional habits and systems that allow us to stay focused, composed and adaptable, not just in key moments, but consistently, across roles, demands and life phases. Sustained performance comes from our ability to activate and integrate internal capabilities under pressure, not just physical output, or mental stamina, but the synergy between them.

Throughout this chapter, we've explored how The Resilience Advantage as one of the three core Calibration Tools, offers a structured, trainable pathway for sustainable high performance. The PROCESS Model provides one way to operationalise that tool, a neuroscience-informed framework designed to help you maintain energy, regulate emotion and support brain performance under load.

But strategy only matters if it holds up when the pressure is high.

So, what happens when preparation meets real-world complexity, when you're under pressure, navigating uncertainty, or performing at the edge of your capacity? That's where we shift from building your system to activating it.

The following strategies show how high performers move from intention to execution. These show how the Calibration Tools are brought to life in the moments that matter most.

1 Performance State Management: Prime Before You Perform

Top performers don't wait for calm and confidence, they create it.

Whether it's a sprinter in the blocks, a surgeon entering theatre, or a leader walking into a boardroom, elite performers use state-priming techniques to access their optimal mental, emotional, and physiological zone. These are intentional interventions, designed to regulate focus and readiness under pressure.

The principle 'Create the state before you operate' comes from elite performance psychology and Neuro Linguistic Programming (NLP). It's one of the most transferable tools for leaders, especially when pressure rises.

Let's explore how two world-class performers use this to their advantage:

Adam Burgess: Predictable Calm and Adaptive Readiness.

Adam prepares for the unpredictability of elite sport with a unique blend of consistency and flexibility. His approach isn't about hyping up, it's about calming down. His rituals are designed to stabilise the nervous system, minimise decision fatigue and preserve energy for the race itself. *"My ritual is usually one of distraction . . . I'll watch things on Netflix that I've already watched. It's real, like a comfort show. It's predictable. There's nothing new. Novelty is a stressor for the nervous system, so I avoid it pre-race."*

Rather than overstimulate himself with last-minute tactics or external cues, Adam deliberately limits new input. He chooses routines and content that are familiar and calming, knowing this helps regulate arousal and sharpen focus.

In his earlier career, overthinking cost him: *"I was warming up and I was yawning . . . I'd been thinking about that start line all week. I never took that moment to calm myself down so I could hit that high again. That was my body saying, 'No'."*

Now, his routine includes flexibility, building in space to adapt if the conditions or schedule shift unexpectedly. When he needs to anchor himself under pressure, he reconnects with: *"The whole path of my life panned out because that 10-year-old Adam just put his hand up. Sometimes I just remind myself of that moment, that belief. The confidence to have a go."*

Adam's strategy is powerful in its simplicity. Manage stimulation, stay flexible and anchor your state in your values and identity, not external circumstances.

Floyd Woodrow: Breath, Anchors and Future-State Visualisation.

Former SAS major and performance strategist Floyd Woodrow enters important moments by aligning breath, thought and emotion through conscious preparation. He combines physiological calm with cognitive clarity: *"I've got everything in place. I'm looking after my body so I can make appropriate decisions mentally. I use breathing techniques to calm myself straight away."*

His mental preparation uses power words, anchors for state and focus: *"So, for me it's courage, resilience, determination. That's always about the opportunity to see how good I could be."*

Using classic NLP techniques like anchoring and immersive visualisation, Floyd trains his mind to step into the desired future state. He explains it's important to: *"Always visualise yourself being at the end of the journey, why you want to be there, how you'll feel, the people who'll be there. The thoughts, the smells. That's what I'm moving towards."*

His approach is proactive, not reactive. He primes his internal system to meet pressure with presence, composure and readiness, not adrenaline.

For me, state priming always begins with a reminder of forward motion. The reality that I'll never be stuck in that one moment, however good or bad it feels, creates a form of safety net. It gives me freedom to step in, to have a go, without fear of being defined by a single outcome.

What I wear also helps trigger the shift. It signals a move from preparation to performance. My children sometimes joke that I'm in 'proper clothes' when I head out to see clients, too used to seeing me in the hybrid comfort of home-based work. Even Stephen, my business partner can tell how I'm feeling depending on whether I dial into our pulse meetings in a hoodie and with a giant mug of tea or something more structured and professional. It's not always intentional, but it's always telling. What I wear reflects and influences my energy, and others pick up on that. That outer shift often prompts an internal one. It's a small but powerful act of readiness.

Because I'm highly visual, mental imagery is also key. I can imagine success, and I rehearse it. I see myself in motion, confident, prepared, engaged. I picture how I'll stand and how I'll speak, what I'll wear and how the room will feel. That vivid internal movie plays like it's already happened, so when the moment comes, I don't have to guess, I simply step into the memory.

2 Decision-Making Under Pressure: Sharpening The Lens

Pressure compresses time. It shrinks your focus, amplifies emotion and tempts reactivity. Resilient leaders train themselves to operate with clarity even under constraint. They build a system for decision-making, one that holds under load.

Key capabilities include:

– **Strategic Intuition:** Recognising patterns quickly without over-processing. This is less about guesswork and more about trained recognition, built through repeated exposure, feedback and reflection.
– **Emotional Clarity:** The ability to separate signal from noise. Regulating emotion in real time so decisions aren't clouded by ego, fatigue or fear.
– **Implementation Agility:** Making the best call available and executing it, despite ambiguity, complexity, or imperfect data.

They are key capabilities you build through practice, anchored in reality-testing, developed in training, refined in transition, and tested in pressure.

Resilience Layer	Primary Focus
1. Daily Operational	Energy management, micro-recoveries, emotional reset, and performance rhythm.
2. Transitional Resilience	Adapting to change, evolving through feedback, reframing failure into fuel.
3. High-Performance Execution	Accessing peak states, staying sharp under load, sustaining excellence over time.

3 Sustaining Performance Over Time: Rhythm, Recovery And Realignment

Resilience means knowing when to run, when to rest and when to recalibrate. This is the difference between momentary excellence and sustainable performance.

We can think of it as three interdependent layers:

Each layer feeds the next. Together, they create your personal suspension system, keeping you moving even when the terrain gets rough.

Ultimately, this is what it means to activate the Calibration Tools:

– Using Emotional Intelligence to regulate your state.
– Using Skilled Communication to lead through complexity.
– Using The Resilience Advantage to sustain momentum and recover rapidly.

This is the architecture of performance. Designed with intention. Lived with rhythm. Refined through reflection.

Next Steps: Bringing Your Performance System To Life

You've now explored the three Calibration Tools that form the heart of the Calibration Model:

– **Emotional Intelligence**
– **Skilled Communication**
– **The Resilience Advantage**

Together, they give you the practical capacity to regulate under pressure, communicate with impact and lead yourself and others with intention. Use what you've read as your personal audit. Revisit the reflection questions, exercises and evidence-based routines woven throughout the chapters. Ask yourself:
− Where am I already strong?
− Where do I need more rhythm, more recovery, or more stretch?
− How can I apply these tools, consistently, not just when it's easy, but when it matters most?

Remember, none of this needs to be perfect to be powerful. This is a process of refinement, not reinvention.

From Tools To Paradigms

Understanding how to calibrate your performance is only half the story. To activate these tools, we need to look at where they apply. After all, sustainable success doesn't just come from knowing how to lead, it comes from knowing what you're leading towards and how your personal and professional drivers interact.

This next section marks a shift away from how to calibrate, to a move towards where it creates impact

In the following chapters, we'll explore the three core paradigms that define a balanced and successful journey:
− **The Money-Mission Paradigm**
− **The Mental-Physical Paradigm**
− **The Work-Life Paradigm**

These aren't abstract theories. They are lived, daily tensions. They shape your decisions, challenge your boundaries, and ultimately define how aligned and fulfilled you feel.

Let's begin with one of the most common and most misunderstood tensions of them all, money versus meaning.

Section Three: **The Money-Mission Paradigm**

Finding Your Sweet Spot: Where Money Meets Meaning

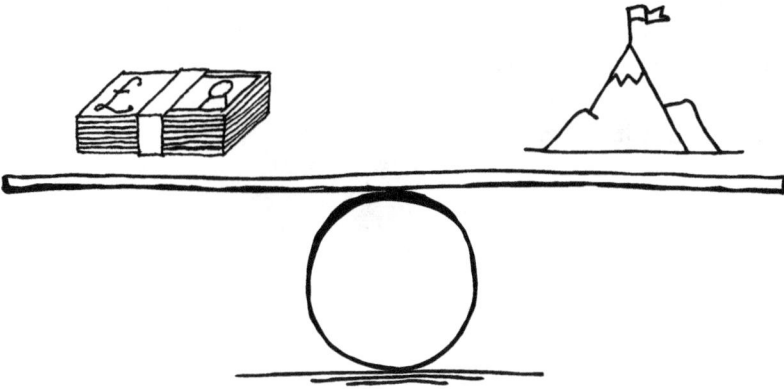

Let's be honest. Most of us are just trying to figure out this whole 'professional success' thing.

Some days, you might be chasing that next promotion or financial milestone. Other days, wondering if there's more to life than just making money. If this is you, you're not alone. I've sat across from hundreds of professionals, from ambitious young executives to experienced business leaders and owners, and heard the same core struggles.

Maybe you're thinking, 'I want to do meaningful work, but I also need to pay my mortgage'. Or perhaps, 'I've achieved financial success, but something still feels . . . empty'. These aren't contradictions. They're completely normal human experiences.

The truth is that your professional journey doesn't have to be a constant compromise between making money and making a difference. It can be both. This mind shift is exactly what we're going to explore in this section.

I'm not about to start guilt-tripping you into some grand social mission and I'm not going to start telling you that money is evil, or that you should sacrifice your financial security for some vague notion of 'purpose'. What we are going to do, together, is explore ways to find your unique balance, a sweet spot where your financial goals and your deeper aspirations work together, not against each other.

Think about it like building a house. You need a solid financial foundation to create something meaningful. But you also need a vision, a purpose that goes beyond just bricks and mortar. This section becomes your guide for constructing a professional life that feels both financially secure and personally fulfilling.

Whether you're driven by ambitious financial targets or a burning desire to create positive change, this section will help you design a professional path that feels authentically, sustainably successful.

Your career is a journey, not a destination. Sometimes, the most important skill is learning how to move forward, with both financial wisdom and personal integrity.

Ready to find your balance?

Chapter 6
Understanding The Money-Mission Paradigm

"I want to do something that matters, but I also have bills to pay."

"I can't complain about the salary, but the work just doesn't inspire me."

"I could earn more elsewhere, but here I feel like I'm contributing to something meaningful."

These reflections, heard from professionals across industries, roles and stages of career, capture a fundamental tension in modern career development, the balance between financial reward and meaningful impact.

This Money-Mission Paradigm goes beyond surface-level job satisfaction or general wellbeing. At its core is a deeper question, how do we build sustainable success that supports both our bank balance and our sense of purpose? In other words, how do we align money and mission, without feeling like we're constantly compromising one for the other?

One person who embodies the Money-Mission Paradigm in action is Anne McClean, Partner, and Head of Wealth at IPS Capital, a Chartered Financial Planner and Certified Financial Planner, Fellow of the Personal Finance Society, and award-winning adviser. She helps individuals and families navigate life's most complex transitions, from business exits to bereavement. But Anne's career didn't begin in finance. When speaking with Anne, she describes her younger self as *"A 13-year-old girl who grew up on a farm in a small village in Shropshire. I had a paper round and milked cows. At school, I was completely rudderless . . . I didn't have a lot of direction or guidance."*

Anne began her career in recruitment. *"I enjoyed the psychology of it,"* she says, *"but I got fed up trying to put people into jobs they didn't want and persuading companies to take people they weren't sure about. It didn't sit right with me."* What did stand out, however, were the interactions she had with financial directors and advisers during that time, people she was helping place into high-paying roles. *"I had two persistent thoughts,"* Anne recalls. *"One, I wouldn't want to have you in front of my mother giving her advice! And two, I can't believe you're earning that much money!"* That contrast, between financial opportunity and ethical discomfort sparked something.

It's a powerful reminder of the value in being exposed early to different roles, not just for what they pay, but for what they reveal about the demands and realities of working life, from character and capability to lifestyle and long-term fit. It showed Anne what was possible financially, but also highlighted a gap. She saw a profession with earning potential with areas where she knew she could do things differently and better than what she'd personally experienced. She saw space to stand out by doing the right thing, not just the profitable thing. So, she pivoted, just before her 30th birthday. *"I decided to change career, undertook lots of study off my own back, took my first exam and got myself a job."* She immersed herself in learning, ordering financial planning books from the US and educating herself before podcasts and online resources were common. *"I just worked and worked."* Along the way, she was fortunate to be supported by a few generous mentors who saw her potential and gave her their time. *"There were a lot of people who looked at clients and just saw pound signs, what's in it for them. I think our industry is tarred with that. But we're not all like that. I've always just been of the opinion that you do the right thing and money will follow. People will refer you. Money will just flow. Just do the right thing."*

Anne's approach to wealth planning, in its most holistic, ethical, and personalised way, is now widely respected and sought after. She describes there being *"great satisfaction in welding technical solutions to people's bespoke values, behaviours and objectives."* Her story is a powerful example of what happens when you combine moral clarity with self-driven action. She didn't enter her field because it was easy, but because it offered a space where she could grow, contribute meaningfully, and build the life she wanted, one aligned with both money and mission.

The Money-Mission Divide: A False Dichotomy

We're often led to believe that money and mission are mutually exclusive, as if pursuing one means compromising the other. This perceived conflict creates to a term known as 'career dissonance', an internal tension that quietly undermines performance, fulfilment and long-term alignment. But this tension is built on out-dated assumptions.

More recent research suggests that leaders who successfully integrate finan-cial achievement with meaningful work report higher career satisfaction, stron-ger leadership presence and more sustainable financial outcomes over time. The real question isn't whether to choose money or mission, but how to align them.

That's the heart of the Money-Mission Paradigm, a shift from 'either/or' to 'both/and'. Instead of treating financial reward and meaningful work as compet-ing goals, this paradigm recognises them as complementary forces. When aligned, they become the foundation for lasting success.

Ali's leadership of the Youth Sport Trust offers a real-world example. Despite the financial demands of running a charity, every decision is grounded in pur-pose. *"Our mission has to lead,"* she says, *"but we still have to pay the bills. That's the daily tension we manage."* Her approach isn't idealistic, it's integrative and it works.

Now consider a client I had, James, a financial advisor whose early career was all about the ladder, earning more, closing deals, growing portfolios. By all external measures, he was successful. The money was great. But something felt off, not broken, just incomplete. At the time, he didn't question it, life was busy, high-achieving and always moving forward. Fulfilment was something for later. Then James became a father. For the first time, the question shifted from what he was building, to why. He realised he had created financial success, but not neces-sarily the kind of life he wanted his child to grow up in. It wasn't a crisis, just a quiet wake-up call. This isn't quite it.

Sometimes, it takes a life event, a change in identity, a shift in perspective, to realise we're craving something more aligned. Not less ambition, but deeper pur-pose. James didn't walk away from his business. He recalibrated it. He started working with clients who wanted more than just wealth, they wanted to use it to shape their families, their futures, and their communities. In helping them build meaningful legacies, James began building one of his own. He became more ener-gised, more connected, and perhaps ironically, more successful. His clients didn't just see him as an advisor, but as a partner in purpose. As his impact deepened, so did his business.

But here's the real shift, as his business grew, James became less busy. He brought others in, built systems, and freed up time, for his health and for his fam-ily. James' journey doesn't just illustrate the Money-Mission paradigm, it reveals something even more powerful. These paradigms don't exist in isolation, they in-tersect and influence one another.

We'll explore that further when we reach the Work-Life paradigm. But for now, let James' story serve as a reminder that sustainable success is built when your ambition and your values walk side by side. When your work creates both income and impact, and when your story is not only profitable, but meaningful.

The Three Dimensions Of Money-Mission Balance

Success isn't only about climbing higher; it's about knowing what you're climbing toward.

Balancing financial goals with meaningful impact is a real and ongoing challenge for driven professionals seeking both prosperity and purpose. As we navigate this tension, three forces come into play. These are value and impact, growth and purpose, and liquidity and legacy.

In the following pages, we'll explore the practical considerations and deeper questions these dimensions raise, and how they shape sustainable success within the Money-Mission Paradigm.

1. Balancing Value With Impact

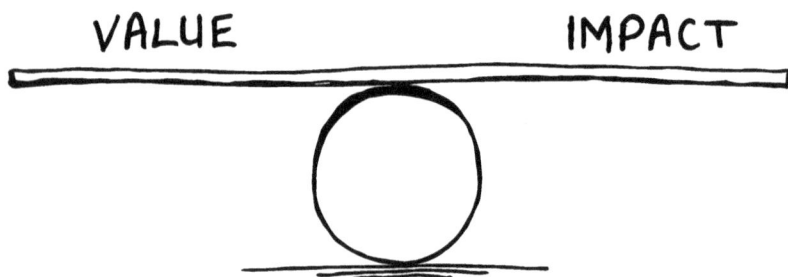

VALUE   IMPACT

Think about your most meaningful achievements, particularly in your professional life. Chances are, the moments that stand out didn't just generate financial gain, but created meaningful, real-world impact. That's not a coincidence. That's alignment in action.

Traditional thinking often frames profit and purpose as opposites, forcing a choice between them. But in reality, when you solve important problems with integrity and innovation, value and impact can grow together.

Take Floyd Woodrow, Founder of the Compass for Life Group. Having already built a portfolio that includes Super North Star and his role as Chairman of the Quantum Group, Floyd had the strategic infrastructure, network and experience to expand his reach. Instead of stopping at high-performance consultancy or fintech incubation though, he launched the Compass for Life Foundation, a philanthropic arm supporting disadvantaged children across the UK. His aim, to help close the educational gap and offer children a roadmap for ambition, resilience and future success.

This wasn't a commercial decision. It was values-led. Because Floyd had first built strong, scalable systems, financially, operationally and reputationally, he had the capacity to act. He didn't keep it quiet, either. He launched a crowdfunding campaign, engaged his wider network, and used his platform to bring others into the mission. The result created ripple effects far beyond what any single business unit could achieve.

That's the synergy of the Money-Mission paradigm at its best. Using commercial success to create deeper impact and using that impact to enhance long-term value.

This philosophy is also embodied by Michael Addison, Academic Director, and co-founder of the International Foundation Group. His relentless focus on quality, placing learner experience and academic integrity above all else, has fuelled sustainable growth. The organisation has expanded into new markets without compromising its core values. Michael proves that scale doesn't have to dilute purpose; done well, it can reinforce it.

Of course, balance is still essential. Growth alone won't secure your mission, and good intentions without viability can't sustain themselves. You need both. Get it wrong and you risk building something deeply meaningful that's commercially fragile, or something highly profitable that's empty and easily replicated.

Value without viability can't grow. Viability without values doesn't last. The sweet spot lies in the synergy.

So, as you reflect on your own work, consider:
How can your strategies generate both financial and social value?
Where are the opportunities to profit by solving problems that matter?
What elements of your mission could unlock new revenue streams?
What foundations do you need to build now to expand your impact later?

When value and impact are aligned, success doesn't just happen, it compounds.

2. Balancing Growth With Purpose

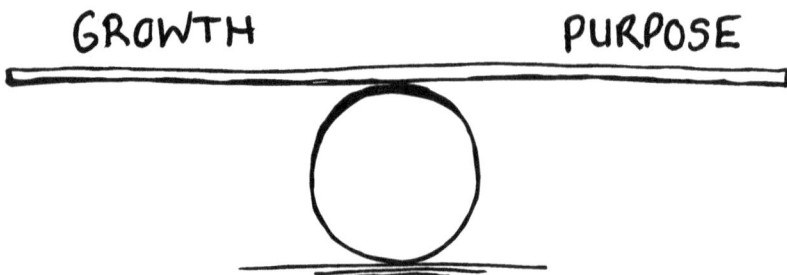

GROWTH   PURPOSE

Leadership development rarely follows a straight line. The most impactful professionals find ways to align their personal growth with a deeper sense of purpose. When learning is intentional and connected to something meaningful, it strengthens both professional value and real-world contribution. In this context, beyond skill-building, growth becomes a force for strategic and personal evolution.

Think of it like flying a twin-engine aircraft, when one side is neglected, the journey becomes unstable.

Tom, a friend, and fellow leadership trainer is a strong example of this principle. With a background in tech and infrastructure, and a deep interest in emotional intelligence, Tom saw a growing tension. As AI advanced rapidly, many leaders were adapting to the tools but losing sight of the human element.

Rather than choosing between innovation and connection, he fused the two. Tom repositioned his business around AI-empowered leadership, helping teams use AI technology to increase their productivity and strategic judgement, whilst also enhancing their creative thinking and empathy. His approach broadened his offer and redefined his role. Today, he's now seen as a technical expert and trusted advisor to those managing the human side of digital transformation. *"The future isn't human or AI,"* he says. *"It's the intelligent integration of both.*

His journey shows that when development is guided by purpose, it opens new territory for career advancement, and for influence and relevance across changing contexts.

This dimension of the Money-Mission paradigm invites reflection:
Which learning opportunities could strengthen both your market value and your contribution?
How might your development support your personal progress, and also meaningful outcomes for others?

What skills or capabilities could extend your impact in the direction that matters most to you?

When growth is guided by purpose, it becomes a lever, influencing both your next step and the legacy you leave behind.

3. Balancing Legacy With Liquidity

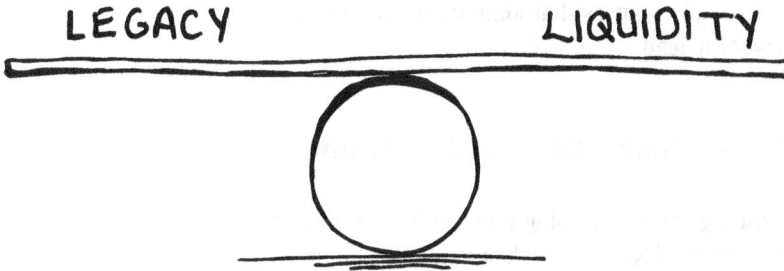

Every professional reaches a point of reflection, a moment where the question shifts from *"What am I achieving?"* to *"What am I building that will last?"*

This dimension explores the tension between immediate financial needs and long-term vision. Balancing liquidity and legacy means meeting today's responsibilities while steadily and intentionally creating something with lasting value.

Take Steph, a senior leader and mum of three. On paper, everything was working. Beneath the momentum of meetings and results though, was a quiet tension, a question, *"is this it?"* She wanted something more. More enjoyment, a way to contribute meaningfully, to support her family and live with more balance. However, she couldn't simply step away, like many, she carried real financial obligations and a strong sense of responsibility.

So, she built a bridge. Instead of taking a leap, she designed a phased transition. She took on consulting projects alongside her full-time role to expand her network, to build her brand and to create a solid bank of results, testimonials and extra earnings. Over time, she saved enough to create a buffer (for her, this marker of success was the equivalent to 1-year salary). Then, with signed contracts in hand and proof of concept, she made the move, stepping forward with intention.

The most powerful part here isn't the leap, it's the structure she built around it. She structured her weeks around three deliberate anchors, income that maintained financial flow, a venture that embodied her mission, and time for writing and thought leadership that expanded her longer-term influence and brought opportunity,

This was a strategic design, earning in the present while investing in the future. A system that respected both liquidity and legacy.

This part of the Money-Mission Paradigm invites reflection:

How are you using today's income to fund tomorrow's vision?

What small shifts could help you move from reactive earning to strategic building?

What structures could allow you to grow your impact without compromising security or stability?

Legacy isn't something you leave behind, it's something you build in motion. It begins with daily choices that align with your future direction and honour the life you want to lead.

The Maslow Connection: Building Sustainable Success

Understanding the relationship between the Money-Mission paradigm and Maslow's Hierarchy of Needs reveals a valuable pattern in how sustainable success takes shape.

Just as Maslow's model moves from essential needs to fulfilment and purpose, the pursuit of financial stability and meaningful impact often follows a similar path. It's not always linear, but rather a dynamic relationship between meeting foundational needs and striving toward aspirational goals.

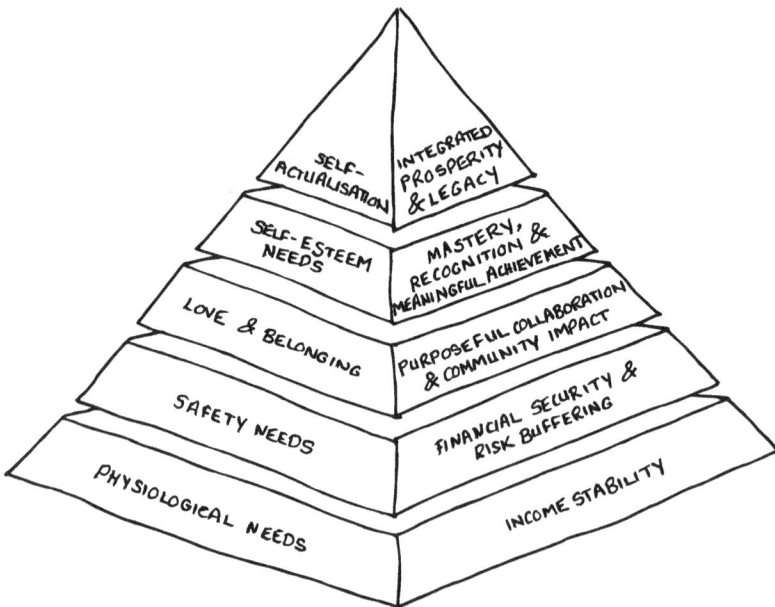

Level 1: Physiological Needs → Income Stability

Before we can make bold, purpose-driven decisions, our basic needs must be met. Just as food, shelter and rest form the foundation of Maslow's hierarchy, in the Money-Mission Paradigm, that foundation is reliable income, the need to have 'enough'.

Take, for example, a recent graduate entering their first job. They may feel strongly about making an impact, but their immediate priority is paying rent and covering essential costs. Purpose still matters, but stability must come first.

L1 Focus: Secure baseline income.

L1 Strategy: Build multiple income streams or reliable employment.

L1 Question: Do I have enough stability to think beyond this month?

Level 2: Safety Needs → Financial Security And Risk Buffering

This level creates breathing space, a foundation of savings, insurance and systems that help you weather uncertainty. With that security in place, you gain the freedom to pursue opportunities that align with your mission, rather than being driven by short-term financial pressure.

For instance, a professional might take on well-paid consultancy work to build a one-year financial buffer (as Steph did in the earlier example). That buffer allows them to transition into more values-led work with confidence without risking burnout or instability.

L2 Focus: Financial protection and freedom.

L2 Strategy: Build a safety net (savings, investments, exit plans).

L2 Question: Can I take a calculated risk without threatening my financial wellbeing?

Level 3: Love And Belonging → Purposeful Collaboration And Community Impact

As a sense of belonging and the need for connection grows, many leaders begin to look for ways to contribute more meaningfully, seeking opportunities for meaningful contribution, whether through their core work, side projects, or community involvement. It's not always about changing careers. Often, it's about redesigning your time and environment to reflect what matters most.

For example, a senior leader may restructure their week to include time for mentoring emerging leaders or contributing to community education programmes. This reflects a shift toward greater alignment, where ambition and purpose move together.

L3 Focus: Integration of contribution and connection.

L3 Strategy: Prioritise time and environments that support meaningful work.

L3 Question: What spaces or relationships help me feel like my work matters to others and to me?

Level 4: Self-Esteem Needs → Mastery, Recognition And Meaningful Achievement

This level is about being seen and valued, not only for performance but for meaningful contribution. Leaders operating here are focused on mastering their craft and driving change that matters, with influence measured by impact as well as outcomes.

For example, a finance director might become known for pioneering ESG initiatives within their company, earning industry credibility and building influence, while contributing to wider change.

L4 Focus: Leadership credibility and meaningful recognition.

L4 Strategy: Pursue excellence in ways that solve real-world problems.

L4 Question: Am I growing my influence in a way that drives meaningful value?

Level 5: Self-Actualisation → Integrated Prosperity And Legacy

At the top of Maslow's model sits the drive to become your fullest self. In the Money-Mission Paradigm, this is where financial autonomy meets life purpose. Leaders operating at this level design businesses, careers, or initiatives as vehicles for long-term impact, while sustaining their own prosperity.

A founder, for example, might build a successful consultancy that reinvests part of its profits into early-stage entrepreneurs. In doing so, they create an ecosystem that merges personal values, commercial acumen, and legacy into one cohesive model.

L5 Focus: Meaningful, sustainable impact.

L5 Strategy: Design long-range models that serve your values and generate ongoing return.

L5 Question: Is my work an expression of who I am and the legacy I want to leave?

You don't need to complete one level before stepping into the next. Most leaders move between them as life and work evolve. Becoming aware of the pattern gives you the ability to plan and progress through them with greater intention.

When you recognise where you are and what you need, you can design your journey to serve both financial growth and meaningful contribution. This is where sustainable success lives, not in trading one for the other, but in learning how to align both intelligently and strategically.

Breaking Through Common Barriers

Integrating money and mission can be challenging. Whether you're leading a team, building a business, or managing your own career trajectory, you'll likely encounter internal and external barriers that make it feel like financial success and meaningful impact are at odds.

Often though, these aren't real structural barriers, they're mindset blocks. High-performing, values-led leaders learn to recognise these internal patterns and dismantle them. In doing so, they unlock new levels of alignment, performance, and fulfilment.

Here are four of the most common Money-Mission blockers, and how to break through them:

1. The Scarcity Mindset: *"It's either purpose or prosperity."*

"If I choose meaningful work, I'll have to sacrifice income."

"If I focus on financial success, I'll lose my impact."

Sound familiar? This is the scarcity mindset, a common belief that financial success and purpose-driven work are in conflict. It's often reinforced by the narrative that doing good means earning less, or that making money somehow dilutes your values.

One leader I worked with in fintech wrestled with this exact dilemma. She was passionate about expanding financial access for underserved communities but hesitated to pursue that path, worried it would mean giving up the stability and the high income she'd worked hard to achieve. Her turning point came when she shifted perspective. Instead of seeing purpose and prosperity as opposites, she saw how her success could fuel her impact. With greater financial freedom, she could invest in what mattered and lead with more choice.

Leaders who shift from scarcity to synergy start making decisions with more confidence. They design work that reflects both their ambitions and their values and create momentum that lasts.

Scarcity is a story. You can choose to tell a different one.

2. The Timeline Trap: *"I'll focus on impact when I'm financially ready."*

One of the biggest traps leaders fall into is delaying their purpose.

They tell themselves: *"I'll give back when I hit this salary," "I'll make a difference when I retire," "I'll explore meaningful work when the kids are older."* But life expands to fill the space. Bigger roles, bigger houses, bigger responsibilities. Before long, the milestone keeps moving and purpose keeps getting postponed. I've experienced this first-hand and seen it play out with many clients. They save, wait, delay . . . only to realise that surplus never feels quite enough. Meanwhile, time is passing, energy is shifting, and their impact is quietly on hold.

Here's the other problem. Money loses value over time thanks to inflation quietly eroding purchasing power. A £10 note in 1987 is worth less than £3 in today's terms. That's the hidden cost of waiting. Without clear intent, we risk holding back our impact while time quietly erodes value. The £10 in your hand today won't stretch as far tomorrow. Purposeful action always beats perfect timing. Value, therefore, must be aligned with timing and intention and smart financial strategy should both build and protect in equal measure.

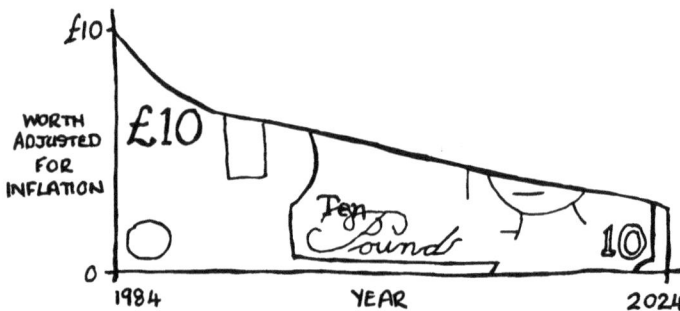

This is why waiting for the right time is risky, because without intention, that time never really arrives. Those who create lasting impact aren't the ones who wait until they feel financially 'ready'. They're the ones who build both in parallel, recognising that financial success isn't a barrier to purpose, but a tool to amplify it.

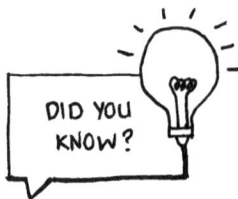

DID YOU KNOW?

The Bank of England aims for a 2% inflation rate, but in recent years, it's been as high as 9%. If your savings grow slower than inflation, your real wealth is shrinking. Even holding large cash reserves can be a risk if not planned intentionally.

When it comes to investing, waiting for the 'right moment' can cost more than you think too. Just like delaying purpose-led action in your career, trying to time financial markets is an intricate process. During periods of economic uncertainty or personal transition, it's natural to hesitate. As Anne McClean points out: *"history shows that those who stay invested, rather than jumping in and out, are far more likely to see long-term gains. Markets recover, but those who delay re-entry often miss out on the best days."*

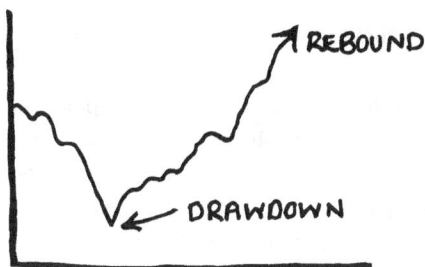

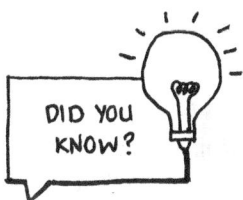

Drawdown is a decline in the value of an investment or portfolio from its peak to its lowest point, often caused by a market crash or economic crisis.

Example: If your portfolio drops from £10,000 to £6,000, that's a 40% drawdown.

Rebound is the subsequent recovery after that low point, when the market bounces back and investments regain (or exceed) their value.

For example: If the same portfolio, then rises back to £9,000, that's part of the rebound.

The key is to understand your personal risk profile in relation to your short and long-term need for access, to both cash and asset value.

The good news? No matter where you are in your journey or what stage of life, you're in, you can review and recalibrate. Change is always possible. You can bring financial success and purpose into closer alignment, through small shifts or bigger strategic decisions. The key is to stop treating them as separate pursuits and start integrating them with intention.

That might mean choosing roles that offer both financial stability and mission-aligned learning opportunities, something younger professionals often prioritise, and a growing consideration in recruitment strategies. It could mean building wealth in ways that actively support your impact goals through investments, philanthropy, or how you structure your business. Or it may involve designing a career path where each move advances both personal and organisational outcomes, strengthening financial return and meaningful contribution in tandem.

When you shift from a linear mindset, *"I'll focus on impact once I'm financially secure"*, to a dual-track approach, you stop postponing what matters most. You start designing a life and career where financial success and meaningful impact grow side by side.

Waiting rarely leads to alignment. Designing does.

3. Misunderstood Value: *"I have a valuable business, don't I?"*

Anne McClean often works with business owners who assume their company is a valuable asset, only to find that without them, the business isn't viable. *"If the business can't run without you, it's not a scalable asset,"* Anne explains. *"It's often more like a job you've built for yourself. I sometimes give it a bank value of £1."*

This can be a confronting realisation, but it's also empowering. Once you see the distinction between income and legacy, you can begin to build strategically:
- Diversify your assets.
- Separate lifestyle income from scalable value.
- Plan for an exit or succession strategy.
- Seek financial guidance proactively, not reactively.

"Not everyone needs a wealth manager," Anne notes, *"but most people need a sounding board."* A good financial advisor isn't just about numbers. They help you translate your ambitions into a strategy, so your impact lives on, even when you step back.

4. The Integration Gap: *"Success looks great but feels empty."*

Traditional career markers, title, salary, bonuses, can project a powerful external image of success, while leaving leaders unfulfilled beneath the surface.

As one senior executive shared: *"I'd hit every goal. On paper, I was winning. But I didn't feel it."* This is the integration gap, the space between what success looks like and how it actually feels.

Bridging that gap starts with redefining success to include both income and impact. One tool I often use with clients is the Personal Prosperity Scorecard. It helps you assess your current path across four core dimensions:
1. Financial growth: Are you secure and scaling in a sustainable way?
2. Mission alignment: Are your daily efforts connected to something that genuinely matters to you?

3. Social impact: Are you influencing lives or systems beyond your own?
4. Learning & leadership development: Are you building skills that strengthen your value and your values?

This multidimensional lens invites a more honest, energising definition of success, one that supports personal clarity and strengthens organisational value.

Ultimately, it helps you design a life and career that feel as successful as they look. Grounded, rewarding and real.

The Financial Map: Timeline And Terrain

Once we break through the mindset barriers, the scarcity stories, the deferrals, and the disconnections, we can start shaping a path that aligns money with meaning in tangible ways.

This means moving from why this all matters, to how it can work. Like any journey worth taking, it needs a map.

Your financial decisions, what to invest in, when to spend, how to structure your income, are all shaped by two major forces:
1. Your stage in life.
2. Your employment status and asset structure.

Whether you're employed or self-employed, early in your career or thinking about legacy, each phase brings its own priorities and blind spots. Understanding this evolving terrain brings focus and flexibility to make better decisions at every stage.

To understand the bigger picture, let's explore the two layers of this map, a timeline of changing priorities and a landscape of structural realities that influence how your financial system functions.

Life Stage Planning Timeline

This timeline outlines how financial priorities typically shift by age and life phase. It provides a practical guide to help you anticipate needs, avoid blind spots, and plan proactively.

Age/Stage	Key Focus	What You Might Need
20s	Foundations	Build budgeting habits, avoid toxic debt, start emergency fund. Consider starting a pension early (employer or private). Learn to differentiate income from lifestyle.
30s	Stability & Growth	Plan for property, children, or business start-up. Protect income (insurance), begin investing and review financial goals yearly. Use windfalls (e.g. bonuses) strategically.
40s	Consolidation	Strengthen pensions, reduce mortgage, consider school/university fees. Reassess investment risk. Address financial habits that no longer serve future goals.
50s	Acceleration & Correction	Maximise pension contributions, review succession plans. Reduce liabilities. Start shaping a realistic retirement plan and timeline. Adjust spending to reflect values.
60s+	Transition & Access	Decide when/how to access pensions. Prioritise estate planning, tax efficiency, potential care provision. Simplify finances and avoid risky late-stage investments.

(Drawn from Anne McClean's advisory experience and best-practice financial planning)

Financial Landscape: Employed vs. Self-Employed

The second layer of the map considers structure. Your employment model plays a huge role in how you need to plan, protect, and invest. Use this comparison to assess where you are and whether your current approach reflects your real risk and opportunity profile.

Category	Employed	Self-Employed / Business Owner
Income	Predictable, easier to budget.	Variable, requires contingency funds and disciplined cashflow management.
Tax & Compliance	Employer handles PAYE, pension auto-enrolment.	Must manage tax returns, NI, pension contributions, often with accountant support.
Pension Access	Employer contributions + tax benefits.	Must self-manage, but more flexibility in pension type and contribution levels.
Sick Pay & Protection	Usually includes sick pay, holiday pay, maternity/paternity rights (though these vary).	Must personally arrange income protection, private health, etc.
Leave & Lifestyle	Paid leave offers guaranteed downtime.	Greater autonomy, but downtime could mean lost income, requires pre-planning and a strategic approach to income generation that isn't dependent solely on own performance.
Investment Opportunity	Often relies on pensions + property. All investment opportunities possible.	Can use business as asset (if structured well) but requires exit or succession plan. All investment opportunities possible.
Support Network	Access to HR, colleagues, structured benefits.	Freedom to design support system, but must create it from scratch (advisors, mentors), or through acquisition.
Blind Spots	May neglect planning because it *"feels covered"* (e.g. pensions running passively).	May overestimate business as retirement plan or delay personal planning until too late.
Upside	Stability allows consistent saving, easier mortgage qualification.	Growth potential can be exponential with the right strategy and support.

(Drawn from Anne McClean's advisory experience and best-practice financial planning)

Which terrain are you walking and are you fully prepared? Consider reviewing these tables with a trusted advisor or partner. Are you clear on the risks and benefits of your current path or is it time to recalibrate your map?

International Moves And Systemic Shifts

Anne-Sophie shares her view on international relocation and the impact of systemic change. When planning a move, especially across countries, it's not just the cost of living that shifts. It's the entire structure of support around you.

Anne-Sophie experienced this first-hand when she and her family relocated from France to the UK with three young children: *"In France, there's significant financial support for families"* she explains. *"When we moved to London, all of that changed. The cost of childcare, transport and daily logistics wasn't just higher, it was almost unsupported in comparison."*

Her experience highlights a critical insight. Your personal income plan must account for the system you're stepping into, or out of. Many professionals underestimate how national frameworks shape real-world financial outcomes, especially when moving for work or family.

Her first UK role, she recalls, barely broke even once nanny costs and travel were factored in. But the decision wasn't purely financial. It was intuitive and mission-led: *"The people, the challenge, the environment, they aligned with what I wanted to grow into, and I knew, even if it didn't work long-term, it was a calculated step forward."*

Anne-Sophie and her partner viewed the move through the lens of adaptive opportunity. If it didn't work, they could return to familiar ground. But it did. That calculated risk became the launchpad for one of the most accelerated phases of her leadership journey.

Her story brings a vital calibration question into focus: *Are you comparing like with like? Have you factored in not just salary, but systems, support, and sustainability?*

Financial planning, especially across borders, requires detailed budgeting, and it also demands an understanding of the whole new terrain.

Managing Unpredictable Income

Systemic change isn't the only challenge. For many professionals, the uncertainty doesn't come from geography, it comes from the nature of their work.

Olympic canoeist Adam Burgess knows this terrain from a different angle. While elite sport might look glamorous, he's open about the financial reality behind the scenes: *"Even at the top of the funding stream, you have to look externally,"* he told me.

His income is a carefully built and managed portfolio of grant funding, a long-term sponsor (JCB), partnerships with manufacturers, paid social media work and a growing breath coaching business. *"It's kind of like I'm building a business,"* he said. *"My performance is the product."*

Managing contracts, negotiating appearances, balancing training with entrepreneurial work, this is modern self-employment in action. For Adam, sport isn't just passion, (one he also happens to be world class at!), it's enterprise. It requires just as much focus and creativity as any start-up venture.

Money-Mission Balance Through Calibration

"A lot of financial decision-making is catastrophe planning or future building," Anne explains. *"They're two sides of the same coin. You're either reacting or you're preparing."*

This shift, from survival mode *("What if everything goes wrong?")* to strategic purpose *("How do I build what I care about?"),* is a defining moment in aligning money with mission. *"You don't need to become a financial expert,"* Anne adds, *"but you do need to take ownership of the story you're writing with your money."*

Balancing money with mission does not require a fixed formula. It's a process of constant calibration, like a tightrope walker adjusting with every step to stay centred and in motion. That's where your Calibration Tools become essential.

Emotional Intelligence is your internal compass.

It helps you notice when your financial choices are drifting out of alignment with your personal purpose. In moments of pressure or trade-off, self-awareness keeps you grounded in what really matters. With emotional intelligence, you also learn to manage stress and regulate your responses, especially when facing important financial decisions. This might mean pausing before saying yes to a lucrative project that feels off-mission or reflecting on how your goals are impacting those around you. Build this muscle through regular emotional check-ins. Journaling, mindfulness, or honest conversations with trusted mentors can help you assess whether your current direction aligns with both meaningful progress and financial outcomes.

Skilled Communication bridges the gap between internal alignment and external influence. It enables you to express your goals with clarity and conviction, connecting financial ambition with deeper mission in a way that feels authentic and persuasive. This is especially important when navigating complex conversations about money, ambition, or your wider career. Whether you're refining your business, pitching to a board, or discussing trade-offs with a partner, communication is how you create shared understanding and sustained buy-in.

Remember, storytelling is an important leadership skill, it's how you invite others to believe in your vision and invest in the journey.

The Resilience Advantage is your energetic engine, your fuel for long-term progress.

It enables you to sustain performance, bounce back from setbacks and protect your drive when challenges arise. Resilient leaders understand that setbacks are feedback, not failure. They prioritise recovery not as a reward for working hard, but as part of the performance system itself. That means embedding practices that protect your energy and sustain your performance. Whether through movement, sleep, creativity, or breathwork, resilience must be a daily investment, not an occasional repair.

As you continue along the executive tightrope, remember, success isn't about perfect balance. It's about progress with purpose.

The most accomplished tightrope walkers don't avoid wobble, they recover quickly, realign constantly, and move forward with intention. That's what your Calibration Tools are designed to help you do.

Keep calibrating. Keep evolving. That's how meaningful success is both built and sustained.

Chapter 7
Making Money-Mission Work For You

You've explored the concept of the Money-Mission Paradigm, the challenge of integrating financial ambition with a sense of deeper purpose. Now, it's time to bring it to life. This chapter translates insight into action, moving you from a place of reflection to integration.

Simply knowing that you want both wealth and meaning isn't enough. You need a way to make this balance real, a way to turn the tightrope into a walkable path.

From Insight To Integration

Understanding your relationship with money and mission is one thing. Living it, daily, is another. It begins with clear understanding. Where are you now? What are your financial realities and responsibilities? What values drive you beyond the numbers?

Think of this chapter as your next foothold. It builds on your inner work and starts to shape the outer world around it. Not through dramatic leaps, but through honest assessment, small experiments and daily alignment.

We'll begin with three essential questions:
1. What are your current financial obligations and aspirations?

2. What is your personal mission and how clearly is it defined?

3. Where is the gap between how you want to live and what you're doing now?

Let's break these down:

1 Financial Reality Mapping

Before planning anything future-focussed, you need to understand your current financial foundation. This doesn't need to be exhaustive, but it should be honest. Look at your income, savings, debts, expenses and most importantly, your relationship with financial risk.

Anne McClean advocates for a deceptively simple but powerful first step: *"Start with a proper balance sheet. Be honest. What is your house 'actually' worth? Not what you wish it was worth! What liabilities do you really have?"*

She adds that this document should include illiquid and liquid assets and distinguish between lifestyle illusions and financial reality: *"Cars aren't assets unless they're rare collectibles, and with businesses, ask: if you left tomorrow, would it still make money? If not, don't count it as wealth."*

RECOMMENDED

Include a section for 'Illiquid / Not Readily Realisable Assets' in your financial plans, this should include business equity, pensions, or property that can't be quickly accessed, alongside your main asset list. This will help you visualise not just your net worth, but your available resilience.

The next stage is where emotional intelligence comes in. Money is rarely just about money, it's tied to our sense of identity, safety, pride and even shame. Acknowledge the emotions that surface because they hold useful data.

First, identify the different financial commitments that you have that shape your life choices, then reflect on the areas where you feel most stretched or limited. Next, consider what fears or assumptions you hold that exist about money that are influencing your life choices and direction?

Here Are Some Of The More Common Fears And Assumptions People Have About Money Include:

"If I don't earn more this year, I've failed." (Money tied to self-worth and achievement).

"Talking about money makes me look greedy." (Assumption that ambition and integrity are in conflict).

"I'll never have enough to feel secure." (A belief rooted in scarcity, not actual numbers).

"Success means having more than others." (Status-driven narrative that may not align with values).

"If I stop working, everything will fall apart." (Fear of losing control or relevance).

"I'm bad with money, so I'll just ignore it." (Avoidance rooted in past experiences or shame).

Do any of these resonate with you?

Here is a simple table you can use to help you map your current situation. You can use the table for annual big picture review and planning or to delve deep into the granular data of daily living.

Financial Area	Current Status	Notes / Emotions / Observations
Income		
Fixed Costs		
Variable Expenses		
Debts / Liabilities		
Savings / Investments That Are Readily Available / Accessible		
Illiquid / Not Readily Realisable Assets		
Risk / Security Feelings		

Use the table to get a snapshot of your numbers and commitments and then go deeper. What do these figures represent emotionally and practically? What do they enable, or limit?

The Three Tiers Of Financial Scaffolding

Anne McClean frames financial wellbeing as a scaffold with three evolving stages:
- **Not Enough:** Where basic needs aren't yet met. The focus is on income stability, debt management and essential budgeting.
- **Enough:** A sustainable stage where security meets flexibility. Planning becomes more strategic, long-term savings emerge and lifestyle starts reflecting values.
- **Plenty:** Where excess can be directed towards legacy, philanthropy, or significant life projects. *"But plenty only works if you've got clarity,"* Anne says. *"Otherwise, you just escalate spending rather than elevate impact."*

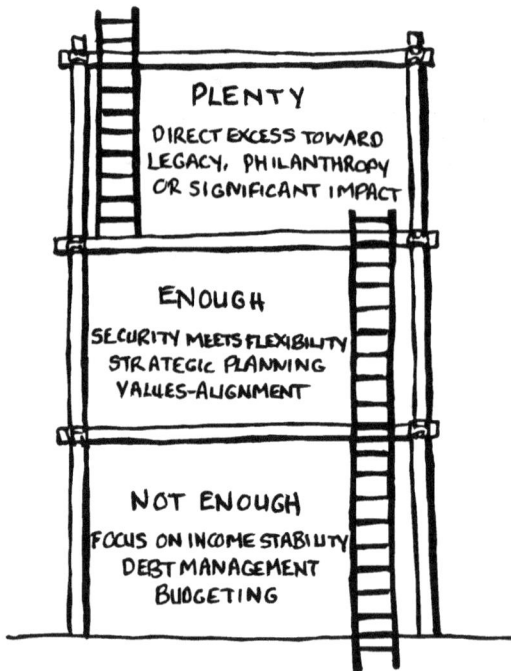

This scaffold is not fixed. Life events, children, health, career change, can move us up or down the tiers. What matters is recognising where you are and planning accordingly.

Anne-Sophie reminds us that meaningful career choices are often about more than money. Reflecting on a pivotal decision early in her career, she shared: *"When I took my first job [in London], I remember financially it didn't really make sense . . . but it was a deliberate choice. I had this wonderful interview, and I thought, 'Let's try it. If it doesn't work, I'll try something else."*

Even later, when the economics of full-time work barely covered childcare and commuting costs, she didn't walk away: *"I chose to work even when my income didn't make a big impact. It was important to me."*

Her story is a powerful example of the 'Enough' mindset, where purpose, autonomy and mission outweigh financial optimisation. For dual-career households and working mothers especially, decisions are rarely black and white. Fulfilment sometimes comes from honouring your sense of self and staying connected to work, even when the spreadsheet doesn't justify it . . . for that moment in time at least.

One of the most overlooked elements of financial wellbeing isn't a number, it's a feeling. How we emotionally relate to money at each stage of the financial scaffold deeply affects our behaviour, decisions and confidence.

Anne McClean observes two recurring patterns:

- *"Some clients who have always had 'not enough' tend to overspend when they finally earn more, it's a survival response."*
- *"Others who have plenty can't bring themselves to spend at all. Even when it's safe to do so, they see the pot going down and feel anxious."*

The fear of losing what you've built, or of never building enough, can quietly govern financial behaviour, even when logic says otherwise. This emotional undercurrent can lead to unnecessary guilt, avoidance or over-correction. That's why Anne helps clients shift not just the numbers, but the narrative. For example, with clients approaching retirement, she designs strategies to convert their assets into income scaffolding, so the money *"sits behind them"* like a springboard, not in front of them like a dwindling pot. This gives them permission to enjoy life without fear or shame.

"You need to build systems that support the life you want to live," she says, *"not just protect the money you've saved."* The key is intention. Whether you're navigating 'not enough', stepping into 'enough', or figuring out what to do with 'plenty', the goal isn't just optimisation, it's alignment.

2 Mission Clarity Assessment

Before aligning your finances to your mission, you need to be clear on what that mission actually is, beyond job titles or generic goals. What does meaningful impact look like for you, in practice? Who are you here to serve? What kind of contribution do you want to be remembered for? Clarity here isn't a luxury, it's a compass. It shapes how you make decisions, where you direct energy and what kind of financial scaffolding will be required to support the legacy you want to leave.

Reflect on the following:
– What matters to me enough to shape my work around it?
– Where do I feel most energised, useful, or 'on mission'?
– What kind of impact would feel deeply fulfilling, now and in the future?

Use the next table to begin mapping that clarity. This is your starting point, something real you can build from:

Element	Clear?	Needs Attention?	Notes
Purpose / Why			
Core Values			
Key Audiences / Beneficiaries			
Legacy / Long-Term Impact			

If elements are unclear or feel confusing, use it as a signal to explore those elements further. You don't need to have all the answers today, but you do need a sense of direction.

3 Integration Gap Analysis

At some point, every high performer needs to ask themselves, is my financial reality aligned with the impact I want to make?

It's not always an easy question. You might be growing your income but feeling drained. Or pursuing meaningful work that leaves your finances on shaky ground. These disconnects don't always present loudly, but they do exist. In your energy, in your decisions, in the trade-offs you keep justifying.

This tool is designed to make the invisible visible. Use the next table to review how your current roles, responsibilities, or income streams are serving both your financial wellbeing and your deeper mission. Doing this creates awareness so your next steps can be more intentional.

Current Action / Role	Financial Impact	Mission Alignment	Notes / Tensions

Once complete, take a step back. Which misalignments are manageable? Which are costing you energy or opportunity? And which ones, if addressed, would create the most forward motion?

Start small. Realignment happens through deliberate shifts, not dramatic overhauls. The more intentional your alignment, the more sustainable your success will become.

Decision-Making In The Money-Mission Paradigm

Making decisions that balance financial success and meaningful impact isn't easy, but it is where real successful leadership lives.

Adam Burgess has lived this paradox in elite sport. For years, he internalised the belief that there was no money in canoeing. But that narrative began to shift when he reframed both his value and his outlook. *"I stopped saying there's no money in sport and started looking for ways to generate value,"* he explains. That mindset shift didn't just attract opportunity, it transformed his entire trajectory. Within weeks, he secured a long-term partnership with JCB. He didn't change his mission. He changed his relationship to possibility.

Alison Oliver, CEO of the Youth Sport Trust, leads one of the UK's most values-driven organisations. But she's clear that vision alone doesn't pay the bills. *"We make values-based decisions,"* she says, *"but we still need a business model that works."* Her leadership is a masterclass in balancing transformational purpose with commercial clarity. Impact without income isn't sustainable, but income without intention is rarely fulfilling.

Whether you're choosing between two job offers, deciding where to invest profits, or building out a team, the real question to ask is does this serve both your financial foundation and your purpose?

Let's take a practical example. You're offered a highly paid role that conflicts with your core values. Through the Money-Mission lens, you'd pause to evaluate:

- Does this support my long-term vision or just solve a short-term problem?
- Will I gain strategic capital or lose alignment?
- What will this cost me, not just financially, but emotionally, ethically, relationally?

This isn't idealism. It's intentionality.

Sustainable success requires us to treat money and mission not as rivals, but as co-pilots. Each decision is an opportunity to align who you are with what you build. As Anne McClean reminds us, *"We all behave differently with money, often shaped more by habit than strategy. What you spend isn't just a decision, it's often a pattern."*

She encourages clients to distinguish between habit and choice. *"Ask yourself, is this spend essential? Is it aligned with your values? Or is it just automatic?"* Financial strategy isn't only about technical optimisation, it's about emotional congruence. When your money choices reflect your mission, you experience both progress and peace of mind.

Anne describes this alignment as *"welding the mechanics of finance to the substance of someone's life."* Her work bridges spreadsheets and soul, reminding us that money is the currency of your values. Every financial decision, whether it's a major investment or your morning coffee, carries meaning.

So, how do we decide wisely? By applying a structured process that evaluates each choice through four key lenses. These are Immediate Impact, Long-term Implications, Stakeholder Effects and Integration & Momentum.

Let's explore each now.

Money-Mission Decision-Making Framework

(Integrated Decision-Making Framework: A four-lens tool for evaluating financial and mission-aligned choices. Based on insights from an interview with Anne McClean, Partner, and Head of Wealth, Chartered and Certified Financial Planner).

Decision Dimension	Key Questions to Ask
Immediate Impact	– What are the direct financial implications, costs, income, opportunity? – Does this energise or exhaust you? What's the short-term emotional toll or reward?

(continued)

Decision Dimension	Key Questions to Ask
Long-Term Implications	– Does this advance your mission today, or divert focus? – Will this support sustainable financial growth or restrict future choices? – How does this align with your long-term vision? Will it build traction or add noise? – Could this contribute to your personal legacy or become a regret?
Stakeholder Effects	– What ripple effects will this have on your relationships, team, or community? – Will it deepen trust and connection or demand trade-offs that need managing? – Are your networks strengthened or stretched by this decision?
Integration & Momentum	– Does this reinforce your existing work, values, or goals? – Can it unlock additional resources, tools, or collaborations? – Is this a catalyst for future growth or a standalone moment?

Use this four-lens tool to evaluate any significant decision, from a new role or investment to a partnership or pivot. This structured reflection helps ensure alignment between your finances, your mission, and your future.

These principles don't only apply to important or pivotal career moves or investment strategy. In fact, the way we spend money day to day reveals and reinforces our values, often more than we realise. As Anne reminds us, money is *"the currency to create the life you want."*

Whether you're ordering lunch or planning a holiday, every decision is shaping a pattern, and that pattern tells a story. These choices might feel small, but they can reflect habits, beliefs, or even blind spots that either strengthen or dilute your alignment.

Consider these everyday examples through the same decision-making lens:

Daily Coffee vs. Holiday Fund: A daily artisan coffee might cost £4. Over a month, that's £120. Over a year, more than £1,400.
Decision lens: Is this a daily joy aligned with your lifestyle, or an unconscious habit? Could redirecting even half of that towards a travel fund enable a meaningful break that supports your wellbeing or family connection.

Dining Out vs. Values-Based Living: Weekly restaurant visits might be easy and social, but the cost can add up fast. What if one in four was replaced with a home-cooked meal using locally sourced food or shared with friends?
Decision lens: Does this shift reflect your health, community, or sustainability values? Would less spending here provide funds for causes you care about?

Clothing Purchases vs. Experiences: *"Buy less, choose well,"* said Vivienne West-wood, and it applies here. When it comes to financial purchases, Anne encourages people to look at patterns. Are you buying clothes or handbags for identity, status, or habit?

Decision lens: Could fewer impulsive fashion buys mean affording that one indulgent one, or increase the saving fund that might save you on a rainy day?

Premium Services vs. Financial Confidence: Do you always go for the premium delivery, luxury gym, or latest phone and plan? These may feel minor, but they set a tone.

Decision lens: Are you using money to shortcut discomfort or to express values? Would switching to 'enough' rather than 'excess' in one category help reduce anxiety or increase your monthly saving buffer enabling you to add to an investment you're committed to growing.

Gifting and Generosity: Do you spend freely on gifts or cover the bill because it feels generous, but end up stretched or resentful?

Decision lens: Is your giving aligned with your mission, or is it masking something (like guilt or pressure)? Could reframing generosity as presence, time, or shared activity offer a more meaningful and sustainable impact?

Mini-Exercise: Pattern Check

For one week, jot down any purchase over £5. At the end, reflect:
- Which of these spending choices align with your values?
- Which supported your long-term mission?
- Which were automatic, habitual, or emotionally driven?

When you start seeing money as a medium for mission, not just a resource to spend or save, you begin to take back control. The smallest decision can become a conscious expression of who you are and what matters most.

Crossroads And Transition Points

Throughout your career, there will be pivotal moments when balancing financial priorities and mission-driven aspirations becomes particularly complex. These moments create critical balancing points; they require heightened awareness, strategic planning, and a clear framework for making confident decisions that align with your long-term success.

During these moments, money becomes much more than a simple resource, it becomes either a stabiliser, or a stressor. Transitions can prompt fear around income, value, and future choices. Anne works with many clients in transition, post-divorce, after selling a business, or while pivoting careers. She explains that people often come thinking they need tactical advice, how to invest, what to sell, how to save. *"But what they really need,"* she says, *"is to reconnect with what life they want next. Then the financial roadmap becomes much clearer."*

You don't need to become financially fluent overnight, but to become successful and to sustain that success, you do need to ensure your financial scaffolding can support your next step. Anne frames it as *"aligning the financial map with a life landscape,"* a mindset that replaces panic with planning and confusion with possibility.

This next table offers a simple but powerful tool to guide your thinking. It will help you anticipate what's shifting, assess the support you need and explore how each transition can serve both your financial health and your broader sense of purpose.

Money-Mission Transition Framework
This table will help you to navigate crossroads with clarity, alignment and confidence.

Category	Considerations
Key Questions For ALL Transition Points	How prepared are you for upcoming transitions? Have you thought through what's changing and what it demands of you mentally, financially and practically? What support systems need to be in place? Do you have the right people, routines, or resources to support this shift, at home and at work? How will you maintain balance during change? What habits, boundaries, or mindset tools can keep you steady while things shift around you? What recovery strategies should you have ready? When the pressure hits, how will you recharge? Is it built into your plan?

(continued)

Category	Considerations
Career Transitions	**Role Changes:** How will this affect both money and mission? Does the new role offer financial progress without losing sight of what drives you? **Industry Shifts:** What new opportunities and risks emerge? Are you expanding your influence, or stepping into the unknown without a clear map? **Entrepreneurial Moves:** How can you maintain both dimensions? How will you protect your purpose while chasing profit, or vice versa? **Organisational Transformations:** What integration possibilities exist? Can this change be used to align business outcomes with personal or team values?
Financial Milestones	**Significant Investments:** How do these serve both goals? Will this investment generate both returns and purpose-driven growth? **Wealth Creation Events:** What mission opportunities emerge? Could this be a moment to give back, build impact, or create something lasting? **Risk-Reward Decisions:** How do you balance both aspects? Is this risk tolerable financially and aligned with who you want to become? **Resource Allocation Choices:** What integration potential exists? Are your resources (time, money, focus) being placed where they can multiply both meaning and results?
Mission Opportunities	**Impact Initiatives:** How can these be financially sustainable? Can you create long-term mission impact without draining your resources? **Moments For Purpose Alignment:** What financial implications exist? Is saying *"yes"* to purpose going to create pressure, or potential? **Legacy-Building Opportunities:** How do you ensure lasting impact? What structures, systems, or strategies will make this stick beyond your direct involvement? **Contribution Crossroads:** What balance needs consideration? How can you show up fully without burning out, or selling out?

Don't forget to visit the WHY-Mapping exercise anytime you want to really drill down into the core reason why you might want to choose to do (or not do!) something. It will help you explore each of these areas at a deeper level to uncover the core drivers behind options, decisions, and best choice of action.

Building Your Support System

Even the most accomplished leaders don't do it alone. Behind every high-impact career is a strong support system, a network of mentors, advisors and peers who bring challenge and wisdom, encouragement, and accountability.

Adam describes his support system to include his coach and several other performance leads including for strength and conditioning, psychology, his agent, lifestyle support and a close group of friends and family. *"If I'm in a difficult phase, they help me recalibrate. I've realised I do best when I feel supported and don't try to do everything alone . . .. We've built a shared language, just by spending time together on the riverbank, in sessions. Sometimes we even come up with silly names for certain techniques or ways of doing things, but it works. It makes things more efficient, and it means we understand each other more quickly."*

Ali's approach to personal alignment is rooted in clarity and openness. She speaks frequently to her support network about her work and its demands. *"If I don't bring people along with me, I risk misalignment at work and at home,"* she says. To strengthen peer support, Ali created a 'supper club' for local CEOs. *"It's not a network,"* she says, *"it's a safe space for people in similar shoes to share honestly."* This kind of intentionally designed peer dialogue offers a real-world example of what it means to build your personal board of advisors, a collective of peers who offer insight and solidarity without hierarchy.

Identify and consider for a moment, three people in your world who appear to live with a strong integration of money and mission. What can you learn from how they work, how they make decisions and prioritise their use of time?

Success isn't just built on talent or effort, it's built on intentional connection. The people who surround you can either accelerate or dilute your progress. In the Money-Mission journey, your support system provides perspective and stable momentum. It enables you to stay resilient and move with greater clarity.

Let's explore what your support system might look like.

Your Personal Board Of Advisors

Unlike a formal boardroom, your personal board of advisors is a diverse, trusted group that helps you stay aligned and accountable. They're the people you can turn to when decisions feel difficult, or when you need grounding perspective.

Your board might include a mentor who's walked a similar path, a coach who challenges your assumptions, a peer who understands your industry, a friend who reminds you who you are, or a financial advisor who helps you plan sustainably

Now that you've seen what intentional support can look like in action, from Adam's multi-layered performance team to Ali's peer-led supper club, it's time to think about your own. We all need a group of trusted people who help us see clearly, stay accountable and stay true to what matters most. Think of it like assembling your own personal board of advisors, not for show, for substance.

This board doesn't need to be formal or official. What matters is that it's deliberate. A group of people you can turn to in times of uncertainty or opportunity, who will bring insight, challenge, and balance across the dimensions of your Money-Mission journey.

Use the table below to map out your current circle of support. Identify who's already in place, what strengths they offer and where you might want to build or rebalance.

Personal Board Of Advisors

Advisor Role	Name / Contact	Area Of Expertise / Value They Bring	Frequency Of Contact	Notes / Actions
Financial Clarity				
Mission / Strategy				
Emotional Support				
Challenging Perspective				

Integrating Those Closest To You

The Money-Mission journey inevitably affects your personal life. Those closest to you, partners, children, family, all need to understand and feel part of the journey. Beyond explanation, you should focus on building shared understanding, mutual respect, and emotional alignment. Leaders with strong family alignment are significantly more likely to sustain integrated success over time. This begins with open, honest conversations and continues with consistent communication and shared vision.

Floyd Woodrow echoes this principle. *"You need people who will be honest, but who also really believe in you. People who'll hold you accountable, not just clap for you."* Across his military and business careers, his inner circle has evolved, but it does always include voices he trusts and relies on for clear thinking and grounded support.

Ask yourself:

How well do my loved ones understand my goals (in a fully integrated sense)?

What concerns or assumptions might they be carrying?

How can I help them feel secure and involved in what I'm building?

What support might they need in order for them to support me?

This is a journey of personal integration, you don't walk it alone. Bring others with you. Invite them to contribute, offer perspective, bring resources, shape what comes next.

A Living System

Work and life aren't separate zones to manage, they're part of a living system. When one-part shifts, the others feel it. If your financial stress increases, your focus drops. If your purpose is unclear, your motivation wanes. If your health is neglected, your performance suffers.

This table provides a way to visualise the interaction and understand the impact:

System Element	Examples	Influence On Others
Finance	Income, debt, investments	Impacts freedom, energy, confidence
Mission / Purpose	Meaningful work, contribution	Drives motivation, resilience
Physical Health	Sleep, strength, stress levels	Affects stamina, clarity, emotion
Mental/Emotional	Self-talk, mood, beliefs	Shapes behaviour, decisions, energy

This is why integration work matters. Success in isolation often creates instability elsewhere. Your world works best when it works together. Keep refining, keep aligning, keep walking forward. You don't need to chase balance; you just need to build it into the way you work and live.

Just a note of warning though, you won't always get credit for the internal shifts you're making. The positive connection of money and mission isn't always visible from the outside and that's okay. Your aim is not to impress, it's to align. You're allowed to care deeply about both, say no to what drains you and structure a life that supports both wellbeing and ambition.

Just remember, integration isn't compromise, it brings clarity and focus for action.

Section Four: **The Mental-Physical Paradigm**

"The mind is everything. What you think, you become." Buddha.

"Take care of your body. It's the only place you have to live." Jim Rohn.

These two pieces of wisdom, one focused on mental mastery, the other on physical wellbeing, have traditionally been treated as distinct. The reality, as modern science now confirms, is that they are two inseparable dimensions of the same integrated system.

Welcome to the Mental-Physical Paradigm, perhaps the most foundational balance of all for modern leadership.

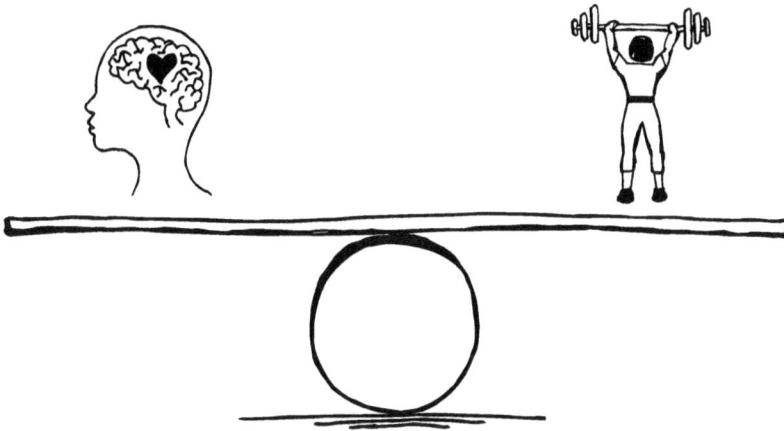

A False Divide

Let's begin by reminding you of a fundamental truth that shapes all performance. Your brain is not just another organ in your body, it is the command centre of your entire existence. It controls literally everything you feel, think, and do. Every decision you make, every emotion you experience, every physical movement you perform, from blinking your eyes to closing multi-million-pound deals, originates in this complex and extremely powerful command centre. The quality of its functioning directly determines the quality of your life and leadership.

When we consider performance of any form (cognitive, emotional, physical), we're ultimately talking about brain function. This is our basic biological reality. Your brain doesn't just influence your performance, it is the source of your performance.

This understanding is strategically essential if you are committed to improving performance and sustaining success in any form, at any level and across any domain of life. For years, many professionals have been conditioned to prioritise intellectual development while overlooking the biology that sustains it. Productivity is often pursued at the expense of sleep. Pressure is endured without adequate recovery. Stress is treated as a mindset issue, rather than recognised for its physiological impact on overall health.

This false divide creates a fragile kind of success, brilliant minds running on empty, and resilience propped up by caffeine and adrenaline. Over time, it breaks down.

The Mental-Physical Paradigm reframes the issue entirely. It recognises that:
–   Your brain and body are not separate systems, they form part of an integrated whole.
–   Physical health directly impacts mental sharpness and emotional regulation.
–   Mental wellbeing influences physical resilience, immunity, and energy.
–   Sustainable leadership depends on strengthening and balancing both.

In the chapters that follow, we'll explore the paradigm in depth and more importantly, translate it into practical strategies for high-performance living and leadership.

Chapter 8
Peak Performance Integration

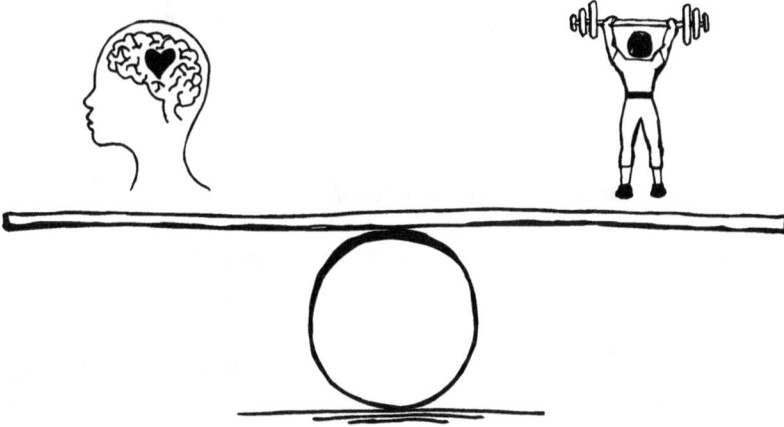

"Performance is health in motion." Dr. John Sullivan.

Picture yourself at your absolute best, thinking clearly under pressure, making complex decisions with confidence, communicating with impact, and sustaining your energy through demanding days. This isn't a fantasy. It's what becomes possible when your mental and physical systems are aligned and working in balance, with purpose and precision.

Peak performance doesn't come from pushing harder or relying on willpower alone. It comes from creating the internal conditions for your brain and body to operate in sync, consciously, subconsciously, and consistently. In The Resilience Advantage, we explored how mental and physical dimensions of leadership aren't just linked, they're biologically interdependent.

This chapter takes it further. What does high-functioning integration really look like in action? How can you align your habits, energy rhythms and leadership demands to sustain high performance over time and not just survive?

Welcome to the practical application of the Mental-Physical Paradigm.

Understanding The Systems: Mental And Physical Health

Sustainable high performance is more than a matter of mindset, it's a full-body endeavour. Behind every sharp decision, calm response, or even powerful presentation there's a biological system working hard to support you. When that system is under strain, it affects your leadership, whether through brain fog, temporary burnout, or more damaging long term emotional volatility, the impact is evident and its one to avoid.

To lead well, especially under pressure, you need to understand the two systems most responsible for driving performance: your mental health and your physical health.

Let's explore both now.

Mental Health: The Engine Of Executive Function

Mental health is often misunderstood. In everyday use, it's still largely associated with mental illness or crisis, a point at which something is 'wrong'. This, however, is a limited view. What we're talking about here is mental wellbeing, a proactive, performance-enhancing state that reflects your focus, emotional regulation, psychological safety, and resilience under stress.

It's the difference between functioning and flourishing. In a leadership context, strong mental wellbeing supports:
- **Cognitive Stamina:** Maintaining focus over long periods without depletion.
- **Emotional Agility:** Navigating change and challenge with calm and flexibility.
- **Executive Function:** Making decisions under pressure, managing complexity, and recovering from setbacks.

It's shaped by thought patterns, habits and your brain's capacity to handle sustained cognitive and emotional load.

Five Mental Health Strategies That Support Performance

We've touched on these throughout earlier chapters on Emotional Intelligence and The Resilience Advantage. Here's a distilled reminder of the most critical strategies that enable high-performance mental wellbeing:
1. **Attention Management:** Protect your prime focus hours. Reduce digital distraction, batch tasks and guard against multitasking.
2. **Emotional Regulation:** Use breathwork, reframing and state-priming techniques to stay composed when the stakes are high.
3. **Sleep Quality:** Prioritise restorative sleep. It's the foundation of memory, decision-making, impulse control and emotional stability.
4. **Recovery Rituals:** Use microbreaks, movement, journaling, or time in nature to decompress regularly, not just after burnout hits.

5. **Purpose Connection:** Re-anchor your daily work to what really matters to you. Purpose increases meaning, stabilises mood and enhances resilience, linking directly to the Mission Paradigm we explored earlier.

Mental wellbeing is at the core of emotional intelligence, the ability to manage your own emotions and respond wisely to others. Leaders with high emotional intelligence create trust-based environments, manage stress effectively and model the behaviours that enable high performance to thrive.

As a final reminder, revisit your energy map from earlier in the book. Where is your mental energy most depleted? Where might a small, deliberate recalibration make the biggest impact?

Physical Health: Your Leadership Edge

In this context, physical health goes far beyond fitness. It refers to the performance of your muscular, cardiovascular, skeletal, hormonal, immune and nervous systems. As Dr. Sullivan reminds us, *"People who are 'just fit' are not elite athletes, military operators, or astronauts. You must look at the full system and context to transfer those insights. Fitness alone doesn't make you elite. If it did, we'd all be in the Olympics."*

High-performance leadership is built on a full-spectrum approach, one that integrates physical conditioning with cognitive stamina, emotional regulation, and strategic recovery.

Physical health is a focus on your body's ability to generate and regulate energy, maintain structural integrity, support immune and hormonal balance, and recover effectively from stress or exertion.

Here's a vital mindset shift. Your brain is part of your body, it does not operate independently. It relies on glucose, oxygen, hydration, sleep, hormonal equilibrium, and movement to function optimally. As the body's most energy-hungry organ, your brain consumes roughly 30% of your calories, even at rest. If your physical system falters, your cognitive and emotional performance will too.

When physical health declines, so does mental clarity, focus and resilience. Likewise, when mental wellbeing suffers, it disrupts sleep, immune function, hormone balance and physical recovery. These aren't separate systems, they are one integrated, high-performance system.

I cannot overstate this: Your physical condition is your leadership platform. Every insight, every decision you make and interaction you deliver draws energy from the same physiological source. Sustaining high performance means actively maintaining the system that fuels it.

Maintaining a strong, stable physical foundation is now a leadership necessity. Let me show you why, through three critical pillars of strength training, cardiovascular conditioning and nutritional support.

1. Strength Training

Strength training does far more than build visible muscle, it plays a central role in long-term resilience, metabolic health and leadership stamina.

At its core, strength training:

- **Enhances Metabolic Efficiency:** Stronger muscles help regulate blood sugar and insulin, reducing fatigue and supporting sustained mental focus.
- **Supports Hormonal Balance:** It helps modulate stress hormones and keeps the wider hormonal system functioning smoothly.
- **Reinforces Structural Integrity:** A strong musculoskeletal system supports posture, reduces everyday aches and keeps you physically capable during long work cycles.

Muscle tissue is metabolically active. It helps regulate glucose, the fuel your brain depends on to stay sharp. It also buffers against stress responses, strengthens your frame and gives you greater physical confidence and control.

After the age of 30, bone density begins to decline. For anyone spending long hours at desks, in meetings, or on flights, this decline can accelerate. Strength training, whether using free weights, bodyweight, or resistance bands, helps combat that, supporting healthy bones and physical freedom later in life. Strength isn't a luxury, it's a form of readiness. It helps you move well, lead well, and stay resilient under pressure.

Take Kelly, a university lecturer who once only enjoyed cardio training. Though she considered herself 'fit', she often felt drained by mid-afternoon and struggled with persistent back ache. She assumed it was simply part of the job, long days of teaching and travel. However, after adding two short weekly strength sessions focused on posture and core stability, she began to notice a real shift. She noticed her energy levels felt better, and her back ache decreased.

2. Cardiovascular Training

Cardiovascular training remains a vital part of physical performance. It improves oxygen delivery, heart health and your body's ability to recover from stress. It also clears mental fog, stabilises mood and can reset your focus in minutes.

Even a 20-minute brisk walk can restore clarity. A longer session, like a 45-minute cycle, swim, or run can help you decompress after a demanding day. Cardio training improves VO2 max, reduces inflammation and helps support the emotional side of performance as much as the physical. The key is balance, not choosing between strength or cardio, choosing both. Training the whole system to cope with varying demands, building real stamina and adaptability over time.

3. The Nutritional Foundation

Neither strength nor cardio can be sustained without fuelling your body well. Nutrition plays a critical role in hormonal balance, energy stability and cognitive performance. A strong nutritional foundation includes:
– Prioritising whole foods.
– Hydrating throughout the day.
– Getting enough quality protein.
– Timing meals and snacks to match energy demands.
– Supplementing only where needed.

Adam Burgess treats nutrition as an evolving tool. He adjusts it depending on his goals and training blocks, but keeps his principles simple, whole foods and conscious fuelling. *"Nutrition isn't about the perfect meal,"*
he says, *"it's about conscious fuelling and consistency."*

If you want to explore more wellbeing and performance insights, you can find additional guidance and support at www.balancing-act.co.uk or by scanning the QR code here:

EXPLORE MORE

MORE CLARITY. MORE TOOLS.
YOUR NEXT STEP.

The Performance Integration Matrix

When your mental and physical systems are aligned, performance is both possible and sustainable. This is underpinned by neuroscience, physiology and what we see in the day-to-day rhythm of high performers.

– Stress elevates cortisol and disrupts immune function.
– Poor sleep impairs emotional regulation and decision-making.
– Physical activity increases levels of brain-derived neurotrophic factor (BDNF) which supports memory and cognitive flexibility.
– Emotional strain triggers inflammation, clouding clarity and slowing thought.

Your brain doesn't operate in isolation, it's part of a dynamic, biological ecosystem. When that system is aligned and well-supported, you think better, feel better, lead more effectively and sustain your energy. When it's out of sync, the impact is swift. The result? Reactivity, exhaustion and poor decision-making.

The Performance Integration Matrix helps illustrate the cost of misalignment and the power of integration:

The Performance Integration Matrix

Mental Capacity	Physical Foundation	Result
High	High	**Integrated Peak Performance:** Sustainable energy, consistent clarity, resilience, productivity and high impact.
High	Low	**Compensated Function:** Strong strategy, but prone to burnout, volatility, and long-term health costs.
Low	High	**Underleveraged Potential:** Good stamina, but dull cognition, slow decision-making, or disengagement.
Low	Low	**System Breakdown:** Chronic fatigue, reactive leadership, poor decisions and increased health risks.

Most leaders operate in the Compensated Function quadrant, fuelled by adrenaline, caffeine and pressure. They stay mentally switched on while ignoring physical needs. Without integration however, performance becomes unpredictable. Sharp one day, foggy the next. Sustainable success means building a system that lets you operate at your best over time. Integration moves you from coping to thriving.

RECOMMENDED

Use the 'Energy Mapping Grid' in your Calibration Toolkit at the end of this book to align tasks with your natural energy rhythms. It's a simple yet highly effective design tool for leaders looking to work with their energy, not against it.

Aligning Mind And Body For Better Leadership

Great leaders don't just build habits, they build systems and architecture that align mental clarity with physical energy. That means understanding that not all tasks demand the same physiological or emotional state. Strategic thinking requires calm and space. Presentations need presence and energy. Difficult conversations benefit from emotional regulation. Matching these to your natural rhythms makes a difference.

Our energy isn't static, it flows in waves. One of the most helpful rhythms to understand is the ultradian cycle, a 90–120-minute pattern of natural peaks and dips. Learn them and you can begin to protect high-focus time and pair the right tasks to the right state. Recovery is part of the performance cycle too. Breathwork, short walks, music, transitions between tasks, these aren't soft extras, they're strategic resets. Ten minutes every 90–120 minutes can refresh your cognitive systems. Quality sleep, anchored by a consistent wind-down routine, enhances learning, mood regulation and emotional control.

Dr. John Sullivan often uses music as a neural primer: *"Anything under 100 beats per minute calms the nervous system. It's not just background noise, it's a tool."* Music can guide your rhythm, shift your state and signal recovery or focus.

Floyd Woodrow designs soundtracks to prepare for transitions, increase focus, or reset energy. He uses rhythm with intent to anchor his mind to his mission.

Olympian Adam Burgess offers two useful strategies:

First, prioritise deliberate recovery. *"We spend most of our time resting,"* he told me. *"What we do with the rest of our time massively influences how productive that time is when we get to train."* For Adam, daily naps, sometimes two, weren't a luxury. *"The majority of my job is resting . . . rest well."* His routine demonstrates that high-performing success isn't built on constant action, it's built on how intentionally we recharge.

Second, protect your state with the familiar. Before race day, Adam doesn't experiment with new media or music, he anchors to the known. *"Nothing new. Same playlist, same film, same feel. It helps me focus. It's a cue for calm."* In high-pressure environments, predictable inputs provide stability and focus.

In my own life, I use small, consistent practices to build similar grounding and discipline. During lockdown, I joined a 25 press-ups-a-day-for-a-month challenge. It felt tough at first, but by the end, it didn't. I stopped once the challenge was over, but a few months later, I realised I wasn't moving enough, so I brought them back. Four years on and I'm still doing them. I've doubled to 50 a day, which I appreciate may not sound like much, but that's the point. It's simple, repeatable, and doesn't require gear or prep. I've settled at 50 as it's always manageable. Even when I feel short on time, I have no excuses. It's a daily commitment, a small, consistent test of discipline and follow-through.

I've used similar mini-practices for willpower and self-regulation, like daily foreign language lessons and monthly no-chocolate streaks, the latter, purely to test impulse control (I do love chocolate). Others I know prefer more structured systems, using fitness apps, productivity trackers, or wall charts to log workouts, screen time, nutritional breakfasts, or even monthly social nights. Different tools, same goal, building awareness and reinforcing habits that support high performance.

These aren't grand gestures. They're micro-acts of mastery, repeated daily to build stamina, discipline and alignment from the inside out.

These kinds of personal commitments tap into The Resilience Advantage Calibration Tool. They also reinforce core aspects of emotional intelligence, including impulse control, autonomous thinking and acting with intention over convenience. You don't need a pressured moment to train your edge. You just need a window in your day and the will to commit.

Anne-Sophie takes a similarly grounded approach to alignment, but hers begins with feeling, not formalisation. She describes her mental and physical health as a dynamic balance, one that ebbs and flows depending on life stages, travel and emotional load. *"I've seen a lot of yo-yos in my mental-physical health over the years,"* she shares. Rather than rigid routines, her approach is guided by how she feels, using intuition, micro-signals, and the support of others to recalibrate when needed.

She maintains a baseline of physical activity, not necessarily structured sport, but walking, running, or even moving through the rhythm of her day. Anne-Sophie's reflection highlights an important recalibration mindset, movement doesn't need to be formalised to be valuable. For her, movement is embedded in the everyday, from walking to work, running errands, baking, or taking the stairs at home. *"There has to be some physical activity,"* she notes. *"Even if it's not sport, it's life."*

On the mental side, Anne-Sophie draws strength from connection, especially in moments of uncertainty or organisational change. *"Going back to my essentials means going back to people,"* she says. *"Talking, just sharing how I feel. Not always for advice, sometimes just to be acknowledged."* She's learned to recognise her personal alarm bells, a drop in patience with her children, silence replacing her usual energy and smile, or colleagues gently pointing out that she's *"not shining the same way."* These are her recalibration cues, and she listens to them. Her coping toolkit is refreshingly honest and human, it includes a good night's sleep, a night out with friends, baking for joy, or simply letting herself cry when she's overwhelmed. *"I don't shy away from saying it,"* she says. *"My body sometimes takes control and releases what's heavy by making me cry over a stressful situation. I've learned to deal with it, to accept it and for others to understand it's part of the natural range of emotions that makes you a caring, engaged and committed leader."*

For Anne-Sophie, the key to sustainable energy is knowing when and how to come back to centre, with honesty, compassion and community. honesty, compassion and community.

Practical Tools For Integration

Here's a week-to-week framework that supports alignment. These are not meant to be rigid rules, they're adaptable tools to support energy, focus and recovery. Add those that resonate to your toolkit.

Strategy	Action	Why It Works
Peak Window Planning	Schedule high-focus work in your energy peaks.	Syncs your sharpest thinking with your most meaningful work.
Power Hour	Block 60 distraction-free minutes daily for specific tasks (admin, networking, marketing, emails).	Builds focus muscle, boosts productivity and creates forward momentum.
Strength Training	2–3 sessions weekly.	Builds hormonal balance, resilience and postural strength.
Cardio Conditioning	Regular aerobic activity.	Enhances oxygenation, mood, and cognitive recovery.
Movement Priming	Walk or stretch before key tasks.	Shifts you into focus and regulates stress.
Micro Recovery Breaks	Pause every 90–120 mins.	Refreshes focus and prevents overload.
Sleep Protection	Prioritise evening wind-down.	Boosts memory, mood and next-day performance.
Smart Nutrition	Hydrate, eat balanced, time protein.	Fuels steady energy and brain performance.

When your mental, physical and emotional systems align, you perform better, and you build a foundation that supports success across every area of your life.

In the next chapter, we'll explore how to embed these principles into your lifestyle, so that integration isn't something you dip in and out of, but something you live. This is how you lead with more clarity, bring more energy to what matters and begin to master the balance of work, wealth and wellbeing, the real formula for true executive success.

Chapter 9
Holistic Executive Wellness

In the previous chapter, we explored how integrating mental and physical systems creates your capacity for excellence in high-pressure, high-importance moments. This chapter introduces holistic executive wellness as a strategic imperative. It is not a luxury or a side note, it's the backbone upon which long-term leadership capacity is built. You are not simply preparing for better days, but for better decades.

Throughout this chapter, we'll look at how to maintain high-level mental-physical integration across the different stages of your leadership journey. We'll consider strategies designed specifically for high-performing professionals and provide practical ways to adapt these to different phases of your career, during international travel, remote or hybrid work and evolving personal responsibilities.

From early-career ambition to late-career legacy, executive wellness must grow in both sophistication and flexibility. We'll also explore how gender and generational differences impact the wellness equation. For example, many women in leadership face unique physical, hormonal and emotional challenges that call for a more nuanced approach. Meanwhile, younger professionals may prioritise balance and meaning over stamina and endurance, whereas those in later stages may focus more on preserving vitality and leaving a legacy.

Executive life rarely slows down and your wellness architecture needs to keep pace.

Let's begin by exploring why standard health advice often fails executives and what a more precise, personal and sustainable approach looks like.

You Are Not Average

If you're in a senior or high-performing role, chances are your days don't follow a simple rhythm. They're filled with competing priorities, fast-changing demands, high expectations and often, relentless travel or screen time. While broad health tips, like 'get eight hours of sleep', 'meditate daily', or 'exercise regularly', are valid and important, they often don't go far enough when it comes to meeting the demands of your unique context.

That's the executive wellness gap. It's not that the advice is wrong, it's that it's not specific or tailored enough. You're not the average population. You are ambitious, you are leading under pressure and you're aiming not just for competence but for excellence. What you need are strategies that translate general principles into actionable, bespoke routines that work for your personal biology, schedule, leadership style and aspirations.

For Ali Oliver, health and energy are grounded in rhythm. *"I was healthier and fitter during COVID than ever in my life because I had routine,"* she shared. *"My job doesn't normally allow me to have any routine."* Recognising this, she led the introduction of 'Active 30', a policy that gives staff 30 minutes each day for movement or reset. *"Whether that's walking your dog or picking up your kids, it's about protecting energy, not just productivity."*

Adam agrees. *"I think sleep and breathwork are the two things I'm most consistent with. That's where my edge is."* His recovery includes naps, active downregulation and structured rest that adapts with his workload. *"It's not about doing less; it's about doing smarter."*

In other words, focus on refining your foundations, make them stronger and then build on them. Think of this next phase as stepping into a more precise, performance-focused form of wellness. One that recognises you're not starting from scratch, rather building a system that fits your world, your stage of leadership and performance and your vision for the mastery of long-term future success.

Designing Your Personal Wellness Strategy

For high-performing leaders, health is about more than quick wins or ticking off habits. It's about building a system that works with your biology, supports your mindset, and fits the rhythm of your real life.

Rather than following broad prescriptions, this approach starts with understanding what works for you, your unique biology and your own performance landscape. Some people thrive with early morning movement, others need longer warm-ups or evening workouts to balance stress. What fuels one executive might fog the focus of another. Knowing your personal operating system is a game-changer.

Start with biological data. If you're serious about optimising performance, consider regular tracking of key biomarkers, blood glucose, hormone levels (especially cortisol and thyroid), sleep patterns and inflammatory markers. These give you objective feedback on how your habits, stress and recovery are affecting your system. Even basic wearable tech can offer powerful insight into heart rate variability (HRV), a critical measure of your nervous system's resilience.

Next, apply contextual adaptation. Leaders often try to apply rigid routines to highly dynamic lives, leading to guilt and inconsistency. Instead, build portable, flexible wellness strategies. If you're flying across time zones, switch to circadian aligned mealtimes and use targeted light exposure and melatonin to adjust. If your schedule collapses, anchor micro-workouts or 15-minute walks between on-line meetings and calls rather than skipping movement altogether. Tailor mind-fulness to your own stress response, some thrive with stillness, others with move-ment-based reflection like yoga or walking meditation.

Then, build implementation architecture, the systems that make health auto-matic. Use habit stacking to embed recovery rituals into daily rhythms, stretching while waiting for the kettle to boil, breathwork before your first email, gratitude journaling before sleep. Create friction against negative behaviours (move the sweets away, install blue-light filters) and reduce resistance to positive ones (lay out gym clothes the night before, preload healthy meals during travel).

Here are some great ways to get started:
- Track your sleep for 7 days and compare it to your mental clarity and mood.
- Schedule one 5-minute decompression pause after your most stressful daily meeting.
- Carry a portable snack that stabilises your blood sugar (nuts, protein bars) to avoid poor choices under pressure.

Wellness Across The Leadership Lifecycle

Just as leadership evolves over time, so too must your approach to wellness. What works in your 30s may no longer serve you in your 50s. The challenges you face early in your career differ from those at its peak, and they will differ again as you transition toward legacy work.

In your 30s and early 40s, you're typically in the achievement phase. Here, wellness is often the first casualty of ambition. Many are juggling career accelera-tion, family growth and identity development. Stress is constant and boundaries are tested. This is the stage to focus on rhythm and recovery. Learn to cycle inten-sity, build your energy reserves, and create baseline practices (like quality sleep, hydration and emotional regulation) that you can rely on.

In mid-career, say 40s and 50s, you're in the expansion phase. You are likely leading systems and people. You're more influential and also likely more exposed. At this stage, the focus isn't simply physical stamina, but cognitive agility and emotional stability. Here, mental fitness becomes critical. Engage in practices that train working memory and cognitive flexibility and practice protecting sleep as a non-negotiable.

In later career or legacy years, often 60 and beyond, the focus moves to sus-taining vitality and preparing for purposeful transition. The body evolves, recov-ery takes longer, muscle tone may reduce, and hormonal shifts become more noticeable. What's needed now is precision, tailored nutrition, resistance work to maintain strength, deep sleep routines and intentional space to reflect and renew. Your wellness rhythm should protect mental clarity and allow for energy that's both steady and impactful.

Across all stages, the principle remains, build the body and mind that can sustain the demands of your current chapter.

Remote Work, Travel, And The Realities Of Modern Leadership

Leadership in the modern world is borderless and so is your exposure to stress. Whether you're constantly travelling or leading from a home office, each context has its own wellness risks and opportunities.

Remote leadership can create a false sense of accessibility. Your desk is ten steps from your bed. Meetings stretch from dawn to dusk, with no commute cues to reset your brain. Emotional isolation is real. To thrive remotely, design clear start-up and shutdown rituals for your day, protect your posture with ergonomic furniture and movement breaks and replace watercooler chats with intentional connection habits (check-in calls, wellbeing prompts in meetings).

Ali Oliver, with a demanding schedule, noticed how easily the calendar can become a trap. *"I've learned to give my Executive Assistant full permission to add recovery space, buffer times after travel, walking gaps between meetings and even 15-minute breathers when we can. It sounds small, but it keeps me grounded and focused."* These micro-strategies protect long-term sustainability.

Frequent travellers face circadian disruption, inconsistent nutrition and environmental stressors. A few strategies to consider include aligning your schedule with your chronotype where possible, early risers and night owls adapt differently; anchor routines like morning stretching, hydration and supplements that travel well and use light and food timing to regulate jet lag and sleep cycles.

In both settings, resilience hinges on adaptability. The more agile your systems, the less you're thrown off when life shifts beneath you.

Leadership Wellness In The Post-Pandemic Landscape

The pandemic didn't just disrupt daily life, it fundamentally transformed how leaders work, connect and recover. It reshaped the leadership environment and introduced new wellness challenges that are now part of our long-term reality.

One of the biggest shifts has been digital immersion. The move to hybrid and virtual work brought a sharp increase in screen time, video meetings and back-to-back digital interactions. This hasn't come without cost. Leaders now how to manage a rise in cognitive load caused by continuous partial attention, reduced non-verbal cues (which can lead to misunderstanding) and constant digital context-switching. Add to that the drain of Zoom fatigue, where prolonged visual focus and self-monitoring deplete mental energy. To manage this, leaders need to get deliberate with digital boundaries, creating tech-free times in the day, choosing voice-only calls when possible, blocking time to process emails in batches and building in short breaks between meetings to let the brain reset.

Work-life boundaries have also blurred. When your home becomes your office, the lines between personal and professional life fade fast. Without the natural transitions of commuting or closing a door behind you, work has a tendency to expand into all available time and space. That's why modern leadership often requires us to create stronger psychological containers, clear rituals to start and end the workday, or parts of it, physical cues like changing clothes or switching environments and redefining what success looks like (not by how available you are, instead by how effectively you manage your energy and output).

Alongside personal wellness, there's been a major shift in team wellbeing leadership. Mental health, isolation and burnout are no longer side conversations, they're core leadership responsibilities. Leaders today must create psychological safety, become more literate in mental health support and model recovery practises themselves. Giving your team permission to pause, encouraging connection, and knowing how to access support has become part of the role.

Yet within all this disruption lies opportunity. The post-pandemic era has opened the door for wellness reinvention. Remote and hybrid work models now offer the chance to better align work with personal rhythms. You can build in more natural movement, access fresh air and nature during breaks, reduce commuting stress and reclaim time that was once lost to logistics. Leaders who embrace these shifts are designing new systems that support both wellbeing and performance in a world that's changed for good.

Leadership Wellness Self-Check

Ask yourself:
- Am I building digital breaks into my day, or running on continuous input?
- Do I have clear transitions that mark the start and end of my workday?
- How often do I model recovery and wellbeing to my team?
- Have I redesigned my routines to take advantage of new flexibility, or am I still operating from old habits?

Small shifts in awareness can lead to big changes in energy, presence and performance.

Generational Considerations In Executive Wellness

Wellness isn't universal, it's shaped by our biology, lived experiences, values and the cultural norms we grew up with. Understanding how different generations and genders approach leadership and wellbeing can unlock more effective strategies, deepen empathy and lead to more tailored support systems.

Younger leaders are redefining success through meaning and mental health. Millennials and Gen Z professionals are entering or advancing in leadership roles with a different lens. Many prioritise purpose, autonomy and a more flexible relationship with work. They expect mental health to be a visible within leadership culture, not treated as an afterthought. Wellness, for them, is integrated by design, built into how they live and lead. Importantly, they're less likely to sacrifice family or mental wellbeing for status or tradition.

At the same time, younger leaders often face change with fewer tools for emotional endurance. While they may excel in areas like innovation and social awareness, they often benefit from mentorship in building emotional stamina, learning how to stay steady during uncertain times and how to recover from setbacks without internalising them.

Older leaders, often Gen X and Baby Boomers, came of age in environments that rewarded self-sacrifice, long hours, and pushing through at any cost. These habits built discipline and drive, but also normalised burnout, emotional suppression, and delayed self-care. Many in this group are now contending with physical changes, joint health, metabolic shifts, disrupted sleep, or cognitive fatigue. Their wellness priorities often focus on preserving executive function, managing long-term stress, and unlearning patterns that no longer serve them.

There's also a quiet identity shift underway. Leaders who've spent decades defined by role and responsibility are now asking, what's next? How do I want to feel while I lead? For this generation, wellness isn't a passing trend, it's becoming key to legacy and freedom.

Ali Oliver captures this transitional awareness clearly: *"There's a new generation coming through. The world is changing and you've either got to be one of those people that's really agile and able to embrace it, able to change really, really well, or you kind of must accept, actually this is now somebody else's era to lead and guide."*

She continues: *"I'm starting to see that the young people coming into the organisation are very different in terms of attitudes and perspectives. Would someone closer to their generation be able to help them become the best version of themselves professionally?"*

Her insight highlights a key shift in leadership, one that values timely transition and evolving influence. Recognising when new voices, values and leadership styles are needed, and being agile enough to support that evolution is becoming increasingly important

When different generations collaborate in leadership teams, wellness can become a powerful bridge. Younger leaders bring fresh perspective and values-driven decision-making. Older leaders offer deep experience, and strategic calm. Shared learning between these groups, around resilience, wellness and sustainable success, benefits everyone.

This is the moment to step beyond outdated models of leadership and build cultures that honour individual rhythms, and the changing nature of performance across time.

Why This Matters For Personal Performance

Understanding how wellness needs shift across gender and generation strengthens more than team dynamics, it sharpens your leadership and enhances personal performance.

When you develop greater awareness of how others function, what energises or drains them, what support they need and how they define wellbeing, you're building emotional intelligence. This is a core aspect of calibrating how you lead and communicate, with empathy, with clarity, and with intent.

It also enhances your ability to apply the Skilled Communication Calibration Tool, expressing your own wellness needs with confidence, while tuning in to the needs of others, even when they differ from your own. Recognising that people thrive under different conditions, and that those conditions evolve over time, allows you to lead with both understanding and adaptability.

This kind of emotional and social awareness deepens connection, it reduces friction, and it helps to protect your own energy. You begin to build environments where performance and wellbeing can grow side by side, starting with your own.

Gender-Specific Wellness Challenges In Leadership

Wellness in leadership isn't one-size-fits-all. Gender can influence how leaders experience pressure, manage recovery, and how their biology supports or challenges daily demands. Recognising these differences helps leaders design systems that reflect their real-world context, instead of forcing themselves into models that don't fit.

For Women: Leading With Biological Awareness

For many women, the overlap of professional, personal and emotional roles creates a distinct set of energy demands. Hormonal transitions, including perimenopause and menopause, can bring reduced energy, and cognitive changes that directly affect leadership presence and decision-making. Tools like cycle-aware planning, targeted nutrition and nervous system regulation can help sustain consistency and resilience.

Understanding hormonal rhythms can be a powerful asset in leadership:

- **Cycle syncing for performance:** Throughout the menstrual cycle, cognitive and emotional capacity shifts. The follicular phase (typically days 1–14) often brings heightened creativity, verbal fluency and social energy, ideal for presentations, brainstorming and relationship-building. The luteal phase (days 15–28) tends to support focused analysis and planning; while energy may dip, detail-oriented thinking often improves.
- **Perimenopause and menopause:** For women in their 40s and 50s, hormonal shifts can impact sleep, mood and mental clarity. These aren't signs of weakness, they're physiological realities that benefit from support. Leaders navigating this stage may benefit from working with specialists in hormonal health, scheduling key meetings during peak energy times, using cooling strategies or environment adjustments, and supporting cognition through nutrition (such as omega-3s, B vitamins, and adaptogens).

Ali refers to herself in this phase as a *"kind of moving into the third age . . . . one that obviously brings with it a lot of choices, both professionally and personally . . . as a female, going through the menopause, there's a lot of things that change personally that affect your perspective, affect your motivation, affect your capacity to continue to work in the same way. Sometimes I'm knackered and I still must show up. That's the job."*

Her honesty highlights the demands of visibility as a female leader and the pressure to stay 'switched on' even through personal health fluctuations. It affirms the need to normalise vulnerability as part of real-world wellness.

- **Balancing the mental load:** Despite evolving gender roles, many women still carry a significant share of emotional and logistical responsibility at home. This hidden labour draws heavily on cognitive and emotional bandwidth. Strategies like decision batching, creating transition rituals between work and home roles, setting 'worry windows', and building supportive delegation systems can help reduce the load and create space for focus and recovery.

For Men: Reframing Wellness And Resilience

While conversations around wellness are evolving, many men still face unique pressures that often go unspoken. Cultural norms around stoicism and self-reliance can make it harder to notice when support is needed, or to respond proactively to physical and emotional changes:

- **Supporting Testosterone And Energy:** From around age 40, testosterone levels begin to decline, a process that can be accelerated by chronic stress and poor sleep habits. These hormonal shifts can lead to lower energy, reduced emotional steadiness, and slower cognitive function. Regular hormone panels (blood tests that track key levels) can offer valuable insight and guide targeted health strategies. Supporting hormone health might include prioritising high-quality sleep (when most testosterone production occurs), engaging in strength-based training (such as squats and compound lifts), and using practices that regulate the nervous system, including breathwork or cold exposure.
- **Breaking The Stoicism Habit:** Even as cultural narratives shift, many male leaders have been conditioned to override physical discomfort or emotional signals. This often leads to unaddressed stress, illness, or reactivity that surfaces only when performance suffers. Reconnecting with internal cues can start simply, through body scanning, reflective journaling, or working with a coach trained in somatic approaches. These practices help tune into early signs of strain, and act before pressure becomes a problem.
- **Redefining Resilience:** For years, resilience has been synonymous with endurance. That mindset is now changing. More leaders are recognising that recovery is part of resilience, it doesn't lower performance, it protects and sustains it. Finding role models who combine strength with sustainability can reinforce a healthier mindset. Shifting away from the 'push through' approach creates space for smarter, longer-lasting performance, and a leadership presence that holds up under pressure.

For All Leaders: Personalised, Context-Aware Wellness

Whatever your gender identity, effective leadership today requires a wellness strategy that fits your reality, not someone else's model. This includes:
- Understanding your unique physiological patterns through regular check-ins or biomarker assessments.
- Tailoring recovery practices to your personal stress response.
- Building a circle of connection and community that offers real support, not just professional, but emotional too.

Leadership wellness is evolving. The most successful leaders are those designing systems that reflect who they are, how they function and what helps them thrive over time.

Small, consistent habits build the foundation. The Daily Calibration Practice in your toolkit (in Chapter 14) offers a quick, practical check-in to help align your daily actions with the future you're working toward.

Wellness As A Leadership Multiplier

Floyd speaks of wellness in terms of readiness. *"You're either getting yourself into the right state, or you're dragging yourself through,"* he says. *"You can't lead well if you're not fit to lead, mentally or physically."*

His approach centres on preparation. Preparing your mental, emotional, and physical foundation for sustainable leadership.

When wellness becomes strategic, when its intentionally designed, personally tailored, and consistently maintained, it stops being something you squeeze in and starts becoming the system that supports everything else.

The goal isn't perfection, it's readiness. When your body is energised, when your mind is sharp and your emotions are steady, you lead differently. You respond rather than react. You notice opportunities others miss. You maintain performance without burning out.

This is the wellness edge. For high-performing leaders, it's no longer optional, it's essential.

Section Five: **The Work – Life Paradigm**

One Person, One Vision

We often separate the language of work and life, as if they belong on different tracks. The reality, however, is that we move through every context with the same system, one body, one mindset. Whether leading others or supporting those closest to us, we rely on the same energy system, the same core beliefs, and the same emotional and physical resources.

Just like a tightrope walker, we move forward step by step and each step demands our full attention. We cannot walk in two directions at once. Every step forward requires us to choose a focus. With each move, we're recalibrating, sometimes consciously, often unconsciously, where our attention, time and energy go. The tighter the rope, the more precise and purposeful our balance needs to be. The more we try to split our weight in different directions, the shakier we become.

We are one person with a single energy system, one set of values, one body and mind. Everything we do, at work, at home, in our relationships, comes from that same system.

Every choice we make in one part of life affects all the others.

This is the heart of the Work-Life Paradigm. It's a reminder that we must see ourselves holistically and drop the outdated idea of balance as a game of time slots and trade-offs and embrace a model that accounts for flow, purpose and sustainability.

Think of how we approach finances, we seek advisors. For our health and strength, we find coaches and trainers, and for performance, we lean into psychology. Yet when it comes to our whole integrated life, where work overlaps with parenting, with marriage, with ambition, with identity . . . where do we go? Who's helping us to successfully design, navigate and succeed across the fuller, much bigger, picture?

This is why your inner circle matters, it provides a mirror and sounding board for the decisions you face across all areas of life. When we're striving for integrated success, we need people around us who understand our whole picture, not just our career goals or parenting demands in isolation. People who can challenge and support us and who remind us of our values when the path ahead feels complex.

Entrepreneur and former Dragon's Den investor Sarah Willingham offers a helpful example. Each year, she plans her time using a pie chart, mapping out family events, school plays, workouts, holidays, board meetings, business ventures and catch-ups with friends. Through doing this, each year she's reminded that there's never enough time for everything. However, instead of reacting in the moment throughout the year, she makes intentional trade-offs in advance. She chooses what matters most, knows why she's saying yes or no and accepts the limits of her energy and time with clarity and ownership.

This is the essence of integration. When we choose consciously, we give more of ourselves to what matters and let go of guilt around what we've chosen to pause or delay. We move forward with alignment, not exhaustion.

In the next chapter, we'll explore what shapes these trade-offs, the career stage you're in, the generational lens you've grown up with, your relationships and your evolving definition of success. These elements influence both what we choose and how we choose, and this is where real, sustainable performance begins.

Chapter 10
Rethinking Success: The Trade-Off Lens

"I'm constantly juggling deadlines at work and my son's football matches."

"I miss breakfast with my family because of morning client calls."

"I haven't taken a proper holiday in years because there's never a good time to take a break."

These reflections, heard from professionals across roles and life stages, capture a fundamental challenge in modern life, how to integrate the demands of work with the needs of the rest of your life. The question is no longer whether you work hard, but whether the way you work still works for you.

This chapter revisits a core question from earlier in the book, what does success really mean to you? Because true success cannot come at the cost of everything else. Building a dream home only to realise your family grew up without you. Landing the big role but missing every school concert. That's not the dream. That's misalignment. It's what happens when we treat work and life as separate systems, forgetting that we are one person, not two.

The Calibration Model encourages integration over balance. Using the tools of Emotional Intelligence, Skilled Communication and The Resilience Advantage, we learn how to perform, relate, recharge and lead in a way that strengthens the whole system.

Let's now explore some different and equally valid approaches to work-life integration. Each one reflects a different set of values, rhythms, and trade-offs. As you read, ask yourself, which one feels most like you? Which one do you aspire to? Is your current model working for you, or do you need to recalibrate?

Time Is The Currency

Anne-Sophie's perspective is a clear example of modern work-life integration. *"What work-life balance means is being able to do what I want to do in the time I want to do it, when and the where are variable."* For her, the key is not a strict routine, it's the freedom to structure each day in a way that reflects her priorities. She thrives on pressure and meaningful connection, traits that once kept her in the office until 7 p.m. most evenings before becoming a parent. Now, she still finds satisfaction in her work, often continuing projects after her children are in bed, her schedule just flexes around the moments that matter. Cooking dinner and sharing a meal remains a non-negotiable anchor in the day, it's *"the bonding time."* For Anne-Sophie, balance isn't static, it changes every day and that dynamic, less-routine lifestyle is part of what she enjoys most.

Intentional Rhythms

For Alison Oliver, balance isn't a perfect split, it's an intentional rhythm, developed over time. Her life involves frequent travel, so she designs structure where she can. *"Sleep's a big thing for me,"* she says. *"Ideally, I'd love eight or nine hours, but if I'm going to have six, I'd rather have six hours every night, so my body gets used to the routine."* That same desire for predictability is evidenced in her exercise habits and work habits. She uses different time zones in her day strategically: *"If I'm driving, it's a thinking task. If I'm on the train, I'll use that time to clear big reports."*

Time is also emotionally coded. Friday nights carry deep meaning, traced back to her dad, who wouldn't go to bed until 3 a.m. on a Friday (or in fact early Saturday morning!) simply because he loved the feeling of the weekend arriving. *"I think it's something you inherit,"* she reflects. *"It gets to about half three on a Friday and I'm not finishing then, but I enjoy knowing the weekend's coming."* There is a contrast between week and weekend that's deliberate. *"I really try not to work on weekends,"* she says. *"When I'm away through the week, I'll work long into the evening if I need to, but when I'm home, I want to protect that time."* She credits her partner's support, walking the dogs, holding space, for making that rhythm possible.

Yet even for someone who loves her job, Sundays remain tough. *"I've never cracked Sunday afternoons,"* she admits. *"It's not because I dread work, I love my job, but it's that gear change. I want to be in my house, with my family, in 'life.' But I feel I've got to gear up and when I try to bring the two worlds together, I feel the conflict."* Alison's story is a powerful reminder that even high-performing leaders have their friction points, but also that rhythm, honesty, and self-awareness can create a work-life balance that can work.

Performance Meets Perspective

Adam Burgess lives for the water, but not only for the wins. A successful GB Olympian in canoe slalom, he describes his perfect day as *"just being on the white water a couple of times a day, especially in the summer."* Even in elite sport, he's conscious of the need for something more. *"It's nice to have balance and something else going on in my life,"* he says. When training disappoints, his breath coaching business keeps him energised. *"It's nice when one side lets you down a bit, the other picks you up."* Adam's not chasing the perfect routine, he's designing the right rhythm, where passion for sport and meaningful side projects coexist. It's this multi-focus approach that helps him thrive in a field known for its emotional highs and lows.

Integration Without Separation

Floyd Woodrow, decorated military leader and founder of Compass for Life, doesn't split his life into compartments. *"I don't separate them,"* he says. *"I look at them being part of me."* His best days are deeply structured and also fluid. He blends breathwork, movement and mental rehearsal in the morning, followed by high-intensity strategic work or deep creative play, like chess, painting, or writing books. *"Every six months, I set challenges,"* he explains, from mastering negotiation to cycling goals. His 'resilience shield' spans physical, mental, emotional, and social domains and he uses his time, not the calendar, as his anchor. *"People on the outside might not know if I'm working or playing. That's the art of living."*

A Balance Of Personas

Personally, I see myself as a professional, a mum of three and a challenge seeker. Which of those comes first depends on who I'm with and what I'm doing, but they're all part of who I am, and they're always present.

I used to thrive on working through the night, the long hours of deep focus with no interruptions. I still enjoy that kind of intensity. When I'm immersed in project work or delivering at pace, I'm all in, and I love it. Since having children, though, I've had to reshape how I manage my time. When I launched my first business, I gained the flexibility to shape how I balanced career and family, and that foundation has guided everything I've built since.

It hasn't always been perfect. I've cancelled holidays when work had to come first, and I've turned down opportunities that clashed with my children's key milestones. It's been an ongoing and evolving process, one that's become more balanced and intentional over time.

Bailey, Darcie, and Brodie are the most important people in my life. They come first, always. I've never missed a birthday, sports day, or school play. Those have always been non-negotiables for me, the trade-offs I've chosen to make. That's not a standard I expect others to follow, and I certainly don't judge anyone for making different choices. We all define what matters most in our own way.

But that doesn't mean I've compromised on ambition. When I commit to work, it's a full commitment, and when I'm with my children, that's just as true. Our household doesn't run on a strict routine, our work lives simply don't allow for it. My husband and I manage the moving pieces together. His calendar is filled with the kids' activities and school events, so we can coordinate and tag in for each other.

Some weeks I'm working long days or travelling, and I love being in that high-performance space. Other weeks, I spend hours on football side-lines or at dance classes and theatre shows, I like the contrast.

For me, work time is shaped by two things, when other people are available for collaboration and when I'm needed elsewhere, by family life or by the challenges I choose to take on. These challenges, whether physical, mental, and endurance-based, are an essential part of the mix. I commit to them fully because they give me space, space away from work, from parenting, from responsibility. They're rare moments where no one else needs me. I can focus on my own energy and mental strength, and often, that's when I do my best thinking. That space is mine and I protect it fiercely.

Each part of me, mother, professional, challenge seeker, requires focus and intentional energy.

Through my work, I get a unique window into how others shape their lives, consciously or otherwise. I've worked with clients who rise early to get straight into work or to hit the gym before the world wakes, using those quiet hours for sharp thinking or high energy tasks, then transitioning into family time or meetings with ease. Others design their week in blocks, working intensely over four days and reserving three full days for family, rest, and wider interests. Some structure their work around biological rhythms, syncing effort with natural energy highs and lows. I've seen couples approach their lives as joint ventures, holding weekly check-ins to rebalance, work and personal goals. Others set non-negotiable time for study or side projects building in growth while guarding against burnout.

These are just a few of the many creative, intentional ways people are integrating their lives and work. The lesson isn't to copy anyone else's model, it's to design your own. One that's built deliberately, based on your energy, your values, your responsibilities, and your personal definition of success.

You might be reading this thinking, *I live alone, I don't need to manage all that.* Or maybe you're dating and wondering, *Should I be learning their daily rhythm already?* Perhaps people say you're 'lucky' because a parent helps out, and maybe that's true, but part of you still wishes you had the capacity to manage more on your own. Or maybe you've already navigated all these phases, made it work however you could, and now you're in a place to support and guide others doing the same.

The point is that success looks different for everyone. There is no single way to 'get it right'. We each work with the time, energy, support, and opportunities we have. The key is using those resources consciously, to design a life that's right for you.

So, pause and ask yourself:

Are you doing that right now?

Career Stage And Life Phase: The Shifting View Of Success

What we define as 'success' is often shaped by both our career stage and our life phase, though these don't always align in predictable or traditional ways.

In the early stages of a career, the focus is often on growth, learning, and building credibility. Mid-career leaders may begin to prioritise influence and autonomy. Later in a career, the lens often shifts toward legacy or lifestyle. However, none of these stages come with fixed timelines.

Some people reach significant milestones early and start asking legacy-level questions in their thirties. Others pivot later in life, driven by curiosity or personal change. Some juggle intense family responsibilities while still early in their careers; others enjoy greater freedom later and reinvent completely.

What matters most is recognising your current stage, not in terms of job title or age, but in terms of what you need, want, and are building toward right now. When you understand where you are, you can recalibrate your definition of success accordingly, and start making trade-offs that align with who you are today, not who you were five years ago, or who others expect you to be.

Our personal vision of success is also shaped by what we've internalised or seen modelled. What feels like a fulfilling risk at one stage might feel draining or misaligned at another. Success is dynamic, and the more aware we are of that, the more intentional and empowered our choices become.

In the early career phase, success might mean visibility, progress, or financial stability. Mid-career often brings a shift toward balance, purpose, or deeper impact. In later stages, reflection becomes more central: *What legacy am I leaving? What really matters now?*

Ali Oliver offers a striking example of legacy-minded leadership. Though still leading the charity, she's already thinking about what might serve it best in the future. *"While I'm moving towards that (age), 'I'm really mindful . . . at some point this will be somebody else's organisation,"* she says. *"If and when inevitably you are going to go, you start to think about laying the foundations or keeping the foundation strong for whoever comes after you."* Her perspective isn't driven by burnout or self-interest, instead by the mission and the people the organisation serves.

It's rare to find a leader so focused on succession planning while still in post, continuously asking what is best for the organisation, not just for me?

In contrast, Adam Burgess is in an earlier phase of his leadership journey. With plans stretching across two more Olympic cycles, he remains open to what might evolve next. As breathwork continues to influence his performance and leadership, he's staying present while allowing space for that practice to organically become part of his next business chapter. His version of success is still forming, dynamic, exploratory and purpose driven.

Floyd Woodrow provides another distinctive model of success. A former SAS officer and recipient of the Distinguished Conduct Medal, Floyd has since built a career as a business leader, author, Chairman of the Quantum Group and Founder of Compass for Life and the CFL Foundation. His work spans elite performance, leadership strategy and education. Floyd exemplifies a fluid career arc, where each chapter layers onto the next rather than replacing it. For him, work isn't something to retire from. *"I don't see a time when I won't be doing what I do. It's part of who I am."*

Anne-Sophie offers a powerful example of how success evolves not only with career progression but with self-awareness and personal values, combining strategic leadership with technical depth, built on a foundation of engineering and chemistry. Her trajectory hasn't followed a rigid blueprint though. Throughout her career, Anne-Sophie has consistently leaned into curiosity and external perspective. Many of her professional transitions were catalysed by others seeing potential in her before she saw it herself. *"My different job changes have been mostly driven by others rather than myself,"* she reflects. This openness, to feedback, sponsorship, and challenge, has played a defining role in her growth. Even when facing fear or uncertainty, she embraces challenge as part of what makes the work worthwhile.

Her current phase reflects a deepening sense of alignment, between her values, her leadership style and what she brings to the organisation. She's not driven by ego or ambition for its own sake, but by a genuine desire to use her strengths to contribute meaningfully. As she's said, it's likely others will help shape what comes next, just as they have shaped her journey so far.

Anne-Sophie's version of success is fluid, relational and guided by intuition and trust. She doesn't define success by position alone, instead she measures it by impact and connection, at work, at home and in herself.

A couple of examples from clients I've worked with illustrate this even further. One client, a Chief Financial Officer, spent two years leading complex overseas acquisitions. The pace and pressure were relentless, she barely saw her family. When the business was eventually sold though, the equity pay-out she received paid off her mortgage and laid future foundations. The sacrifice was intentional, time-bound, and ultimately liberating.

Another, an international recruiter, decided to leave his full-time role and set up his own agency. He now earns more in commission than he did in any of his salaried positions, while working far more flexibly and with greater autonomy. His trade-off wasn't about working less, it was about working on his own terms, with the freedom to choose how and when to deliver (and be remunerated for it accordingly).

These decisions weren't easy, but they aligned with the individuals' evolving definitions of success and what they were willing to trade to get there.

And then there are my own chapters. I set up my first business while on maternity leave, when I thought I'd have the time (I know, I laugh as I write that . . .). I did it as a way to build flexibility into my career. Later, I moved into international work, where I enjoyed the travel and quite literally lived a double life, full-time focused professional while away, full-time focused mum on my return. That experience taught me how to weave integration through the chaos. Now, as someone leading multiple ventures, I've found a rhythm that feels more balanced. Not always perfect, but increasingly intentional. Each chapter bringing me closer to my North Star, with greater focus and momentum.

As these stories show, recognising your life and career phase helps you make trade-offs with perspective and stay aligned with your evolving vision of success. The key here is intention. Trade-offs will always exist, mastery of success comes from choosing with purpose, alignment, and conscious intention.

Generational Influence And Workplace Identity

Success is also shaped by the generational stories we carry. Many Gen X and Baby Boomer leaders were raised on ideas of endurance, sacrifice and 'making it'. Millennials and Gen Z are reshaping that narrative by placing greater value on meaning and wellbeing. Neither view is wrong, they're just different. When we don't understand and acknowledge this difference, misalignment and conflict, can occur.

Cross-generational teams thrive when they share their success criteria. It builds empathy, encourages dialogue, and invites deeper collaboration. This is where the Skilled Communication and Emotional Intelligence Calibration Tools come to life. When we understand the story behind what someone values, we open the door to mutual understanding and shared motivation.

Each generation brings its own lens to the work-life conversation, shaped by the economic, technological and cultural forces of their formative years:

Baby Boomers (born 1946–1964): Largely pioneered the concept of work-life balance, challenging the all-consuming work cultures they inherited. Many sought to create clearer demarcation between work and personal life, often seeing them as separate but equal priorities.

Generation X (born 1965–1980): Built on that foundation, leveraging emerging technologies to create more flexible arrangements. As working parents, they were often the first to negotiate remote options, adjusted hours, and alternative career paths to accommodate changing family dynamics.

Millennials (born 1981–1996): Questioned the very separation of work and life. Entering the workforce during economic instability and rapid digital transformation, they prioritised purpose, fulfilment, and alignment between values and vocation, blending personal and professional identity more fluidly.

Generation Z (born 1997–2012): Has accelerated this shift, with strong expectations for authenticity and value alignment. They see rigid structures as outdated and expect flexibility, inclusivity, and digital enablement as the norm.

These generational perspectives don't exist in isolation. Most workplaces now include three or even four generations working side by side, each with different expectations about how work should relate to life. That diversity brings complexity, but also huge opportunity.

The key isn't to rank one generation's view over another, but to recognise that each brings something valuable. The loyalty and dedication of Baby Boomers, the adaptability and realism of Gen X, the purpose-driven mindset of Millennials, and the authenticity and self-awareness of Gen Z all contribute to a richer, more integrated conversation about how life and leadership can evolve, together.

The Digital Revolution: Enabler Or Disruptor?

Technology has fundamentally transformed the work-life paradigm, creating unprecedented opportunities for integration while also introducing new challenges.

The digital revolution has eliminated geographic constraints allowing work to happen anywhere, created asynchronous communication possibilities reducing the need for simultaneous presence, provided tools for automated organisation scheduling and task management and enabled new forms of collaboration that transcend physical workplaces. Yet these same technologies have also blurred boundaries between work and personal time, created expectations of constant availability, increased the cognitive load through notification overload and introduced new forms of monitoring and surveillance

The result is a complex picture where the same technologies that enable integration also undermine it. The key differentiator isn't the technology itself, it's how it's implemented and governed. Organisations that establish clear digital boundaries, like no-email periods, notification-free zones, or asynchronous work protocols, enable their people to leverage technology without being consumed by it. Individuals who develop personal practices around digital hygiene, such as dedicated device-free times, strategic notification management, or clear communication about availability, are better positioned to use technology as an integration enabler rather than a disruptor.

Organisational Culture: The Integration Enabler

While integration ultimately happens at the individual level, organisational culture plays a crucial role in either supporting or hindering it. The most integration-friendly cultures share several characteristics:

Results Focus Over Presence: Organisations that measure outputs rather than inputs, what people accomplish rather than when or where they work, create space for personalised integration. When performance is judged by impact rather than activity, individuals gain the autonomy to structure their work in ways that complement rather than conflict with personal priorities.

Clear Expectations: Integration flourishes when expectations are explicit rather than implicit. Cultures that clearly articulate performance standards, availability requirements and communication protocols eliminate the uncertainty that often drives overwork and boundary confusion.

Leader Modelling: When leaders demonstrate integrated approaches to their own lives, leaving visibly for children's events, taking proper holidays, talking openly about personal priorities, they create permission for others to do the same. Conversely, leaders who project an always-on, work-first mentality, regardless of their stated policies, create cultures where integration is discouraged in practice even if promoted in principle.

Support Infrastructure: Integration-friendly organisations build systems that enable flexibility, from collaborative technology platforms to cross-training that prevents single points of failure. They recognise that integration is more than a philosophy, it's a practical approach that requires structural support.

Flexibility With Boundaries: The most effective cultures balance flexibility with clarity. They provide autonomy within defined guardrails, creating enough freedom for personalisation while maintaining enough structure for coordination and collaboration.

It's worth noting that these characteristics benefit everyone, not just those with family responsibilities. Whether you're caring for children, pursuing education, managing health challenges, or simply seeking a more balanced approach to life, these cultural elements create space for sustainable success. If you hold any kind of leadership responsibility, consider how you can implement and reinforce these elements in your own sphere, perhaps through how you manage your team, through the influence you have over policy, or through the behaviours you choose to model. The more we normalise and actively shape integration-friendly practices, the more they become part of the wider culture, not just personal exceptions.

Dr. John Sullivan reinforces that culture isn't built on policy, it's shaped by behaviour and communication. *"Everybody matters . . . or nobody matters,"* Equity in attention, respect and inclusion is not just ethically right, it's a performance advantage. He goes further: *"Our messaging really matters. All businesses need a sincere communication plan and a culture of support, one that provides clarity and freedom to act."*

In high-performing environments, communication is leadership. Whether articulating vision, setting expectations, or offering support, the clarity and sincerity of your message directly impacts trust and long-term performance.

The Role Of Relationships In Sustainable Success

At 16, Adam Burgess left home to train full-time. *"I didn't really understand how much support I was walking away from until I didn't have it,"* he says. Over time, he built a network of teammates, coaches and housemates who became family. *"That emotional scaffolding helped me thrive."*

Floyd Woodrow similarly credits the relationships around him as central to sustainable leadership. *"I've been incredibly lucky in the people I've had around me,"* he said. Whether in the military or business, he consistently surrounds himself with people who share his values and challenge him to grow. *"My circle has always included people who can be honest with me. Sometimes, you must move away from people who don't align with where you're going. That's tough, but it's necessary."*

Family relationships also form a vital but often overlooked part of a high-performing life. While this book explores leadership and success, through the mastery of work, wealth and wellbeing, these themes ripple through our personal worlds too. Parents balancing ambition and presence, siblings negotiating legacy and autonomy, or adult children navigating responsibility for ageing parents, each dynamic demands recalibration. The success of one doesn't have to mean sacrifice for another, it does though require conversation, and conscious design.

Michelle Obama recently spoke on a podcast (Diary of a CEO) about marriage, parenting, and success. She shared a powerful insight about the shift that happens when two ambitious people, both out 'slaying dragons' and building their empires, become parents. Before children, time together is filled with fun, conversation, connection and momentum. After children, time becomes logistics. Conversations revolve around sleep schedules and feeding plans. What once felt energising can become exhausting if it's not proactively nurtured.

This doesn't always present a problem, but it does require intention and a proactive recalibration. Relationships, romantic or otherwise, need shared vision, emotional alignment, and clear roles. For some couples, that might mean formal discussions around parenting and domestic roles. For others, it may involve building a rhythm of regular check-ins and shared rituals. Some clients I've worked with have even engaged in marriage or relationship counselling before having children, not because there was something wrong, but to voice concerns and identify blind spots in advance. That's wisdom, not weakness.

We often say we're attracted to people who share our values, but how do those values express themselves day to day? Do you both value education? Great, but how will that fit into evening and weekend routines if taken alongside work? Do you both want a healthy lifestyle? Excellent, but how do you divide time to make it happen? Alignment in vision doesn't mean sameness in task, it means shared ownership of outcomes.

In relationships that thrive through challenge, partners don't just understand each other's goals, they feel invested in them. They see their contribution to each other's success. Whether that's logistical, emotional, or motivational, it matters. It requires communication and honesty about what you want from life, your career, and your shared future. You don't need to see each other all the time, when you do though, let it be connective, not just operational. Check in often and ask if the vision still feels good. Adjust your expectations when needed. If you're both contributing to a shared life, it's vital to ensure you're still aligned on what that life is meant to look and feel like.

Whether you're in a romantic partnership, co-parenting relationship, or leading a team, relationships are the core of sustainable success. They fuel your energy. They ground your mission, and they hold up the mirror to your values.

Ali puts it this way: *"When you're really clear on your values, you're not drained by the job, even when it's hard. Because you know you're in the right place, doing the right thing. That's where energy comes from."*

Building Your Portfolio Of Wealth

By now, you'll have seen this theme woven throughout the book: success isn't one-dimensional. The life you're building is made up of more than just a job title or a bank balance. Your real wealth lives in your energy, your time, your health, your relationships, your sense of purpose and your ability to enjoy it all while you're living it.

Think of it as your 'Integrated Wealth Portfolio', a personal blend of six core assets that power your performance and define how well you're really doing:

Money: Financial wellbeing, freedom, security. Are you building stability and opportunity that supports your life and legacy?

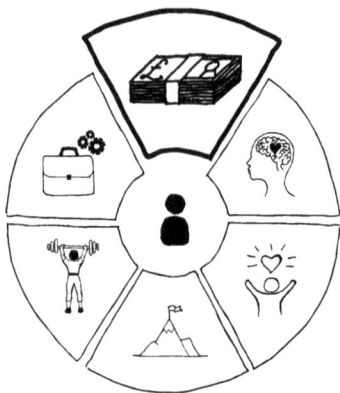

Mission: Purpose, contribution, meaningful work. Does what you do each day align with what you care about most?

Mental Health: Clarity, calm, emotional agility. Are you mentally resourced to lead, connect and sustain performance?

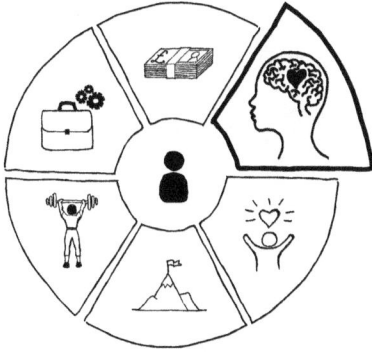

Physical Health: Strength, stamina, vitality. Is your body enabling your ambitions or asking for more care?

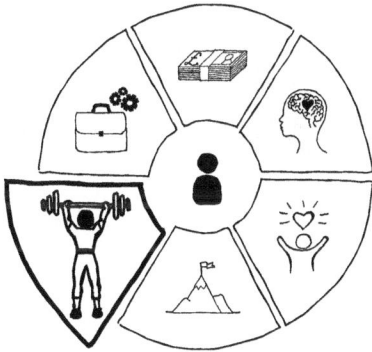

Work: Structure, growth, professional fulfilment. Are you shaping work that supports your wider vision of success?

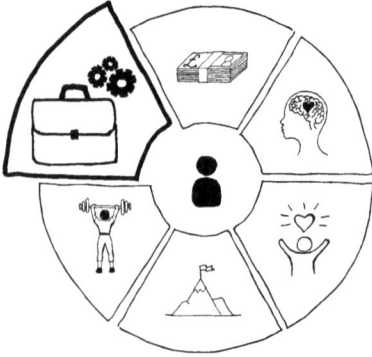

Life: Joy, relationships, rest, exploration. Is there enough space for what you love and who you love?

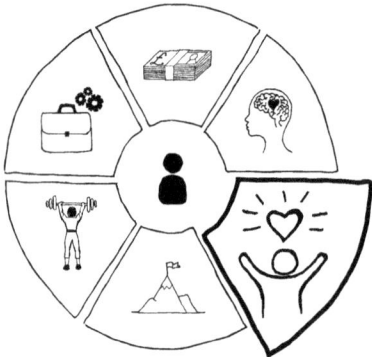

You'll already be building parts of this, even if unconsciously. Now's the time to take a step back and look at the whole. Are you investing in all areas? Are you protecting and replenishing what matters most? Are you growing one part while unintentionally depleting another?

There's no fixed formula, just the invitation to make more intentional choices. When you say yes to something, what are you saying no to in return? And are you happy with that trade-off?

Success evolves. Your vision at 25 might feel very different at 45. That's okay, it's healthy and it's the reality of your changing priorities and wider world. The goal isn't to freeze your idea of success, it's to keep recalibrating it as your circumstances shift. A portfolio built five years ago may not reflect what you need or want now and that's the prompt to pause and re-align.

Checking Your Inner Circle

You've probably also noticed how much we've talked about your environment, your network, and your support systems. These matter because they shape what feels normal, what feels possible and what gets reinforced, subtly, or loudly, every day. We'll explore this a little closer in the next chapter, for now, here's a useful check-in:

– Who are you spending the most time with right now?
– Who are you learning from, leaning on, or unconsciously modelling?
– Who gets to influence your definition of success?

Think of this like reviewing your personal board of advisors. The people closest to you shape your standards, your energy, and your priorities. Do they align with the life you're working toward? Are they encouraging the version of success you're now defining for yourself? Or are they tied to an older version you've quietly outgrown?

And what about you? Have you shared your evolving definition of success with them? Do they know what you're building now? Sometimes our inner circle needs refreshing, not because of conflict, but because you're growing. Different seasons call for different support and if you're in a leadership role, this goes one step further. You're influencing others every day, whether you realise it or not. The way you work, rest, communicate and prioritise will shape the culture around you. You have the chance to be the kind of leader who models integrated wealth, not just peak performance in one area.

Before we move on, here's your gentle nudge, take stock, revisit your own portfolio, reassess what success means right now, reflect on who's helping you shape it and whether those influences are still the right ones for this next chapter.

Make choices that strengthen your full system, so that the life you're building really does feels like the one you want.

Chapter 11
Fear, Identity And Our Inner Operating System

Why Fear Belongs In The Work-Life Paradigm

Fear of failure is one of the most powerful and often unseen forces shaping how we engage with both work and life. It rarely stems from personality or professional ability, instead it stems from deeper roots, childhood messages, early role models, school environments and cultural expectations. Over time, these influences become embedded in our internal operating system, quietly guiding our decisions, shaping what we pursue and influencing how we define success.

This theme sits within the Work-Life Paradigm because fear of failure can affect the full breadth of how we experience the world, how we manage relationships, interpret feedback, and imagine future possibilities. Unless we bring it into awareness, it can keep us stuck in patterns that no longer serve us.

This chapter is about bringing that fear into the light and learning to use it to move forward.

Failing Forward: A Lesson In Self-Awareness

One of the most significant mindsets shift in my work-life journey happened during time on my MBA at the European Summer School for Advanced Management in Aarhus, Denmark. We were a diverse cohort, students from many countries and sectors, each bringing a different lens on leadership, success, and failure.

Professor Mike Shaner, an award-winning academic from Saint Louis University, was delivering our first leadership session. He entered the room with energy and insight. His session began with familiar tools including DiSC profiles, team dynamics, leadership reflections, but it soon moved deeper, asking us to consider how our beliefs are formed? How does culture, upbringing and experience shape our response to pressure and setbacks?

At the end of the session, Mike added something quietly profound: *"I'll be at the bar later if anyone wants to chat, but you'll have to come to me. I'm an introvert."* That simple comment stuck. In many environments, introversion is still misunderstood, however here was someone confident, engaging and widely respected, showing that being quieter doesn't mean contributing less. Mike explained that teaching was a kind of performance, not inauthentic, but intentional.

He gave his energy to the room, then gave himself space to recover and re-fill. That wasn't a flaw, it was a strong sense of self-awareness.

As someone whose energy tips more toward the introvert end of the spectrum, his approach gave me something to reflect on. I had worked hard to become a confident facilitator and speaker and his words reinforced what I'd come to understand through experience, you can lead powerfully and recharge privately. This insight deepened my interest in emotional intelligence and communication, the foundations of the Calibration Tools.

I've since been asked, especially when delivering leadership training days or team profiling sessions, *"But how do you do this if you're not an extrovert?"* My answer is always the same, labels don't tell the whole story. There's a scale, yes, but more importantly, there's context. Energy can be expressed outwardly while remaining inwardly authentic. Emotional intelligence begins by being curious about others' maps of the world, not judging them by surface behaviours.

Reframing Fear: From Paralysis To Progress

Mike's philosophy, what he called *"failing forward,"* left an even deeper imprint. He taught us that it's rarely the failure itself that derails us. It's the fear around it. Not fear in a vague sense, fear specifically of being exposed or judged.

He said it simply: *"You freeze because you're afraid. But you're not stuck unless you stop moving."* That became a lens through which I began to view challenge. In coaching and leadership development, I've seen it again and again, when people hit a wall, it's rarely a lack of capability, it's fear, fear of not measuring up, fear of disappointing others, fear of proving an inner criticism true.

Fear of failure, as research shows, is rarely about the failure itself, it's about the shame or judgment we fear will come with it.

The fear of failure is often rooted in a narrow definition of success. Win, or lose, yes or no, pass or fail. Real growth doesn't always fit into binary boxes, in high-performance environments, whether sport or leadership, the pressure to 'deliver' can obscure more meaningful forms of progress. That's why it's essential to recalibrate how we interpret results.

I see this play out with my children in sport all the time. Brodie, my youngest, started football in a team that rarely won. He was just six and over time we noticed he stopped talking about the score altogether. Instead, he'd tell us how he played, where he passed the ball, how much he ran. Without realising, he was connecting more to the process than the outcome. Now that his team win, draw and lose in equal measure, we've come to see that his mindset hasn't changed, and it was probably the right one all along. Success lies in building a strong, sustainable team, not just in tallying goals.

Bailey, my eldest, played as goalkeeper for Port Vale's academy. Some days the team would win, and he'd barely touch the ball. Other days, they'd lose, but he'd have made 28 saves from 31 shots. (Yes, I counted!) What does success look like there? The answer depends on your lens. If success is about personal performance, contribution, and the application of superior skill, then that day he 'lost,' he actually delivered an outstanding performance.

And then there's Darcie, my daughter, a competitive gymnast who once won a regional title at just eight years old. Before a big competition this summer (the same competition 2 years later), she had the option, play it safe or add in a more difficult move, one that excited her but lowered the predictability of her score. She chose risk. She didn't win. She nailed the move and walked off prouder than ever. To me, that moment held more value than any medal. She removed the fear of failure by reframing it and she made it part of the process.

Failure can often lead to behaviours like procrastination, over-preparation, or withdrawal, and it isn't because we don't care, more often, it's because we care too much, or more accurately, we care about the wrong thing. The first step in reframing fear is recognising when we're operating from a limiting belief. Sometimes it's overt *"I always mess up under pressure."* More often, it's subtle, perfectionism, delay or even avoidance. These beliefs often stem from early life experiences, from homes where only success was celebrated, or failure was quietly ignored.

As Dr. John Sullivan reminds us, *"We need mistakes and failings . . . they matter."* Learning happens on the edge of discomfort. Innovation and growth don't come from perfection, they come from environments that allow us to try, reflect and recalibrate and improve. Athlete Adam Burgess described this beautifully: *"You've got to be able to train on your own. You've got to sit with it sometimes and just figure it out."*

This is where emotional intelligence becomes a survival skill. The ability to notice fear, understand it and keep moving anyway is the start of real growth. When our efforts are connected to a clear mission, fear loses its grip. Failure becomes part of the process, not the end of the story.

When Ego Edits The Story

For a time, I had a pattern I didn't fully recognise. I would take on big challenges, physical, professional, personal, and I'd keep them quiet. It felt safer that way. If no one knew, I didn't have to succeed. If I didn't finish, there was no one to disappoint.

In my early career days, I would apply for jobs, even attend some interviews, and not tell anyone in advance. The very first time I attempted the SAS Fan Dance challenge; I only told a few people. When I completed it, I felt pride, but also regret. Why hadn't I shared more of the journey? Why had I hidden the effort, the doubt, the training? The truth? It was ego. Not the loud, boastful kind, but the quiet, protective one. The voice that wants to appear competent, unshakable, and always fully in control. It wasn't fear of failure itself. I believed I could do it. I just didn't want others to see me fail, just in case. Which, when I stepped back, was absurd. My track record suggested I would achieve it. Ego isn't logical though, it's self-preserving.

It's a pattern worth checking. Are our actions aligned with our intentions? Are we bringing others with us, or are we editing the story to avoid vulnerability? Floyd once said to me, *"When we speak it out loud, we hold ourselves accountable, but we also open the door for others to help."* He's right. If we don't share what we're working toward, how can we possibly know who might have the tools, insight, encouragement or even the much needed resources to support us?

Now, I make a point of telling people what I'm doing, from major goals to personal challenges. Not for recognition, but because I've learned that secrecy often serves the ego more than the outcome and because the journey becomes richer and more resilient when we invite others to walk alongside us.

So how about you? What are you working on in silence? What might shift if you let yourself be seen before you succeed?

How Our Models Shape Our Map

So where does fear of failure come from?

This is where modelling matters. In NLP, modelling refers to the unconscious absorption of behaviours, beliefs and emotional patterns. As children, we learn by watching how adults and peers manage pressure and respond to setbacks, how they define success and how they carry failure. These early lessons form our internal map of the world. Not an objective reality, but our own version of it. That map influences how we judge what's acceptable or off-limits, what we pursue or avoid and how we see ourselves in relation to ambition, risk and worth.

Maybe your parents worked every weekend, maybe rest was rare, risk was discouraged, or achievement was everything. These things don't make your map wrong, but they do form part of it. If your map is outdated or limiting, it needs redrawing.

Our relationships often reinforce it. Sometimes, even well-meaning comments like *"Should you really be working today?" "You're lucky to have help," "Why don't you just work more hours so you can afford it,"* reflect someone else's map.

The question is, are you living yours?

Floyd Woodrow described it well in our interview, explaining that everything you do toward a goal teaches you something, even the path you don't stay on brings value. As he says, there's no failure, only feedback. Understanding your map means becoming aware of whose voice shaped it and whose voice you want to keep, and therefore who's you may also want to quieten or let go of forever.

The Fear Of Success: A Hidden Counterpart

Fear of failure gets more attention, fear of success though, can be just as limiting. It sounds counterintuitive, who wouldn't want to succeed? Success brings visibility, it brings expectations, responsibility and change. For many, this creates quiet resistance, modest goals that don't stretch too far, delayed launches and opportunities that are avoided. We don't fail, but we don't quite fly either.

This presents in entrepreneurs who stall growth, in leaders who downplay ambition and in professionals who self-sabotage. It often stems from fear that success will change relationships, stretch identity, or expose inadequacies. Success doesn't just ask us to be capable, it asks us to be seen.

Sarah Willingham once said to me, *"You're always two decisions away from bankruptcy."* It was a reminder that risk is ever-present. Resilience means developing systems and mindsets robust enough to carry risk, not deny its existence.

The key, again, is awareness. What might happen if you succeed? And which of those outcomes are real and which are imagined?

The Invitation: Reframe, Recalibrate, Reimagine

Fear isn't something to erase. It's something to understand. When we name it, we neutralise it. When we work with it, we grow. Fear is part of the leadership landscape, not a flaw in it.

By now, you've explored every part of the Calibration Model, your relationship with money and mission, mental and physical health, work-life patterns, and the Calibration Tools that help you communicate, lead, and live more consciously.

Before you move forward, here's a different kind of check-in. Are you really focused on what matters, or are you unintentionally masking fear of failure (or success) by staying too busy?

Use the Calibration Tools to pause and recalibrate:

– **Emotional Intelligence:** What's really driving your energy and attention right now? Are you filling your schedule as avoidance, or choosing aligned action?

– **Skilled Communication:** What aren't you saying (to yourself or others) about what you fear?

– **The Resilience Advantage:** How do you recover your focus and clarity when distraction creeps in?

This is where the model becomes diagnostic. Map how you divide your time, track how you're spending your energy and check if you're investing in what matters, or hiding from it?

This chapter is your final pivot point. It asks, what are you still holding back and what fear is ready to be reframed?

In the next chapter, we bring it all together. Not as a checklist, but as a dashboard for intentional, aligned living.

Section Six: **The Calibration Model**

Through the book you've explored what it means to live and lead well across work, wealth and wellbeing. You've challenged assumptions, deepened your awareness, and considered what sustainable success looks like for you. Now, we move from exploration to application.

The Calibration Model offers a practical structure to support high performance and long-term alignment. It gives you the tools to make informed decisions, adapt and stay focused on what matters most, regardless of the complexity or pace of your world.

This is Balancing Act in motion, the full integration of work, wealth and wellbeing. The real formula for executive success lies in your ability to calibrate consistently and act with purpose across all domains. In the pages that follow, you'll revisit the model in its entirety. You'll see how to apply it to strategic planning and short-term decision-making, and you'll find exercises designed to help you work through each segment in your own time and way. These tools are here for you to return to, again and again, as your context evolves.

Before we close, you'll hear from those who've helped shape this book. In the Advice Wall, they share their reflections, lessons, and personal messages to their younger selves. Their voices add something essential, the reminder that success is never static, it's lived, recalibrated and uniquely your own.

Let's return to the Calibration Model and look at how everything fits together in practice.

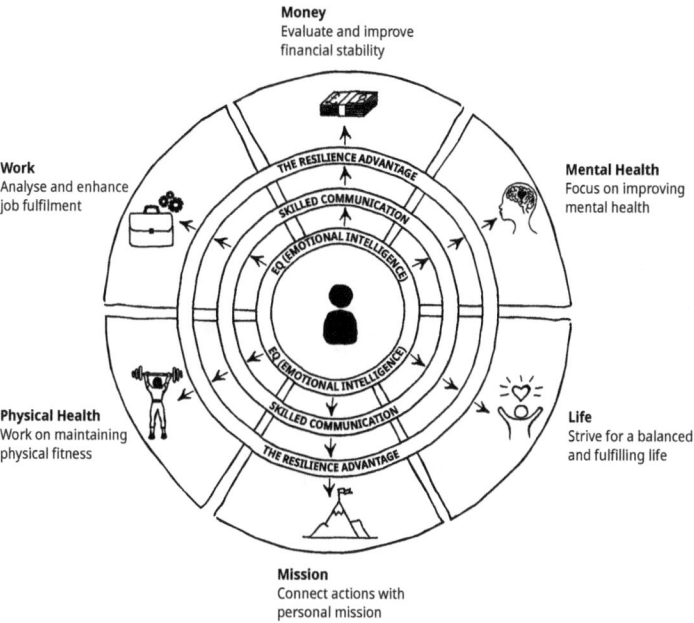

Money
Evaluate and improve financial stability

Work
Analyse and enhance job fulfilment

Mental Health
Focus on improving mental health

THE RESILIENCE ADVANTAGE
SKILLED COMMUNICATION
EQ (EMOTIONAL INTELLIGENCE)

Physical Health
Work on maintaining physical fitness

Life
Strive for a balanced and fulfilling life

Mission
Connect actions with personal mission

Chapter 12
Mastering The Balancing Act

Recalibration In Practice

When we first introduced the Calibration Model, it served as a guide for understanding sustainable success across six life segments, three essential paradigms and three core tools of calibration. Now, having explored each component, from emotional intelligence to energy mapping, from purpose-led decision-making to resilience under pressure, it's time to bring it all together.

The Calibration Model is a tool you can apply to long-term planning, short-term decision-making, or daily alignment. The goal now is deliberate application.

Before moving forward, it helps to reconnect with the three core Calibration Paradigms that shape the model. Each offers a distinct but connected focus and when applied together, they provide the clarity and rhythm needed to lead with intention.

Money-Mission: Money provides the foundation, it funds your focus, fuels your freedom, and enables the mission that motivates you. When financial clarity is paired with a strong sense of mission, it becomes easier to make aligned decisions and invest your energy with purpose.

Mental-Physical Health: Performance is built on wellbeing. Mental strength and physical vitality work in tandem to fuel sustainable success. Health and resilience act as essential assets for leaders who want to stay sharp and perform under pressure.

Work-Life: How you spend your time shapes how you experience your life. Balancing work and life means designing a daily rhythm that reflects what matters most. Success includes the people you love and the moments that matter. High performance holds the greatest value when it's part of a life you actually enjoy.

These paradigms work in connection with one another. They evolve with your seasons, reflect your priorities, and shape the daily decisions that support long-term success. Alignment across these areas creates the foundation for consistent, sustainable performance.

Let's return to the model and explore how to use it in a way that works with your goals and reality.

Using The Model: Two Key Applications

One of the most powerful ways to use the Calibration Model is as a dual tool, both for long-term strategic planning and for regular check-ins that keep you aligned and adaptive. This is where you connect your journey with your destination.

STAGE 1. Long-Term Model Of Success Planning

Begin with each of the six segments, Money, Mission, Mental, Physical, Work and Life.

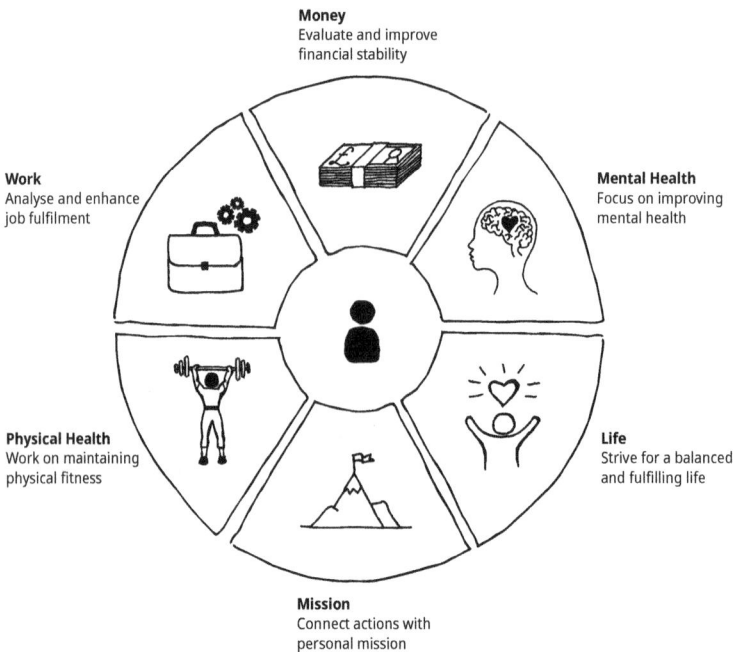

Money
Evaluate and improve
financial stability

Work
Analyse and enhance
job fulfilment

Mental Health
Focus on improving
mental health

Physical Health
Work on maintaining
physical fitness

Life
Strive for a balanced
and fulfilling life

Mission
Connect actions with
personal mission

For each one, ask yourself:
1. What do I want to achieve here over the next 3–5 years (chose a specific time frame that suits you and your life plans and use the same one for all segments)?
2. What does success look like for me in this segment?
3. What would make this area feel meaningful, energised, or aligned?

This is where your North Star Vision and WHY-Mapping exercises come into play. Use them to map your aspirations more deeply, or simply jot down headline goals if you're short on time. The key is to make it yours. This is about usefulness, not perfection, and while time can be tight, if you're serious about mastering success across work, wealth and wellbeing, then this process is worth making space for.

STAGE 2. Your Current Snapshot

Now repeat the process, but for where you are right now.

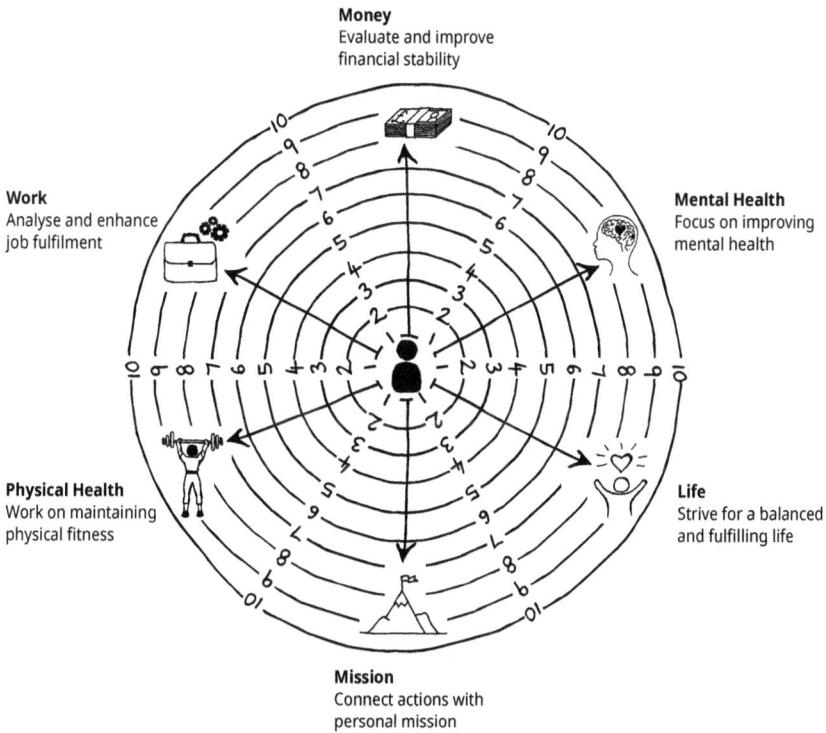

Money
Evaluate and improve
financial stability

Work
Analyse and enhance
job fulfilment

Mental Health
Focus on improving
mental health

Physical Health
Work on maintaining
physical fitness

Life
Strive for a balanced
and fulfilling life

Mission
Connect actions with
personal mission

For each of the six segments, score yourself out of 10:
–   10 = I'm achieving exactly what I want here. I'm on target, in balance and focused.
–   0 = I'm completely off track or deprioritising this area right now.

This gives you a snapshot of your current Balancing Act. In my experience, there's often a visible tilt, one side of the model (such as Work, Money and Mental) showing more attention than the other (such as Physical, Mission and Life). If this is evident, it might not present a problem for now, but it is an important signal for your 'later'.

STAGE 3. Overlay And Recalibrate

Now place your two models' side by side, long-term and current. Whether you've drawn them, printed the templates, or used the digital tools, the insight comes in the comparison.

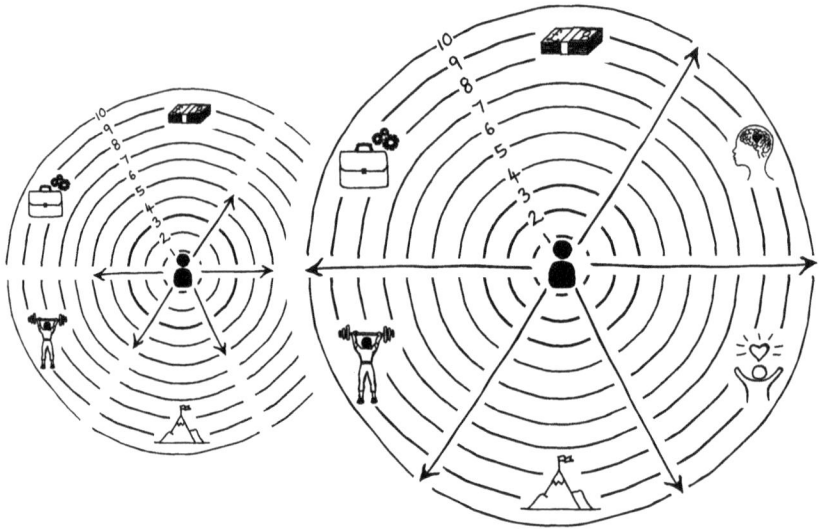

This is your recalibration moment.
 Where the gaps appear, ask:
-   What needs to shift, now, sooner, or later than I'd planned?
-   What goals need refining, removing, or reframing?
-   Where do I need support, energy, or resource to rebalance?

This is where planning becomes strategy and intention turns into action.

As the (slightly controversial) quote from Bonnie and Clyde goes: *"Every-body's got dreams. I got plans."* It stuck with me. My eldest son Bailey had his first lead role in that musical and hearing that line land on opening night reminded me how often we all do this, we carry dreams, but never quite get to the plan. The Calibration Model is your plan. It's your pocket tool. It doesn't ask for perfection, it asks for presence, alignment, rhythm and commitment.

During my study of sport science I used data, biometrics and performance analysis to examine movement and outcomes in granular detail. The data was only ever part of the picture though, context mattered too. What was the athlete trying to achieve? How did one player's movement affect the whole team? Similarly, your Calibration Model gives you data, about time, energy and focus, but it's what you do with that data that creates impact. Are you investing in the right things, or are you unconsciously filling your time to mask fear of failure, or fear of success? Use the Calibration Tools to investigate. Map how you divide your time. Track your energy flow. The insight is there if you're willing to look.

Ali Oliver describes this kind of recalibration as essential leadership awareness. She acknowledges that her deep sense of responsibility sometimes drives her to try and do everything, but experience has taught her the power of prioritisation. Here she shares her approach: *"I know I can't do everything at the same level. I know when I get short-tempered, when I can't make decisions quickly and clearly, or when I'm trying to write something, and I can't articulate it straight away. I know that all those signs tell me something . . . I need to cut back and prioritise . . . I look at what I must do and decide what's an A, what's A/B and what's B/C. All of these are a pass, but not all need to be an A."* Her insight offers a powerful check-in prompt, if the quality of your thinking or energy is shifting, the next step might not be about working harder, it might be time to recalibrate and decide where your time and energy are best focussed. Where will you get your greatest return on investment?

Anne-Sophie's path reflects a powerful recalibration, not in pace, but in perspective. Early in her career, she followed a more structured, goal-oriented route, choosing engineering because it offered a prestigious and stable future. *"Where I grew up, it was the royal path to success,"* she says. *"So, I followed it, with purpose. I studied for good grades, for a good university."*

Her career advanced rapidly, moving from technical roles into consultancy, client leadership and eventually into a senior executive position. But while her trajectory remained ambitious, the way she approached progress began to shift. Her decisions became more values-driven, shaped not just by the next opportunity, but by what worked for her, her family, and the teams around her. *"I realised I could still stretch myself professionally while making choices that supported my family life and aligned with our shared priorities,"* she reflects. *"And I didn't need to do it all alone. I've been lucky to work with diverse, collaborative teams where different perspectives genuinely shape the way we lead."*

This evolution didn't mean pulling back, it signalled a shift in planning. Her approach became more fluid and responsive, anchored in who she is and what matters (most and to her). Her story shows how recalibration can open the way to more conscious and connected leadership.

As you analyse the gap between where you are and where you want to be, remember that closing the gap isn't always about better time management or clearer goals. Sometimes, what's needed is capacity and capability, the inner resources that enable sustainable performance. This is where your three Calibration Tools come in.

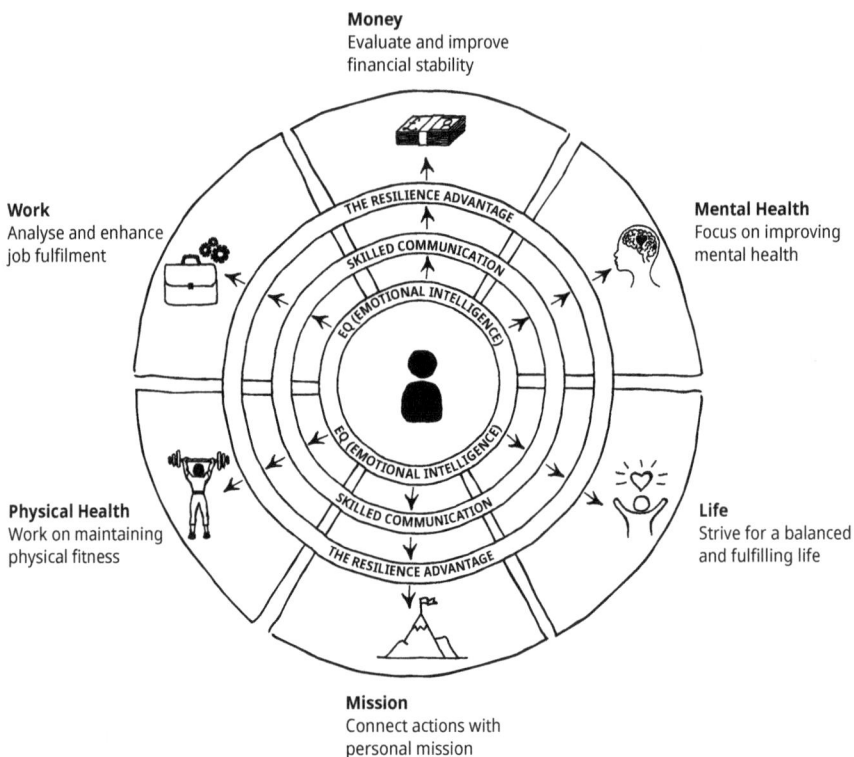

Money
Evaluate and improve financial stability

Work
Analyse and enhance job fulfilment

Mental Health
Focus on improving mental health

Physical Health
Work on maintaining physical fitness

Life
Strive for a balanced and fulfilling life

Mission
Connect actions with personal mission

Emotional Intelligence, Skilled Communication and The Resilience Advantage are the capabilities that enable you to engage fully, stay grounded, make informed decisions, and sustain your energy over time. If your scores are consistently low in a particular area, it may not be a question of effort, but of focus or capability. Recalibration involves both realigning your priorities and actively developing the tools that support meaningful progress.

You can use the Calibration Toolkit at the end of the book to track how well you're balancing across the three paradigms each month. The exercises provide a quick and powerful pulse check that can prevent subtle imbalances from growing into larger issues. Use them to track specific goals and ensure your steps forward are both productive and sustainable.

As Dr. John Sullivan often reminds his clients, even micro-stressors can become tools for growth, if you use them wisely: *"In sport, I make some athletes drive home in peak traffic to learn to manage their emotions."* That deliberate exposure strengthens psychological flexibility, one of the core traits of high-performance leadership. Think about what controlled stressors you might use in your own environment to build similar strength.

Making It Work For You

Ali, whose leadership journey has always been values-led, puts this into practice through regular self-checks: *"I'm forever evaluating and re-evaluating, questioning, does this organisation need a different skill set? A fresher perspective? Am I still the best person for this role?"*

This level of ongoing internal review is a form of leadership calibration, for personal performance and for longer-term impact.

Floyd reassesses his main goals every six months, using daily check-ins to maintain alignment between his everyday habits and the future success he's working toward.

Anne-Sophie and Adam both bring others into their journey regularly, drawing on feedback from colleagues, friends, coaches and mentors to help guide their balance and momentum.

Planning doesn't need to always be done on your own. In fact, it's better when it isn't. When I'm working with my team on strategy for Illuminare, or running sessions with businesses or teams, we often use sticky notes to map out KPIs, milestones and action steps, covering entire walls with intent. The finished plan has value, but the real impact comes from the process, the physical act of placing a sticky note on that wall, committing to it, collaborating on it. That creates investment. It engages active learning, and it turns abstract goals into shared direction.

You can apply the same principle in your own life, leadership, or wider business planning. Bring in your personal board of advisors. Ask for perspective on blind spots you may not see. Share your goals with those closest to you, and also with those who can help you to build, challenge, or reshape them.

Strategy built in conversation holds deeper roots. There's no one right format. For example, you might choose to:
- Revisit your Calibration scores monthly.
- Use the Daily Prompts for morning clarity and evening reflection.
- Set quarterly reviews to recalibrate across your six segments.
- Or simply return to your North Star and ask: *"Am I still heading there in a balanced, self-aware and purposeful way?"*

The value lies in the consistency of recalibration, not the complexity of your method. Your version of balance may not be perfectly symmetrical, it simply needs to align with your priorities, values, vision of success and current season of life. Choose that balance with intention, so a version you didn't plan for can't knock you off course or carry you somewhere you never meant to go.

You now have the model, you've sharpened the tools, and you've heard from leaders who apply this rhythm daily. This is where your version of executive success takes shape, one that's deliberate and sustainable, shaped by your vision and by the people who help hold it steady.

Chapter 13
Final Reflections: The Advice Wall

Before you close this book or jump ahead to the exercises and templates that follow, pause here. What comes next is something to carry with you; the voices of those living the Balancing Act. People who test it, shape it, and continue to redefine success on their own terms.

Beyond theory, these are reflections grounded in real experience. Each insight comes from a different stage of the journey, yet they share one thing in common, a commitment to building a balanced, sustainable, high-performing life, on their own terms.

Adam, Alison, Floyd, John, Anne-Sophie, Anne, and I, each speak to our younger selves, and to you.

Adam Burgess
Olympic Medallist | Breathwork Educator | Resilient High-Performer

What Adam Would Say To His Younger Self: *"If I could speak to 10-year-old Adam, the kid who raised his hand in class and said yes to trying canoeing, I'd say thank you. That moment shaped my life more than I could've known. He had no idea where it would take him, and I still carry that spirit with me. That openness, the joy, the quiet courage, it's there when I need it . . . Especially just before the start of a race, when the pressure peaks, I come back to 10-year-old Adam and the way he just went for it."*

"I don't give advice to that version of myself, I take it from him. Just keep being. Keep trusting what feels right and stay close to what comes naturally. That mindset still guides me through high-performance environments and helps me reset when pressure builds."

Mantra: Return to what you love, then perform from there.

Adam's Top Tips For A Sustainable, High-Performing Life:
- Do what comes naturally. If it constantly feels like a grind, it probably isn't right long term.
- Be open to opportunities, even unlikely ones. If it's natural and authentic, that has value.
- Be adaptable. Holding too tightly to plans can blind you to opportunity or risk.
- Focus on what you can control, your intention and where you place your attention.
- Practice recovery. Your performance relies on it.

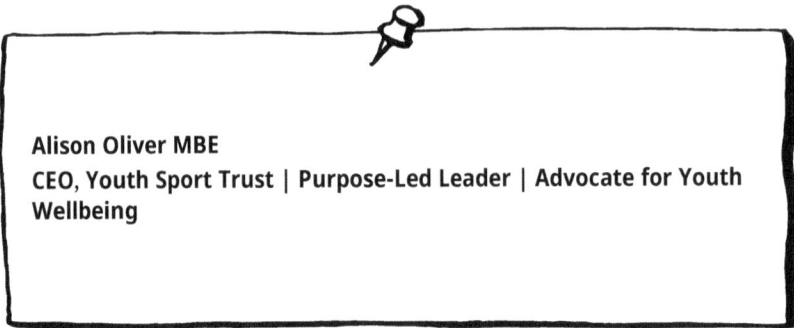

Alison Oliver MBE
CEO, Youth Sport Trust | Purpose-Led Leader | Advocate for Youth Wellbeing

What Alison Would Say To Her Younger Self: *"You won't always feel like you belong and that's okay. I was never part of the popular crowd growing up, never in a gang, always a little different. I spent more time on my bike or volunteering at the local old people's home than trying to fit in. At the time, I didn't think too much of it thanks to strong parenting, but looking back, I know there were moments when I just wanted to blend in."*

"What I've learned is this, the thing that makes you different now might just become your superpower later. Being comfortable in your own skin, even when it feels unfamiliar to others, will serve you as a leader more than you can imagine."

"Also, look ahead. Find people who are 10 or 15 years older and ask them questions. Their hindsight can become your foresight. I had great role models around me, but I didn't always stop to ask the deeper questions. I'd do that differently now."

Mantra: Work hard, make yourself useful and seize opportunities.

Ali's Top Tips For A Holistically Successful Life:
- Define success for yourself and use that as your benchmark.
- Anchor your career in something you care deeply about.
- Stay endlessly curious, ask, learn, question, grow.
- Seek out role models early. Learn from where they've been.
- Don't hide your differences, they might just be your edge.

Floyd Woodrow MBE DCM
Elite Military Leader | Founder, Compass for Life | Chairman,
Quantum Group

What Floyd Would Say To His Younger Self: *"Learn who you are, faster. That's what I'd say. Your strengths, your patterns, your natural instincts, those are your edge. You don't need to wait until everything is perfect to start. Fear will show up and that's okay. When you acknowledge it, it loses its power. Accepting that truth was the biggest shift for me."*

"You'll also learn that you don't need to carry the journey alone. Your clarity, your 'supernova', is yours to own. But the route? That's something you build with others. Get people around you who challenge and support you and be deliberate."

Mantra: Start with your supernova. Then take the next right step.

Floyd's Top Tips For A Purpose-Driven Life:
– Know your purpose and let it pull you forward.
– Build the right team, success is a joint effort.
– Plan with precision, especially your first few wins. Focus on facts, figures, detail, no emotion. Stick to that.
– Speak clearly about your mission, it attracts the right people.
– Align mentally, physically, and spiritually, performance follows purpose.

Dr. John Sullivan
Clinical Sport Psychologist | Sport Scientist | Creator of the PROCESS Model

What John Would Say To Anyone Pursuing High Performance: *"There's one principle I've seen hold true across every elite environment I've worked in; the brain always wins. If you override it, ignore its signals, push through fatigue, you will pay for it. Performance begins with biology, and it ends with strategy."*

"If you want to lead, create, or endure; honour your neurology. Don't just push harder. Listen better. Build recovery into your rhythm. That's where resilience lives."

Mantra: The brain always wins. Make sure it's on your side.

John's Top Tips For Resilient, Evidence-Informed Performance:
- Recovery isn't indulgence, it's the foundation of high performance.
- Build micro-rest into your daily systems.
- Emotions drive thoughts, not the other way around, regulate them first.
- Focus on influence, not control.
- Real change is feedback-led. Create your own feedback loops.

Anne-Sophie Amiot
Global Energy Executive | Vice President, Sales & Strategy | Advocate
for Women in Engineering

What Anne-Sophie Would Say To Her Younger Self: *"Success is deeply personal. It's not the same as the person next door. You must define what it means to you and the earlier you do that, the clearer your journey becomes. I followed leads instead of actively searching for what I really wanted. I'd change that. Be bolder in your pursuit. Trust your instincts."*

"Also, understand that wealth isn't just about money. It's about family, contribution and meaning. Aligning your work with those values makes success far more satisfying. Also, don't regret the detours, they add depth."

Mantra: Be open to the nudges of those you trust to guide you and, over time, learn to understand, define, and own your strengths so you can know and guide yourself.

Anne-Sophie's Top Tips For A Meaningful Career And Life:
- Know what success looks like for you. Not someone else.
- Align your work with meaning, it fuels longevity.
- Wealth includes purpose, connection, and contribution.
- Don't wait to be invited, pursue what you want.
- Every step counts, even the sideways ones.

Anne McClean
Partner and Head of Wealth | Chartered Financial Planner and
Certified Financial Planner | Specialist in Strategic Financial Planning

---

What Anne Would Say To Her Younger Self: *"Start early. Put more into your pension. Understand the stock market. Learn what assets really mean. These things might sound dull at first, but they create real security and security gives you freedom. It gives you choice."*

"Sometimes you'll feel like you're standing still, but you're not. You're setting up for a leap. That matters. Don't judge your progress by someone else's finish line, take pride in the small steps. No one sees the full journey; they just see that you arrived."

Mantra: Lay the foundations early, your future self will thank you.

Anne's Top Tips For A Financially Empowered Life:
– Join the pension. Even a little early makes a big difference.
– Learn financial literacy, stock markets, equity, cashflow.
– Avoid debt. Understand your inflows and outflows.
– Invest in yourself, studies, skills, and confidence.
– Love what you do, it sustains everything else.

And finally, here's mine.

This book has been built on the stories, strategies and insights of others, but also my own. Everything within these pages has been tested in the field, through coaching, leadership, parenting, failing, learning and growing. I've walked these models myself. So, this final reflection comes not only as an author, strategist, and coach, but as someone still navigating the Balancing Act.

Sarah Brennand
Executive Coach | Strategic Educator | Performance and Leadership Specialist

What I Would Say To My Younger Self: *"Start sooner. You don't need to feel older, know more, or wait for the perfect moment. I delayed starting my first business because my informal board of advisors all looked, lived, and thought the same. Choose variety. Ask questions early. Find people doing what excites you and ask them how they got there."*

"Don't let others box you in, not into a role, a level, or a ceiling. Corporate structures can do that if you're not careful. Don't let them limit your potential or slow your growth."

"Say yes more. Take the opportunity. Try the thing. You don't know what you don't know. I surprised everyone (myself included) when I signed up for the Duke of Edinburgh Award at school. I wasn't outdoorsy back then, but that one decision sparked a love for ultra-hikes and solo mountain challenges that still shape who I am today. Curiosity gives you courage. Open the door."

Mantra: Role model who you want your children to see and believe what they see in you.

My Top Tips For A Balanced, Brave Life:
- Seek out diverse role models and ask bold questions.
- Don't wait to be ready. Start anyway.
- Build financial security, it enables risk.
- Keep moving forward. Test yourself, that's where growth happens.
- Remember you are role-modelling every day, especially to the people who matter most. If you wouldn't say it to your child, don't say it to yourself.

Let our voices sit with you. Take what resonates. Return to them when you need to. Our insight is now part of yours.

Wherever you're heading next, you're not starting from scratch, you're building from experience.

Keep calibrating. Keep moving. On your terms. For your future.

Chapter 14
Your Calibration Toolkit

This section brings together the key tools referenced throughout the book, now in one place for ease of access and consistent recalibration. Whether you complete them now or return to them over time, they're here to guide you from insight to implementation.

Each template is designed to be flexible. You don't need to follow them perfectly. Use what resonates, adapt what helps and revisit as your needs evolve. This toolkit is meant to grow with you.

Template Index

1. **The Calibration Model:** Your tool for alignment and action. Begin here. This whole-life model gives you a clear visual of where you are and where you want to be. It works at any stage, whether you're planning long term or recalibrating in real time.
2. **Defining Your North Star:** Clarify your future direction and define success across all six life segments. Use this to create a compelling vision if you don't yet have one, or to develop a more detailed version of your existing goals. It gives your Calibration Model a long-range destination to anchor around, supporting strategy, motivation and meaningful measurable, progress.
3. **WHY-Mapping:** Discover what's really driving your goals and strengthen your emotional connection to them. Layer this under your North Star and Calibration Model to check for alignment, motivation, and paradigm balance.
4. **Paradigm Calibration: Monthly Progress Check-In:** A structured scorecard to track your progress across the three core paradigms. This helps you spot imbalance early and adjust before you veer off course.
5. **Milestone Calibration: Monthly Goal Check-In:** Plan and track tangible milestones while maintaining equilibrium across your life. Break your North Star into achievable steps, without tipping into burnout.
6. **Daily Calibration Practice:** A quick daily rhythm for intention-setting, reflection, and recalibration. Small habits, done consistently, build the strongest foundation for long-term alignment.
7. **Energy Mapping Grid:** Track your energy patterns across the week and match your tasks to your natural rhythm. Build performance through design, not depletion.

Note: All tools are available for download or print at www.balancing-act.co.uk, where you'll also find additional resources to guide you.

1 The Calibration Model

Begin here. This is your foundational alignment tool.

The Calibration Model brings together the six life segments of Money, Mission, Mental, Physical, Work and Life and overlays them with the three Calibration Tools of Emotional Intelligence, Skilled Communication and The Resilience Advantage.

This model helps you:
–   Map where you are now.
–   Define where you want to be.
–   Identify what needs to shift for sustainable progress.

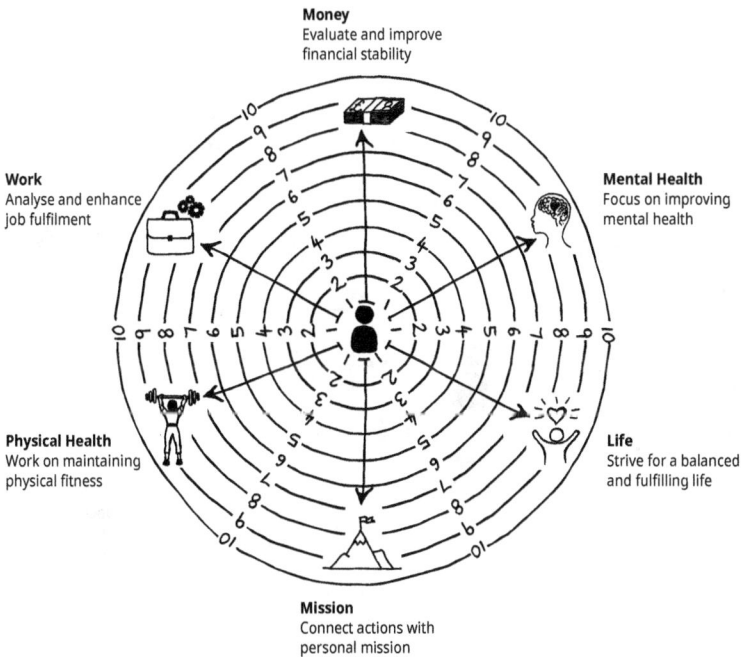

Money
Evaluate and improve
financial stability

Work
Analyse and enhance
job fulfilment

Mental Health
Focus on improving
mental health

Physical Health
Work on maintaining
physical fitness

Life
Strive for a balanced
and fulfilling life

Mission
Connect actions with
personal mission

There Are Three Key Applications:

1.   **Long-Term Model Of Success:** Set your direction by mapping what success looks like across each life segment over the next 3–5 years. Use this to visualise your North Star, clarify priorities and create meaningful goals.

2.   **Current Snapshot:** Rate your current state across each segment using the 0–10 scale provided. This gives you a quick insight into where attention is needed right now.

3.   **Overlay The Two Models:** Your vision and your present, to highlight gaps, patterns, and opportunities for recalibration.

This process can take as little as 15 minutes or be explored more fully using the accompanying tools in this chapter. The point isn't perfection, it's the creation of clear and meaningful focus.

Recommended Revisit: Every 3–6 months, or during times of change or decision-making.

Use the visual templates to complete both your Long-Term Model of Success and Current Snapshot, then overlay them to guide your recalibration.

Calibration Model Tools

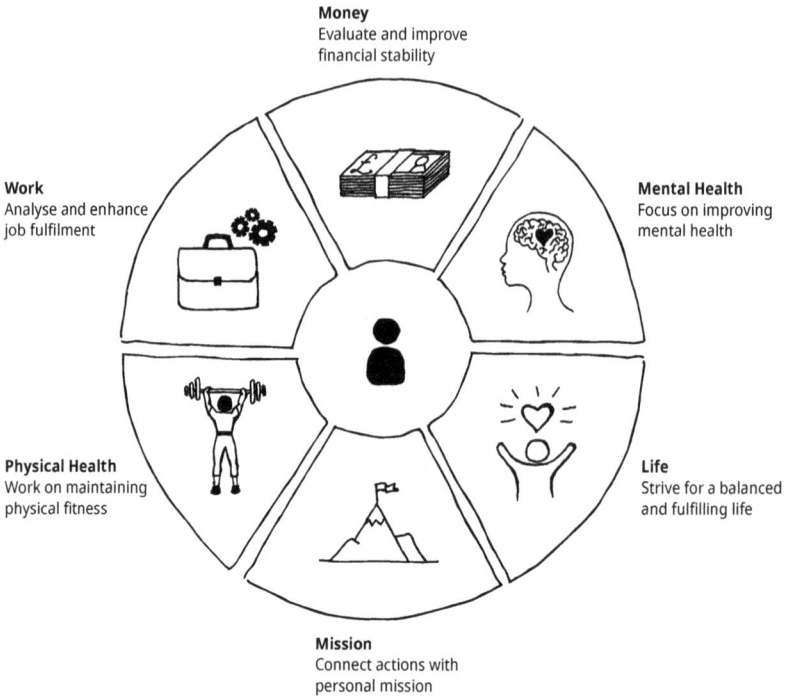

Money
Evaluate and improve financial stability

Mental Health
Focus on improving mental health

Life
Strive for a balanced and fulfilling life

Mission
Connect actions with personal mission

Physical Health
Work on maintaining physical fitness

Work
Analyse and enhance job fulfilment

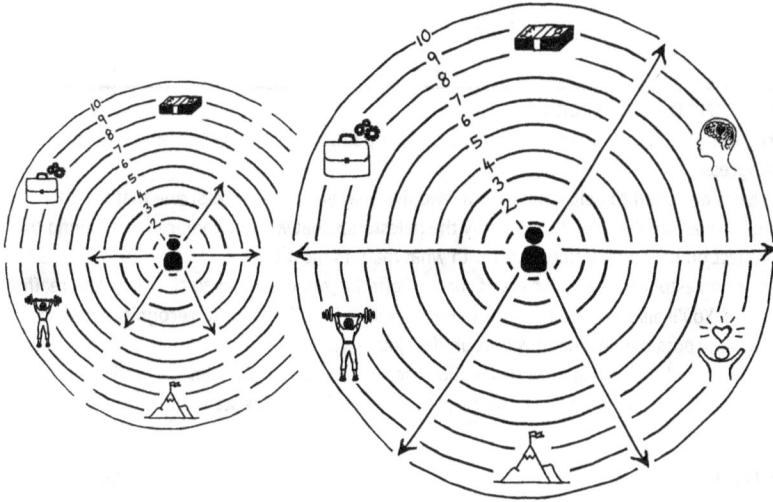

2 Defining Your North Star

INTRODUCTION TO THE EXERCISE

Your North Star is the destination that illuminates your path, fuels your actions, and gives meaning to your progress.

This exercise is designed to help you shape a vivid five-year vision of success, one that's both aspirational and actionable. You'll also clarify the milestones that will mark your journey along the way and reflect on how your vision aligns with what matters most to you.

These shorter milestones act as markers of success, offering opportunities to celebrate and reaffirm your progress. You'll also explore how this vision fits into a broader context, recognising that this is just one of many possible destinations in your life's journey.

For now, focus deeply on making this destination meaningful to you. The aim is to activate both emotional and cognitive commitment, the inner clarity that drives consistent, purpose-led action.

INSTRUCTIONS   **Suggested**
                                                                Time: 30 Minutes

Part 1: Vision Crystallisation

1. **Future Success Visualisation**
   – Find a quiet space where you can focus without distractions.
   – Close your eyes and project yourself five years into the future, visualising the success you plan to achieve.
   – Visualise a day where everything aligns, where you feel successful, purposeful, and balanced.

2. **Vision Mapping Across Paradigms**

Write detailed responses for each paradigm:

a) **Money-Mission**
   1. What financial achievements will define this success for you?
   2. How are you creating meaningful impact?

b) **Mental-Physical**
   3. What mental state characterises your success?
   4. How does your peak health feel?

c) **Work-Life**
   5. What does your ideal day look like?
   6. Who shares in your success?

(continued)

Part 2: Mapping Markers of Success

Now that you've envisioned your destination, let's translate that into measurable steps. These are your calibration points, indicators that keep you aligned.

1. **Markers of Success**
   - **For Each Paradigm (Money-Mission, Mental-Physical, Work-Life), identify:**
     - What must you achieve to reach your vision?
     - What are the shorter milestones along the way?
     - How will you know you're on the right track?

Here are a few milestone examples to guide your thinking:

- **A Financial Milestone** (e.g., reaching a specific income or funding goal within 2 years).
- **A Health Improvement Milestone** (e.g., being able to run 10k or reducing stress).
- **A Work-Life Balance Milestone** (e.g., committing to regular family time or vacations).

2. **Celebration And Recognition**
   - **For Each Milestone, Decide:**
     - How will you celebrate this achievement?
     - What will you do to recognise yourself and others involved in the success?
   - **For Your North Star Destination:** Plan a special celebration or event to honour your hard work and commitment.

(continued)

Part 3: North Star Alignment	**Suggested Time:**
1. **Congruence Check**	**10 Minutes**

Use the checklist below to assess how strongly your vision aligns with your values and energy. Rate each statement from 1 (strongly disagree) to 5 (strongly agree).

–   This vision energises me.
–   The goals stretch yet inspire me.
–   Success includes meaningful impact.
–   The vision balances all paradigms.
–   I can clearly articulate why this matters to me.

2. **Impact Analysis**

Purposeful goals often create ripple effects. Let's explore the broader impact of what you're working toward.

For each major goal, answer:

–   Who benefits besides me?
–   What broader impact does it create?
–   How does it align with my values?

Part 4: From Vision To Execution, Planning Your Milestones	**Suggested Time:**
1. **Milestone Mapping**	**20 Minutes**

Create a timeline for achieving your vision:

–   90-day action steps.
–   1-year milestones.
–   3-year achievements.
–   5-year vision realisation.

2. **Balance Integration**

For each milestone, reflect on how to maintain balance across your life domains. Consider time, energy, health, and support.

For each milestone, identify:

–   Required resources.
–   Potential challenges.
–   Support needed.
–   Balance maintenance strategies.

Part 5: Broader Vision Reflection	**Suggested Time:**
1. **Recognising the Bigger Picture**	**15 Minutes**

–   Reflect on how this vision is one of many potential destinations in your life.
–   Consider that there may be other, longer-term goals that stretch beyond five years.

(continued)

2. **Why This Vision, Now?**
    –   Write a short paragraph on why this particular destination is the most important to you right now.
    –   How does it energise and inspire you to take action?
3. **Commitment**
    –   Describe how focusing on this vision will spark your motivation and guide your decision-making.
    –   Write a short commitment statement to reinforce your intent. For example:

"I commit to pursuing this vision because it reflects what matters most to me right now [insert reason]."

You're On Your Way!

By defining your North Star and identifying the milestones that lead to it, you've created both a compelling vision and a practical roadmap. Along the way, don't forget to celebrate your successes, recognise your progress, and recalibrate as needed.

Your North Star isn't fixed. It evolves as you grow. Today though, it gives you direction, a purpose-driven map for the next stretch of your journey.

Need inspiration or extra support? Scan the QR code or visit www.balancing-act.co.uk to access completed examples, downloadable templates and additional guidance to help you bring your North Star to life.

EXPLORE MORE

MORE CLARITY. MORE TOOLS. YOUR NEXT STEP.

3 WHY-Mapping

WHY-Mapping: Your Motivation In Motion

Reframing The Power Of WHY: From Problem-Solving To Purpose-Finding
INNOVATION INSIGHT
While Toyota's famous 5 Whys model has been used globally for decades to investigate problems, I've reimagined this powerful technique into something equally transformative, a proactive tool for purpose discovery and sustained motivation.
The original model, developed by Sakichi Toyoda in the 1930s, became foundational to Lean thinking and Six Sigma methodology, asking *"Why?"* five times to reach the root cause of a problem.

WHY-Mapping Inverts That Logic.
Instead of looking backwards to uncover what went wrong, it looks forward strengthening what's right. It helps you:
- Discover your deeper motivations.
- Strengthen commitment to your vision.
- Ensure balanced energy allocation.
- Maintain forward momentum.

Where the original fixed what's broken, this version fuels what moves you.

INTRODUCTION TO THE EXERCISE
Knowing your destination is powerful, but it's your WHY that keeps you moving. WHY-Mapping is a calibration tool designed to strengthen your emotional connection to your goals and sustain your motivation over time.

Suggested Time:
15 Minutes

Use it to:
- Validate your direction.
- Strengthen and reconnect with your purpose when motivation dips.
- Spot imbalance across life paradigms.
- Recalibrate energy and commitment as needed.

HOW TO MAP YOUR WHY
1. Place your North Star vision in the centre of a blank page.
2. Draw 3–5 major goal branches radiating outward. Use the three paradigms to guide you (Money-Mission, Mental-Physical, Work-Life).
3. For each goal branch, ask:
   - *"Why is this important to me?"*
   - Then take that answer and ask *"Why?"* again.
   - Continue until you've asked *"Why?"* five times.
4. Circle the answers that resonate most deeply.

(continued)

5. Reflect on your answers:
    -   Does this WHY genuinely energise you?
    -   Will it help you stay committed and balanced?
    -   If not, what needs to change? your goal, your approach,
        or your allocation of time and energy?

CALIBRATION TIP: Use colour-coding for each paradigm (e.g. green = Work-Life, blue = Mental-Physical, gold = Money-Mission). This will help you spot imbalance or over-concentration.

IMPLEMENTATION SCHEDULE:
-   Initial use: Right after defining your North Star.
-   Monthly check-ins: Use for reflection and course correction.
-   Quarterly reviews: Ensure ongoing strategic alignment.
-   During major transitions: Career shifts, personal life changes, burnout, or recalibration periods.

This five-layer questioning method activates deeper motivation centres in the brain, strengthening the link between daily action and core purpose. The more you revisit your WHY, the stronger the neural connections and the easier it becomes to stay aligned and engaged

4 Paradigm Calibration: Monthly Progress Check-In

Paradigm Calibration: Monthly Progress Check-In Template

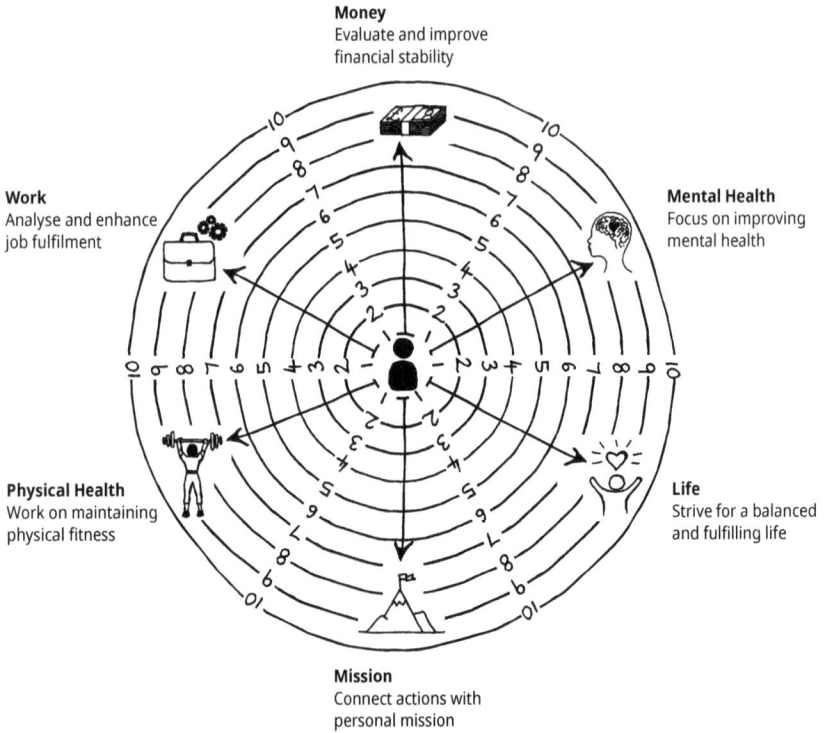

Money
Evaluate and improve
financial stability

Work
Analyse and enhance
job fulfilment

Mental Health
Focus on improving
mental health

Physical Health
Work on maintaining
physical fitness

Life
Strive for a balanced
and fulfilling life

Mission
Connect actions with
personal mission

Track your progress across the three core paradigms and spot imbalance before it builds.
Use this template to stay aligned with your goals, maintain balance, and stay on track toward
reaching your destination. It will identify imbalances and enable you to recalibrate before it's too
late!

INSTRUCTIONS
- Give a score of **0–10** for each sub-paradigm. **0** being the lowest and **10** being the best you can
  award.
- **Notes:** Use this space to jot down reflections, challenges, or insights that might be helpful for
  your next steps.
- **Action Needed:** After each section, write down any actions you'll take to recalibrate or improve
  in that area.

(continued)

DATE

MONEY-MISSION Paradigm	Sub-Score	Notes
Financial Progress (0–10)	/10	
Mission Impact (0–10)	/10	
Integration Level (0–10)	/10	
Total Score For Money-Mission Paradigm	/30	

Action Needed (What's the one thing that would create the most impact here this month?)

MENTAL-PHYSICAL Paradigm	Sub-Score	Notes
Mental Clarity (0–10)	/10	
Physical Wellbeing (0–10)	/10	
Energy Levels (0–10)	/10	
Total Score For Mental-Physical Paradigm	/30	

Acton Needed (What's the one thing that would create the most impact here this month?)

WORK-LIFE Paradigm	Sub-Score	Notes
Professional Achievement (0–10)	/10	
Personal Fulfilment (0–10)	/10	
Relationship Quality (0–10)	/10	
Total Score For Work-Life Paradigm	/30	

Acton Needed (What's the one thing that would create the most impact here this month?)

OVERALL CALIBRATION SCORE	/90
PRIORITY ADJUSTMENT REQUIRED	

5 Milestone Calibration: Monthly Progress Check-In

Milestone Calibration: Monthly Progress Check-In Template

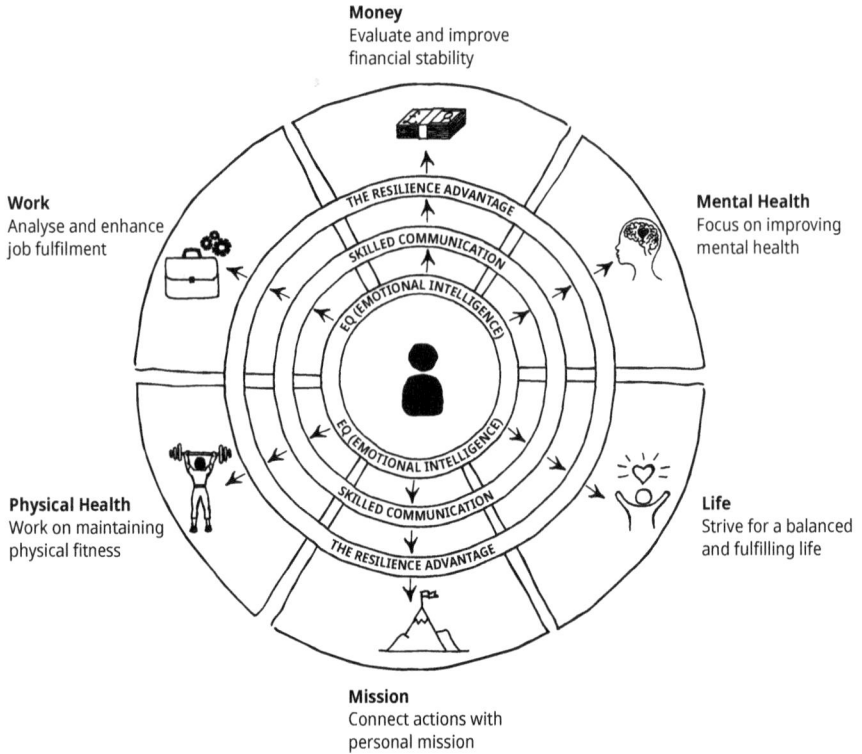

Money
Evaluate and improve
financial stability

Work
Analyse and enhance
job fulfilment

Mental Health
Focus on improving
mental health

Physical Health
Work on maintaining
physical fitness

Life
Strive for a balanced
and fulfilling life

Mission
Connect actions with
personal mission

PURPOSE: Create practical strategies for maintaining balance while pursuing goals.
INSTRUCTIONS: For each milestone in your plan, complete the table below.

Milestone	
Target Date	

Resource Requirements	
Time Needed	
Energy Required	
Support Necessary	
Financial Investment	

(continued)

Potential Challenges	
1.	
2.	
3.	

Balance Maintenance Strategies	
Money-Mission	
Mental-Physical	
Work-Life	

6 Daily Calibration Practice

Daily Calibration Practice

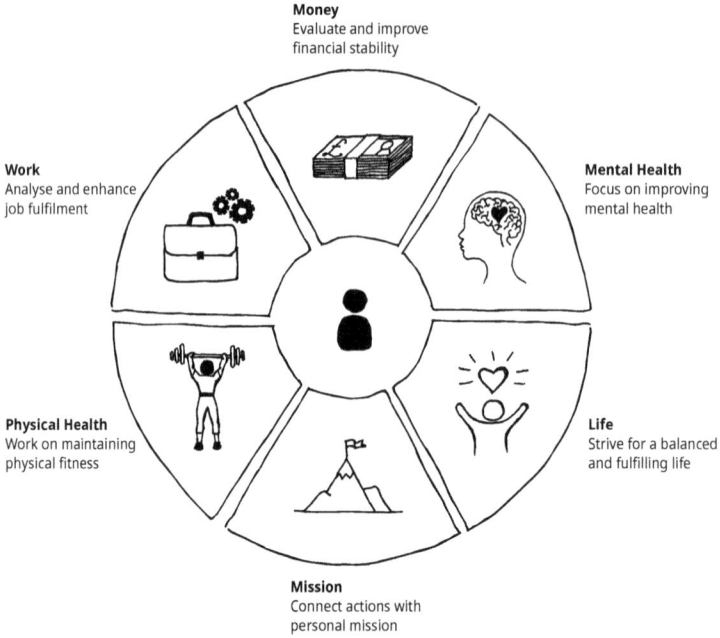

Money
Evaluate and improve
financial stability

Work
Analyse and enhance
job fulfilment

Mental Health
Focus on improving
mental health

Physical Health
Work on maintaining
physical fitness

Life
Strive for a balanced
and fulfilling life

Mission
Connect actions with
personal mission

PURPOSE: Maintain awareness and make micro-adjustments for optimal balance. Use both morning and evening entries or adapt to one daily check-in depending on your rhythm and capacity.

INSTRUCTIONS: Complete brief morning and evening reviews (maximum 5 minutes for each review).

Morning Review And Planning	
Energy Level (1–10)	
Top 3 Priorities	1.
	2.
	3.
Balance Focus Today	

Evening Achievement Review	
Progress Made	
Balance Maintained	
Recalibration Needed	

(continued)

Tomorrow's Preparation	
Key Focus	
Potential Challenges	
Support Required	

7 Energy Mapping Grid

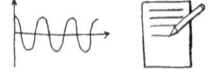

PURPOSE: Track your peak cognitive and emotional energy across a typical week. Match task types to energy rhythms. This practice turns fatigue into feedback and enhances resilience by design.

INSTRUCTIONS

Step 1: Rate each domain from 1 (very low) to 10 (very high). Use the notes section to capture observations.

Step 2: Reflect and Adjust:
- When did you feel most energised?
- Which activities drained you or lifted you?
- What changes could help you better align your tasks with your energy peaks?

Day	Time of Day	Physical	Mental	Emotional	Purpose	Notes
Monday	Morning					
	Afternoon					
	Evening					
Tuesday	Morning					
	Afternoon					
	Evening					
Wednesday	Morning					
	Afternoon					
	Evening					
Thursday	Morning					
	Afternoon					
	Evening					
Friday	Morning					
	Afternoon					
	Evening					

(continued)

Saturday	Morning					
	Afternoon					
	Evening					
Sunday	Morning					
	Afternoon					
	Evening					

Epilogue: The Balance Is Yours To Define

Sustainable success is a dynamic process of calibration. This book has offered tools, reflections and voices from real people managing the same tension you face: how to balance ambition with wellbeing, pressure with purpose and achievement with joy.

No single model or mentor can prescribe your exact route. With focus, self-awareness and the courage to adapt, you can keep aligning your work, wealth and wellbeing in ways that feel right for life far beyond your title. Define what you want. Make purposeful choices about how you use your time, it's the one resource you can't get back. Let each decision reflect what you value, not just what you're expected to pursue.

You've met the cast. You've explored the frameworks. Now it's your move. Keep adjusting, stay close to what matters and remember that balance isn't static, it's a rhythm you learn to feel and apply.

Your Resource Hub Awaits

The end of this book is just the beginning.

If BALANCING ACT has sparked insight, challenged your thinking, or shifted your sense of what's possible, now is the time to build momentum.

Scan the QR code or visit www.balancing-act.co.uk to access:
- Templates & downloadable tools.
- Explainer videos.
- Extended leader interviews.
- Strategy guides & practical examples.
- The Calibration Model in action across industries.

The Resource Hub is your evolving performance ecosystem, built to strengthen your personal architecture, help you find better balance and master the art of work, wealth and wellbeing.

EXPLORE MORE

MORE CLARITY. MORE TOOLS. YOUR NEXT STEP.

References

Best, T., & Dye, L. (Eds.). (2015). Nutrition for Brain Health and Cognitive Performance. CRC Press.

Carlson, N.R. & Birkett, M.A. (2017). Physiology of Behaviour. 12th ed. Harlow: Pearson Education.

Conroy, D.E. & Elliot, A.J. (2004) 'Fear of failure and achievement goals in sport: Addressing the issue of the chicken and the egg', Anxiety, Stress & Coping, 17(3), pp. 271–285.

Davidson, R.J. & Begley, S., 2012. The Emotional Life of Your Brain. New York: Penguin.

Duchek, S. (2020). Organizational resilience: a capability-based conceptualization. Business Research, 13(1), 215–246.

Goleman, D., 1995. Emotional Intelligence: Why It Can Matter More Than IQ. New York: Bantam Books.

Knight, S. (2020). NLP at Work: The Difference That Makes a Difference in Business. 4th ed. London: Nicholas Brealey.

Kouzes, J.M. & Posner, B.Z. (2017) The Leadership Challenge. 6th ed. Hoboken, NJ: Wiley.

Luthar, S. S., Cicchetti, D., & Becker, B. (2000). "The construct of resilience: A critical evaluation and guidelines for future work." Child Development, 71(3), 543–562.

Masten, A. S. (2001). "Ordinary magic: Resilience processes in development." American Psychologist, 56(3), 227–238.

Matthews, G., Zeidner, M. & Roberts, R.D., 2002. Emotional Intelligence: Science and Myth. Cambridge: MIT Press.

Mosconi, L. (2018) Brain Food: The Surprising Science of Eating for Cognitive Power. London: Penguin Life.

Salovey, P. & Mayer, J.D., 1990. Emotional intelligence. Imagination, Cognition and Personality, 9(3), pp.185–211.

Schein, E.H. & Schein, P.A. (2017) Organizational Culture and Leadership. 5th ed. Hoboken, NJ: Wiley.

Southwick, S. M., Bonanno, G. A., Masten, A. S., Panter-Brick, C., & Yehuda, R. (2014). "Resilience definitions, theory, and challenges: Interdisciplinary perspectives." European Journal of Psychotraumatology, 5(1), 25338.

Sullivan, J. & Parker, C. (2025) The Brain Always Wins 2. London: Chiselbury Publishing.

Valcour, M., 2018. Work-life integration: Challenges and organizational responses. In: T.D. Allen and L.T. Eby, eds. The Oxford Handbook of Work and Family. New York: Oxford University Press, pp.463–481.

Webster, K. E., et al. (2021). Goal Setting Improves Cognitive Performance in a Randomized Trial of Chronic Stroke Survivors. Stroke, 52(2), 569–577.

Woodrow, F. (2023) The Warrior, The Strategist and You: How to Find Your Purpose and Realise Your Potential. London: Elliott & Thompson.

Index

www.ingramcontent.com/pod-product-compliance
Lightning Source LLC
Chambersburg PA
CBHW061155240326
R18026400001B/R180264PG41519CBX00003B/5